ADAM MICHNIK [is a] historian and
political[...] [f]ounders of KOR
(Wo[...] [o]rganization of
diss[...] [wi]th the independent [...] [w]ay for the emergence [...] [S]olidarity in the 1980s. His
essays have appeared in the *New York Times*, *New York
Review of Books*, *The N[...]*
DAVID OST [...]

The Church and the Left

THE CHURCH
AND THE LEFT

ADAM MICHNIK

EDITED, TRANSLATED, AND WITH
AN INTRODUCTION BY

DAVID OST

THE UNIVERSITY OF CHICAGO PRESS
CHICAGO & LONDON

ADAM MICHNIK is a Polish historian and political writer who was one of the founders of KOR (Workers' Defense Committee), the organization of dissident intellectuals that paved the way for the Solidarity trade union in the late 1970s. His essays have appeared in *The New York Times, The New York Review of Books, The New Republic,* and *Harper's.* DAVID OST, assistant professor of political science at Hobart and William Smith Colleges, is the author of *Solidarity and the Politics of Anti-Politics.*

The University of Chicago Press, Chicago 60637
The University of Chicago Press, Ltd., London
© 1993 by The University of Chicago
All rights reserved. Published 1993
Printed in the United States of America

02 01 00 99 98 97 96 95 94 93   5 4 3 2 1

ISBN (cloth): 0–226–52424–8

Originally published as *Kościół, Lewica, Dialog* and as *L'Eglise et la gauche* (Paris: Editions du Seuil, © 1979).

Grateful acknowledgment is made to the Alfred Jurzykowski Foundation, Inc., New York, for its generous contribution toward the publication of this book and to the Central & East European Publishing Project, Oxford, for its generous assistance with the translation.

Library of Congress Cataloging-in-Publication Data

Michnik, Adam.
    [Kościół, lewica, dialog. English]
    The church and the left / Adam Michnik; edited, translated, and
with an introduction by David Ost.
        p.   cm.
    Translation of: Kościół, lewica, dialog.
Includes bibliographical references and index.
    1. Communism and Christianity—Catholic Church—Poland.
2.Catholic Church—Poland—History—20th century. 3. Church and
state—Poland—History—20th century. 4. Poland—Church
history—20th century. I. Ost, David. II. Title.
BX1566.2.M5313 1992
322'. 1'0943809045—dc20   92–20503

                                                              CIP

CONTENTS

Afterwords, 1977–1987

TRANSLATOR'S FOREWORD

Alan Thomas, my continually supportive editor at the University of Chicago Press, first proposed the project to me. Nina Gładziuk, my closest friend and co-thinker in Poland for more than a decade, convinced me to accept it. This project would not have been done without them.

In the course of translating a book filled with so many styles (not only Michnik's but those of the numerous authorities, both secular and religious, that he quotes so liberally), I went to several people with my questions. A special thanks goes to Anna Kłobucka, who was particularly generous with her time, helping me work through difficult passages and assisting greatly in the production of the glossary. Lillian Vallee read the entire translation and offered numerous good suggestions. Stanisław Barańczak, Clifford Green, Ewa Hauser, Nina and Antoni Hoffman, Jerzy Jedlicki, Helena Kaufman, Dunbar Moodie, Anna Popiel, and Roman Stachyra also provided valuable assistance; as did Grażyna Stando and especially Beata Ryczkowska at Michnik's newspaper, *Gazeta Wyborcza,* in Warsaw, and of course Adam Michnik himself. I benefited from consulting the fine previous translation of excerpts of this book, by Olga Amsterdamskaya and Gene Moore (in Frantisek Silnitsky et al., eds., *Communism and Eastern Europe* [New York: Karz, 1979]). Robert Hullot-Kentor's thoughtful essays on translation, published in *Telos,* helped me rethink my own methods in very useful ways. Andrzej Walicki offered useful criticism of my Introduction.

For institutional support I am grateful to the International Research and Exchanges Board (IREX) for funding my 1990 stay in Poland, which enabled me to research the Introduction; to Abby Collins and the Center for European Studies at Harvard University for the postdoctoral fellowship in 1990–91, which gave me time to complete the final draft; and to Hobart and William Smith Colleges for offering regular support and a stimulating home base. Finally, I would like to thank Randy Petilos and my manuscript editor Kathryn Kraynik at the University of Chicago Press, and Dawn Feligno and Sue Yates at Hobart and William Smith Colleges.

•   •

The original Polish title of this book is *Kościół—Lewica—Dialog,* or "Church—Left—Dialogue." Michnik's commitment to the last element of the triad is visible virtually on every page: not only in his attempts to reconcile apparently irreconcilable viewpoints but in his regular practice of naming names. Michnik will begin speaking of a certain school of thought and then, as a way of demonstrating just how many different people are central to Polish culture, simply reel off up to a few dozen names as notable representatives. Naturally, this presented problems for the translation. Should every name be identified in a glossary? Should those that make only fleeting appearances be eliminated in order to make the text read smoother? Neither solution seemed appropriate. The first would make the glossary unwieldy, while the second would be unfaithful to the original. Listing so many names slows the flow of the argument in Polish too, but Michnik felt that this way of emphasizing the principles of dialogue and inclusion outweighed any desirable elegance of parsimony. In the end, we decided to leave all the names in the text and to identify many of them, but not all, in a glossary. We began with the glossary included in the 1979 French edition of the book *(L'Église et la Gauche* [Paris: Editions du Seuil; translated by Agnès Słonimski]). Anna Kłobucka translated it and did some initial updating. I then edited and expanded it, adding many names. I also benefited from consulting the excellent glossary in the Russian-language version of the book *(Polski Dialog* [London: Overseas Publication Interchange, 1980; translated by N. Gorbanevskaya]).

The original Polish version (published in Paris in 1977 and in a semilegal domestic edition in 1981) was divided into three parts labeled simply I, II, and III. For this edition, I have divided the book into chapters. All chapter titles, subheadings, and introductory notes were written by me. Michnik frequently quotes other authors. For these passages I have used already existing English translations when available, with only occasional corrections for clarity. This volume includes both Michnik's footnotes as well as my own explanatory notes. I should point out that the original text, not an academic work, contains gaps in the footnotes—a publisher's name might be missing, or precise page numbers. I have often, but not always, been able to track down the missing information. As a result, the footnoting here is not always consistent.

No extensive note on translation is necessary. I will just mention a few terms. Where the text reads "national-chauvinism," this is almost always a rendering of the Polish term *nacjonalizm*. The English word "nationalism" inadequately conveys the connotation of the original. *Integryzm*, which Michnik uses in his discussion of conservative tendencies in the Roman Catholic Church (referred to throughout simply as the Church), has been translated as "fundamentalism" rather than "integralism." While the latter term is often employed in historical studies of the Church in Europe, the former is more common in American usage, and especially fits Michnik's use of *integryzm* in his 1987 essay "Troubles." Lastly, *ojczyzna* is usually translated as "fatherland" to convey both the root and the frequent moral connotations of the Polish original. Sometimes, however, the Polish term is used in a very neutral way, and "fatherland" seems a bit heavy. In those cases the word is translated the same way as *kraj:* "country."

Finally, I would like to dedicate this translation to the memory of Kimberley Kinast, 1955–1989, with whom I began the long road leading up to this. An endlessly creative thinker about everything, Kimberley found Polish political thought as fascinating as I did, even for her own very different life as a student, dancer, one-time New York City taxi driver, and just beginning as a lawyer who actually took ideals of justice seriously. And as everything about her just glowed, so did everything she took an interest in. It is no surprise that so many of her values, and her questions, are reflected so precisely on these pages.

PREFACE TO THE ENGLISH-LANGUAGE EDITION

I confess to a certain fear in offering this book to the American reader. The United States is a country of many religions. It is multi-ethnic and pluralist; multicultural almost by definition. The principle of separation of Church and state is accepted by all. Thus, American debates about abortion, for example, have a different political context than they do in Poland: they are debates about the limits of life, not the limits of the Church. There are no religious parties in the United States. Nor does the United States have historical experience of religious wars, or of bitter conflict between Church and state, or of an atheist and totalitarian communist dictatorship, or even of a sense that one religion is somehow more American than another. That is why I fear that my view of the Polish experience may somehow be untranslatable. Nevertheless, urged by my friend David Ost, let me say these few words about the book to my American readers.

I wrote this book in 1975–76. It was originally intended to be part of a special issue of the émigré quarterly *Aneks*, edited by my friend Aleksander Smolar. Our aim, together with other contributors such as Jan Józef Lipski, Antoni Macierewicz, and Father Jacek Salij, was to reexamine the complex relationship between the Catholic Church and the secular intelligentsia. We wanted to shed light on the new way each side was looking at the other. At about the same time, writing under a pseudonym, Jacek Kuroń published "Christians Without God" in the Catholic monthly *Znak*. My book was thus situated in a context of encounters and conversations between people far removed from the Church who, in the course of their involvement in the political opposition, were discovering that the Church was itself a source of democratic and humane values.

The Church at the time focused its efforts on defending its own identity and institutional freedom. It was led by Cardinal Stefan Wyszyński, now called "Cardinal of the Millennium." One may dispute such a grandiose label. One may not, however, doubt that the cardinal rendered great services on behalf of the opposition.

At the time I was writing, the democratic opposition was at the beginning of its road. Small groups of people, mostly intellectuals, sought to break the widespread barriers of fear and inertia. Attitudes to politics were still haunted by shadows of 1968 and memories of December 1970. We tried to convince people that apathy and the prevailing sense of helplessness only served to legitimize the powers that be.

Contrary to what has often been suggested, my book was no attempt to forge a political alliance with the Church. I was not so naive as to believe that the Church would embrace isolated intellectuals as real allies. My intention was only to propose a new way of thinking about the Church and its place in the world. I wanted to familiarize a wider audience with the ideas of modern Catholic intellectuals. I wanted to suggest a new approach to religion.

What exactly is religion? That was the question I asked myself while working on the book. I had come to believe that interpretations of religion as "ideology" or "false consciousness" were weak and inadequate. The opposition would do better to understand religion as an absolute, as mystery, as *sacrum*. This was part of a more general point. The opposition could survive, I felt, only by grounding itself in the culture at large. We had to be able to formulate our questions and values in the context of that culture.

In the formation of independent public opinion, literature played a decisive role. Miłosz and Konwicki, Brandys and Herbert, Barańczak and Zagajewski, Kołakowski and Gombrowicz, Solzhenitsyn and Havel—without a close reading of their works it is impossible to understand the moral and intellectual dilemmas of Polish oppositionist thought.

Reading the Holy Scriptures and reflecting on religion, the opposition asked questions that were simultaneously political and existential. We asked about the meaning of life and suffering, and how to relate to enemies. We were grappling with the relative and absolute nature of values, the meaning of tolerance, the law of love. And all of these questions informed concrete decisions that each of us had to make. For choosing to fight the dictatorship was not a decision to be taken lightly. It was a major decision and exacted a high price. Surely we could not at the time seriously believe that so many of us would be able to trade in our prison cells for the swank offices of state dignitaries. Our questions and reflections on religion thus had a very specific undertone. These were questions about how to live under a dictatorship. About how to avoid the temptations of "normality." In the name of what, we asked ourselves, were we ready to make our own lives and the lives of our loved ones so miserable?

Today I feel my book is no longer relevant—and yet relevant all the same. We live in a new era. Many of the ideas that I then considered great discoveries today seem commonplace or outdated. Some have been substantiated, others invalidated. We might best begin with the concept of the "Secular Left," which today's proponents of a Catholic state continue to pounce upon so eagerly. That is a completely historical concept. I used it to refer to those who opposed the regime in the name of leftist and secular values and did not identify with the Catholic Church. With their antitotalitarian ideas, these people would go on to become active in the Workers' Defense Committee (KOR), and then in Solidarity, the underground, and the Round Table negotiations of 1989. Many of them, eventually, also went on to embrace the Church, finding there something more than just an ally. A uniquely Polish synthesis of Christian and democratic ideas seemed to be forming.

Over the last two years, the rapid resurgence of right-wing rhetoric has raised new questions for this group. In my book, I wrote about Charles Maurras and his instrumentalist attitude toward the Church, about the "Julianic" Church trying to regain past privileges, and about the dangers of using religion for political aims. Today, all these issues are again of enormous importance.

One senses a conflict in the Polish Church today between two ways of thinking about religion: the so-called "French" way and the "Sarmatian" way. The former harks back to early times, when the Church lived together with pagans in a common state and did not seek to use the state to convert them. The latter finds its model in the later Middle Ages, when the Church tried to construct a confessional state. These two kinds of Catholicism reflect two deeply rooted tendencies of Polish culture: the European and the ethnocentric. We need only look to Cardinal Stefan Wyszyński to understand their force.

There was always a certain ambiguity in the cardinal's pastorship. Like General de Gaulle, he was a great anachronism. His greatness consisted in his flawless decoding of the nature of communism and his brilliant strategy of resistance. In this the cardinal was remarkably modern. But this modernness of practice went together with an anachronistic rhetoric and doctrine. His was the anticommunism of a conservative. He could defend himself effectively against the attacks of the communist state, but he distrusted Vatican II and was less than eager to engage others in dialogue. Cardinal Wyszyński was a man of monologue, cut from the old model of the Church. Modernity and the language of human rights left a foul scent for him, as if part of some devious Masonic plot. He had little interest in intellectual Catholicism. He believed instead in the Church of the masses, the rural Church, rooted in the traditional world of paternalism and particularism.

Karol Wojtyła's world was quite different. A poet, philosopher, and man of theater, Wojtyła was the hope of intellectuals. He shunned nationalist rhetoric yet remained deeply rooted in the national tradition. He opposed communism in the name of human rights, broadly understood, yet maintained strong reservations toward the Western model of a tolerant society in a secular and democratic state. Here we see the contradictions of Wojtyła, both as Archbishop of Kraków and as Pope John Paul II. In Poland, we greeted him as a great friend of freedom. Western Europe saw him as a conservative trying to stop the Church's progressive work. These two faces of Wojtyła were not masquerade. It is just that on the two sides of Europe, different things were considered important. The message and emphasis, heard one way in the East, sounded another way in the West.

•　　　•

The Church has not yet found its place in the postcommunist era. Today it stands at a crossroads. Does it seek institutional privileges and special rights for itself? Should it try to use the state to impose Christian values? Does it seek special influence on governmental policy? Or will it see its place as metapolitical, free from the temptations of party alliances and electoral campaigning; shunning the pursuit of official privileges and eschewing the power to shape state legislation? If it chooses the first road, the Church risks becoming a political pressure group, opportunistically supported by some, strongly challenged by others. If it opts for the second road, it may rapidly become like the churches in Western Europe.

Postcommunist societies are today doggedly moving in the direction of the market. But is the free market really some magic wand to solve all problems, as was once thought about the planned economy? Can the market, with its cult of wealth and initiative, its contempt for weakness and poverty, really provide answers to the new questions of the day? The Church does not yet want to offer a definitive reply. It would seem, however, that the social sensibility formed by the Church cannot permit an unequivocally affirmative response. The Church will never fully endorse the ruthlessness of the market. While it tends to support the market against the proponents of liberation theology, the approval comes with eschatological reservations: the market may be a necessary mechanism, but it must be adjusted to take into account the principles of love for thy neighbor and the brotherhood of man.

Unfortunately, in the postcommunist era, the Church and its supporters are unlikely to be satisfied by the role of "eschatological opposition." They will probably prefer to have concrete influence on state policy. This is what seems to be happening today. Thus, the Church's encounter with the world is being formulated anew. The Church once again speaks as if it were a besieged fortress. One hears a tone of fear in recent Episcopal statements, as if the forces of the Antichrist were amassing for another attack on the Lord's vineyard. Yet this time the Antichrist is liberalism and secular humanism, not atheistic communism.

In the great black hole after communism, part of the Catholic hierarchy sees the secular state as such as the new Public Enemy Number One. In this view—one hears it frequently nowadays—the aggressive atheism of communist society is being replaced by the practical atheism of consumer society. Western liberalism thus fills the recently vacated slot as the apocalyptic enemy of Catholicism.

In the language of the besieged fortress, dialogue is replaced by anathema. And indeed, the Church no longer speaks in the language of dialogue. Instead, there is monologue, spoken from the pulpit and printed in the pastoral letters: a monologue of warning against the dangers of liberalism.

As the Church tries to legislate evangelical values, it is time to concentrate again on the need for dialogue. For the problem today is that the aggressive language of the Church tends to elicit an equally aggressive language *against* the Church, a kind of gutter atheism, primitive anticlericalism. Thus, while the Church rails against liberalism, we hear others charge that the Church is trying to create a police dictatorship and to replace Marxism-Leninism with Catholic doctrine.

And so we have a struggle between two contradictory fundamentalisms: clerical and anticlerical. What is one to do?

The answer, I think, is that one should do as always: defend truth, common sense, and dialogue as opposed to hatred. One must remember that real participation in politics and true meaning in life can only be provided by the three Christian values of faith, hope, and love. And of these three, the most important is love.

•   •

Finally, in ending, one personal note. Recently a volume of Father Henryk Jańkowski's sermons was published. Jankowski is pastor of St. Brygida's Church in Gdańsk, the Solidarity stronghold and unofficial headquarters during martial law. That was a period when people of the anticommunist opposition met regularly in church cellars. It was a time when no one demanded religious declarations from anyone. What united us was a community of a different kind, a community of commitment. I remember one sermon from June 1985. Władysław Frasyniuk, Bogdan Lis, and I had just been sentenced to prison for our activities on behalf of Solidarity.[1] Father Jankowski, pastor of the Gdańsk shipworkers, spoke as follows:

> In every society, laws created and accepted by the community are intended for the safeguarding of human rights. Such is their function, and thus do people come to respect the collection of rules stating what is permissible and what is not. Nevertheless, history supplies no shortage of examples where the law has been applied for other purposes. . . . Today, a verdict has been laid down that pains the heart of every Christian and Pole. Bogdan Lis, Władysław Frasyniuk, and Adam Michnik have been condemned to prison. For what? For being loyal to the cause of human solidarity in Poland. For being loyal to a Poland of our ideals, a Poland, as Adam Michnik has written, "based on Christian values and social justice, . . . capable of compromise and moderations, realism and partnership, but incapable of servitude and spiritual surrender, unable to live in spiritual subjugation."
>
> This is the kind of Poland in the hearts of those who are the co-creators of August 1980. Bogdan Lis—a worker and signer of the Gdańsk Accord, Adam Michnik—an intellectual and member of KOR, Władysław Frasyniuk—a worker from Silesia and a leading Solidarity official: these three were punished for belonging to Solidarity's Provisional Coordinating Commission; punished, that is, for holding views different from the official ones. There was no proof of guilt. The unprecedented pattern of recent years is that

1. Frasyniuk and Lis were leading Solidarity activists from Wrocław and Gdańsk, respectively. The three stayed in prison until a general amnesty in 1986.— TRANS.

people go to jail solely on the testimony of secret policemen who, citing national security, reveal nothing about the sources of their "evidence" against the accused. . . .

This trial was different from the one for the murderers of Father Jerzy Popiełuszko.[2] Those defendants had an open trial. They were allowed to speak as much as they wanted. They could defame with impunity the name of the one they brutally murdered, and even besmirch representatives of the Church hierarchy. The newspapers reported every word. Things were quite different for Lis, Michnik, and Frasyniuk. The court did not allow them to make full statements, nor were their lawyers permitted to do so. The verdict was delivered in an atmosphere filled with threats. Militia virtually surrounded the court building, the corridors were closed off, the trial was secret, and the accused, their families and their lawyers were all searched upon entry, allegedly in the interests of courtroom security. The authorities no longer even took care to maintain appearances. The trial became pure fiction, a way to keep the defendants in jail and society in fear.

Yet the defendants maintained inner peace. For they are free, despite their external constraints. Freedom of spirit is the measure of human dignity. In his final words, Adam Michnik said, "To my slanderers and framers, I forgive you." He spoke this way, on behalf of all the accused, in the spirit of Christian truth. For their pain is guiltless. Theirs is like the suffering of Job, for whom torment was a sign not that Job had done wrong, but that he was special.[3]

Adam Michnik
January 1992

2. In October 1984, Popiełuszko, a pro-Solidarity priest from Warsaw, was kidnapped, tortured, and killed by Polish security police. Those who carried out the crime were tried and convicted and sentenced to up to twenty-five years in prison.—TRANS.

3. Ksiądz Henryk Jańkowski, *Z tej drogi zejść nie mogę: Wybór Kazań 1983– 1991* [This Road I Cannot Abandon: Selected Sermons] (Gdańsk, 1992), pp. 210–11.

INTRODUCTION by David Ost

There are at least four reasons why, for a Western audience, this book is more relevant today than when it was written in 1976.

1. In the past fifteen years, Poland has experienced one of the most remarkable social and political upheavals of the twentieth century, precipitating the collapse of Communist rule in Eastern Europe, and both Adam Michnik and the ideas expressed in this book played a significant role in bringing this about.

Michnik has been present at both ends of this experience, as a key leader in the pre-Solidarity opposition and as a central player in the 1989 Round Table negotiations that finally brought Communist rule to a close. Michnik's chief impact has been on intellectuals, not workers. He was not involved in the creation of Solidarity and, in fact, initially opposed the demand for free trade unions as unattainable. But he was crucial in helping shape the attitude of a generation of intellectuals that contributed so much to the Solidarity movement as a whole.

The Polish upheaval has been the most fascinating but perhaps the most confusing of all the Eastern European "revolutions." Here we saw a social movement packed with all the symbols usually associated with the Left, yet with a stocky religious underpinning that seemed part of a different drama altogether. Workers occupied factories and called for a society of social justice while priests conducted mass in the Lenin Shipyard for thousands. The confluence of the secular and the religious, of the modern and premodern, seemed unsettling to many in the West but entirely acceptable to liberal Polish intellectuals who had not long before been as anticlerical as any other European intelligentsia. No other book explains the basis or rationale for the intellectuals' turn to the Church as well as Michnik's does. Nor does any other work make clear the differences still remaining,

1

differences which become more prominent today. *The Church and the Left* gives us a key to understanding many of the developments of this extraordinary recent period in Polish and Eastern European history.

2. Like the rest of Eastern Europe, Poland is now trying to build a new democratic political system—an uncertain political project that requires the precise meaning of democracy to be created anew. Through Michnik's superb discussions of liberalism and nationalism, of secularism and clericalism, as well as through the critical reactions his arguments have elicited in Poland (discussed later in this Introduction), the book teaches us a great deal about the contending sides in the internal struggles now rocking Eastern Europe. *The Church and the Left* illuminates political problems of the present and future in a way that could not have been anticipated in 1976.

3. In the 1970s everybody seemed to treat religion as a mere relic of the past, waging a losing battle against progress and mercilessly cast aside by the irrepressible pull of secular modernity. Even the experts considered Ayatollah Khomeini's struggle for power in Iran a curious sideshow to the "real" struggle between the monarchy and the political Left. Today, on the contrary, the widespread feeling that secular progress, whether in its liberal or communist variants, only destroyed communities instead of creating the better ones it had promised (whether in the name of market prosperity or classless harmony), has led to a revival of religion and to a questioning of the notion of progress throughout the world. Including, of course, Poland, where the Church felt strong enough in 1991 to propose the repeal of the constitutional separation of church and state and admonish Poles against succumbing to the temptations of Western liberalism.

In light of this, the relationship of religion to politics needs to be examined more closely than ever. Few contemporary writers do so as thoughtfully as Michnik. While emphasizing the specifics of the Polish situation (thus introducing us to the milieu that so fundamentally shaped Pope John Paul II), Michnik offers valuable observations on this relationship relevant to various countries with differing political systems. Likely to have been read in the West in 1976 as a mere political curiosity, *The Church and the Left* can now be seen as an important contribution to an exceedingly urgent discussion.

4. Finally, publication of *The Church and the Left* is timely today simply because it was written by Adam Michnik. Through a wide body of writing over the past fifteen years, and an unswerving polit-

ical commitment that took him from prison to parliament and leaves him today as the chief editor of Poland's most important daily newspaper, Michnik has earned a place as one of the most influential and innovative European thinkers of our time. His words have been translated into many languages and published in journals from Argentina to Russia and Japan. In the United States, his essays have been published in *The New York Times, The New York Review of Books, Dissent, Telos, The New Republic, Harper's,* and elsewhere. In 1989 he was named "European of the Year" by the French journal *La Vie.* But until now, English-language readers have only had short essays on which to base their assessment of his work.[1] *The Church and the Left,* Michnik's first book, is the first publication in English to provide a systematic account of the author's basic ideas and approach. We have here a seminal work of a seminal thinker who will no doubt play an important part in conceptualizing whatever kind of European order will replace the one that ended in Poland in 1989.

Born in 1946, Michnik grew up in a family of veteran Jewish Communists; his father was a radical who felt far more comfortable as a communist without power, fighting for justice, than as the representative of a system supposedly implementing the Just World. Consequently, Michnik grew up with a respect for the radical Left traditions of the past and a deep distrust of the institutionalized leftism of the ruling Party.

If the older generation of radical intellectuals Michnik discusses were shaped by the experiences of the 1930s and 1940s, Michnik and his generation of Polish intellectuals were shaped by 1968. Apart from the Prague Spring and Soviet invasion in Czechoslovakia, apart from the radical spirit pervasive throughout the world, what was most important for this group was the experience of the student protests in Poland and the way they were suppressed. Students had gone on strike in March to protest government restrictions on free speech and other democratic rights, rights that these students, like all other student radicals in 1968, considered central to what "real socialism" was all about. They did not doubt they would meet repression, but they certainly did not expect what actually ensued. The government responded to the protests by launching a veritable *Külturkampf* against the intelligentsia, jailing students, firing professors, and blaming the trouble on Jews, most of whom were now pushed out of

1. Adam Michnik, *Letters from Prison and Other Essays,* translated by Maya Latynski (Berkeley: University of California Press, 1985).

the country. The Party organized goon squads and sent them into action, dubbing this an example of "good patriotic Polish people" repelling an assault of "Zionists," "Trotskyists," and other "alien" elements. In other words, it responded to the students' challenge by appealing to the worst sort of nationalist xenophobia, tapping the classic paraphernalia of native fascist traditions.

Previously, one of the ways the Party defended its power was to claim that only it could prevent the reemergence of right-wing nationalism. The Communists had identified the Church as the main bearer of such values, and, as Michnik notes, most non-Communist intellectuals of the Left had agreed. Characteristic for this latter circle were Leszek Kołakowski's early criticisms of Catholic "obscurantism," or Witold Jedlicki's withering attacks on the Church as a reactionary institution willing, for a price, to collaborate even with Stalinists against democratic rights.[2] But 1968 changed that. The events showed the Communist party tapping fascist traditions while many in the Church defended the students. Soon, blacklisted authors, including many Jews, could find nowhere to publish *except* in the Catholic press. The lessons of 1968 seemed to be that the Party had abandoned its last vestiges of leftism and that the Church was not the enemy of liberalism it had been in the past. As Michnik sat in jail, the world as he knew it seemed to come apart. The experiences of 1968 demanded a rethinking of old concepts and strategies, a rethinking of the meaning of the Left, and a rethinking of the nature of the Church.

The Church and the Left is a result of this rethinking. Or, perhaps more accurately, it is part of the process of this rethinking and a plea for others to do the same. For although Michnik firmly places himself in the camp of the secular liberal Left, his point is not to argue in favor of his views and against those of others. Indeed, sections of this book are so critical of the Left that it is hard to believe they were written by someone claiming to be part of it. But that is his point: our old concepts just won't do anymore. Neither those on the Left nor those allied with the Church have a program that can bring about a world both will feel comfortable in. That can only be achieved through "dialogue," which Michnik understands, following Tadeusz Mazowiecki (who in 1989 became postwar Poland's first

2. Kołakowski's views are discussed at length by Michnik in the text. Jedlicki's views are expressed in his history of the intellectual opposition in the 1956 period, *Klub Krzywego Koła* [The Club of the Crooked Circle] (Paris: Instytut Literacki, 1963; reprint, Warsaw: Solidarni, 1989), esp. pp. 38–39, 69–73.

non-Communist prime minister), as "a readiness to understand the validity of someone else's position, . . . a method by which an ideologically diverse society can learn to live together." In the end, Michnik's is not so much a politics of the Left as a politics of dialogue.

In this sense, his politics is visible on every page. For the book is a spectacular example of what Michnik has always done best: mediate differences, mitigate conflicts by accepting the truths on both sides, and locate a space where opposing sides can work toward a common goal. Dialogue is the real hero of the book.

Socialism and Liberalism

It is in *The Church and the Left* that Michnik most clearly articulates the groundwork of his political philosophy. Much confusion stems from the fact that he gives labels to his beliefs. He consistently speaks of himself and his co-thinkers as part of the "secular Left" and states forthrightly that he is in favor of "democratic socialism." Michnik has regretted using these terms ever since, saying they simply confuse issues, as they undoubtedly have. Nevertheless, he did use these terms, and central to understanding Michnik is explaining why he did so and what they meant for him.

The labels came naturally to Michnik. They were not only part of his family background but central to the radical milieu of his time. Michnik has often referred to himself—sometimes with pride, sometimes with resignation—as a child of the 1960s. As he notes in the book, he felt a camaraderie with radical protesters in the West who envisioned a world that would combine the participatory ethos of democracy with the egalitarian commitment of socialism. As late as 1988, in an interview with Daniel Cohn-Bendit (of France '68 fame), Michnik said he still felt "loyal to the whole anti-authoritarian project" of 1968.[3] Radicals in the East, however, never had any illusions about the Soviet claim to embody socialism. That had been undermined not only by Leon Trotsky in the 1920s but by a series of Eastern European "revisionist Marxists" in the 1950s and 1960s, who persistently stressed the democratic principles so central to the thought of the young Marx and the practice of non-Leninist Marxists.[4] Michnik saw a commonality between this Eastern European

3. *Kontakt* (Paris), nos. 74–75, July–August 1988, p. 54.
4. See, for example, Gajo Petrović, *Marx in the Mid-Twentieth Century: A Yugoslav Philosopher Reconsiders Karl Marx's Writings* (Garden City, NY: Anchor, 1967).

tradition and the radicalism of new leftists in the West. Both Czech proponents of "socialism with a human face" and French '68 proponents of the "left-wing alternative" were anti-Soviet, anti-authoritarian, and committed to popular participation in political decision making. Equating socialism with democracy was thus no bold innovation for Michnik.

Actually, Michnik here seems to understand socialism to mean little more than liberal democracy—one of the reasons he has since been able to shed the socialist affiliation without changing his views too substantially. With his occasional criticisms of capitalism and strong support for welfare guarantees and social justice, he manifests a moral preference for a welfare state. But he is not terribly concerned about property forms and does not claim to have the answer for how poverty and injustice can be eradicated. Theoretically, he demands nothing that could not be accomplished through a primarily market economy and Western parliamentary structure.

As expressed in this book, Michnik's "socialist" politics are what we might call liberal communitarian. The liberal aspect is most clearly on display in his ardent defense of individual rights, freedom of expression, and full religious and political tolerance. Michnik appeals to John Stuart Mill as his authority, not Karl Marx or anyone from the socialist tradition. No political ideology could even be considered socialist if it did not have a communitarian aspect to it. What is special about Michnik's communitarianism, however, is that it too is of an essentially liberal pedigree. He is decidedly unsympathetic to the communitarianism of Leninism and the old Left, with its focus on organic unity between state and society, its vision of a state embodying the needs and interests of all citizens. Michnik recognizes the totalitarian implications of such communitarianism and rejects fundamentalist Catholicism for having similar organicist aspirations. Michnik's communitarianism is based in a free and active citizenry participating extensively in discussing and legislating the issues that confront them. Community is generated through the process of politics, not in its outcome.

Michnik's view of democratic socialism thus comes from classical ideas about the democratic *polis*. It is a view liberal theorists once shared. But they finally abandoned the notion that widespread citizen participation in politics was a good thing after World War II, when they reinterpreted the chaos of the prewar period as being due precisely to the mobilization of masses in politics. Liberals thereupon became enemies of popular participation, ceding this old liberal aspiration to radicals and socialists.[5] Western new leftists used it against the liberal systems of the West while Michnik and others used it against the communist systems of Eastern Europe. Authorities in both parts of the world preferred managerial rule instead.

Finally, the connection between liberal democracy and socialism is particularly strong in Poland because of Poland's specific history. It is here that the foundations of Michnik's thought are most likely to get lost in translation—not from Polish to English, but from Eastern European experience to the Western experience. For readers in the West may be surprised that Michnik's socialism is little more than a defense of liberalism and individual rights. In the modern capitalist countries of the West, socialists speak usually of the flaws of individualism. They usually want to protect and empower those that market individualism leaves behind. But this only points to a fundamental difference between Eastern Europe and the West that is central to understanding Michnik. For whereas modern secular liberalism is the starting point for political conflict in the West, it is still largely the object of struggle in the East. With their emphasis on individual rights and reason ("dialogue"), Michnik and his co-thinkers were very much children of the Enlightenment. But whereas such values go unnoticed in the West, where virtually all political tendencies claim to share them, they still constitute a partisan battle cry in Poland: the battle cry of the Left. Michnik is identified in Poland today as a leftist not because he is a socialist but because he is a liberal, and liberal ideals in Poland have always been championed by the Left.

Poland has had a historical experience quite different from the experience of the West. No smooth transition from feudalism to capitalism here. No easy evolution from a social system revolving around Church and faith to one based on science and reason. No natural progression from premodern communitarianism to modern secular individualism. That linear path of historical development— formulated first by Marx but most persistently argued, paradoxically, by anti-Marxists, right up to the modernization theorists of today— bears little resemblance to Poland's historical evolution. The Reformation ultimately failed in Poland. Like most of Eastern Europe, Poland did not develop an indigenous bourgeoisie. In its first indus-

5. Probably the two most influential statements of this postwar liberal antipathy to citizen participation are Joseph Schumpeter's *Capitalism, Socialism and Democracy* (New York: Harper and Row, 1950), and Michael Crozier, Samuel Huntington, and Joji Watanuki, eds., *The Crisis of Democracy* (New York: Trilateral Commission, 1975).

trialization periods from 1880 to the Second World War, Poland's capitalists tended to be Germans and Jews, both reflecting and contributing to the "alien" reputation business activity had acquired. Without a strong competitor for the loyalty of elites, the Roman Catholic Church remained uncommonly strong. Not even the state posed a threat to the cohesiveness of the old Church. On the contrary, the Polish state was so weak that by the late eighteenth century the country was simply annexed by Austria, Russia, and Prussia and would not regain its independence until more than a hundred years later, in 1918.

Such history, naturally, produced political configurations quite different from those considered normal in the West. Most important, as far as the book is concerned, it retarded the emergence of modern secularism and liberalism.

The modern tradition from the Enlightenment to liberalism largely defined itself against the Church. It challenged Catholicism through its emphasis on reason and progress, its conviction that the world was knowable and that progress on earth was possible. In Western Europe, the new ideology was embraced by the emerging bourgeoisie, anxious and able to assert its rights against the Church and landed gentry. There, anticlerical liberal values fit in quite well with the new nationalism. With an indigenous class of people committed to a dynamic expansion of the economy, the new secular ideas seemed to be a precondition for developing strong modern states.

In Poland, however, without a strong Protestant or bourgeois past, liberalism could not develop such a following. The long periods of foreign occupation not only kept the traditional Church intact but solidified the view that a conservative Church was indispensable to national survival. Those leading the fight against the Church in Poland in the nineteenth and early twentieth centuries were not the domestic bourgeoisie but the foreign occupiers. For more than a hundred years, Polish myths and the Polish language were kept alive by a Roman Catholic Church that resisted all modern and secular encroachments. Whereas liberalism helped consolidate strong nation-states in the West, it was *illiberalism* that kept the national identity intact in Poland.

If the nation is identified with a premodern Church and there is no native bourgeoisie to conduct a struggle against it, where were modern secular liberal ideas to come from? In Poland they came from the socialists. The party that sought to transcend liberalism in Western Europe sought to introduce liberalism in Eastern Europe, particularly in Poland. From its foundation in 1895 until its dissolution by the Communists in 1948, the Polish Socialist Party was the most consistent defender of liberal democracy in the country. It opposed the establishment of Catholicism as the state religion and almost solely championed the rights of national and religious minorities. In the interwar years of 1918 through 1939, the socialists often stood alone in their defense of parliamentary rule, arguing against the European vogue for a "strong leader." Indeed, it is only thanks to the socialists that newly independent Poland decided on free elections and parliamentary government at all.

In Poland, therefore, the fight for liberal values and institutions has always been led by the Left. This legacy is a crucial background to Michnik's book. When Michnik appeals to the socialist tradition but in fact puts forth an essentially liberal program, he is only being loyal to the mainstream of the Polish left-wing tradition. Defending this tradition puts him at odds with Catholic nationalism as well as with Communism. It does not put him at odds with the Left.

Michnik thus supports the Church, but he is choosy. He defends it against the Communists, but warns against a return to the kind of Church that prevailed in the pre-Communist period. He sees in the Church a powerful ally in the fight against the Communists' antidemocratic rule, but is wary of the Church that is still committed to its own form of premodern antidemocratic rule. What is central to Michnik is the separation of realms. He fights for the Church's rights in the realm of religion but opposes any attempt to impose Church rules on the autonomous realm of politics. Just as he feels that the Communists' desire to subordinate all public and private life to the Party inexorably leads to totalitarianism, he fears that the lingering Catholic tendency to seek a dominant role in social and political life poses similar dangers. Michnik thus defends the Church as a social institution that has an inalienable right to pursue its pastoral mission for the faithful, but warns against the fundamentalist tendency to establish Catholicism as a state religion and deny others the same rights it reserves for itself. He defends a liberal Church, not a fundamentalist one.

One of the main goals of his book is to promote the evolution of this liberal Catholic variant. He champions the "social Catholic" tendency represented by Jerzy Turowicz and the weekly *Tygodnik Powszechny* in Kraków, and by Tadeusz Mazowiecki and the monthly *Więź* in Warsaw. Increasingly prominent in intellectual circles even while scarce among the hierarchy, strongly influenced by the "personalism" of French theologians like Jacques Maritain and Immanuel Mounier, this tendency claimed for Catholicism the liberal values of openness, tolerance, and diversity. Michnik favorably counterposed this kind of Church to the Church of righteousness, xenophobia, and rigid dogma. Among books written by secular liberal Polish intellectuals, Michnik's is unprecedented in its openness and goodwill toward the Roman Catholic Church, but in the end he wants only a Church that will abide by modern liberal rules. Not all in the Church were ready to go along.

Reactions to Michnik

Most readers of this translation will probably agree with the book's main argument: only through dialogue between secular and religious forces can a good and desirable democratic order be constructed. Yet the book has been quite controversial in Poland. While his secular intellectual audience hailed it as a profound contribution ("our Bible," one intellectual called the book, with barely a trace of irony, when I asked him about it in 1981), the Catholic hierarchy and those who felt little sympathy with Michnik's "Left" received it with considerable skepticism and mistrust. For the critics, Michnik had defended the Church precisely in a way it did not need to be defended. They saw condescension in his approach. They rejected his distinction between a good Church to be commended and a dangerous Church to be rebuked. Who was he to make such judgments? How can a self-proclaimed leftist presume to so lecture the Church?

This criticism elicited by the book is interesting not just for the light it sheds on the ideological diversity of the old opposition, but because it presages in many ways the attacks on Michnik and other liberals in the postcommunist period that have now put liberalism on the defensive.

The first critical response came from the pen of Zdzisław Najder, the prominent literary critic and acclaimed biographer of Joseph Conrad who has lectured in elite universities throughout Europe and the United States. In the 1970s and early 1980s, Najder also wrote, under pseudonym, political essays in the émigré journal *Kultura*. With his own claims of sympathy for the prewar socialist tradition, Najder would seem likely to be a Michnik admirer. But unlike many other successful Polish intellectuals of his generation, including those Michnik praises so highly, Najder rejected the Communist tradition from the beginning. And Najder believed Michnik was still too stuck in that tradition, even as he tried to distance himself from it.

Najder's suspicions stem from Michnik's understanding of "the Left." On the one hand, Michnik's attempt to claim for the Left all the good things in life—democratic values, openness, tolerance, commitment to "freedom, equality, and independence"—would seem to remove the Communist legacy from the Left. Yet elsewhere, notes Najder, Michnik seems to applaud that legacy, as when he approvingly quotes Antoni Słonimski ("my teacher," Michnik calls him) saying that in the prewar period the Church was "reactionary" and communism "progressive." Either way, says Najder, Michnik is wrong. In the first version he misreads history and monopolizes virtue for the Left; in the second, he defends a prewar communism that may have spoken fine words about freedom and justice but that in its insistence on the subordination of the individual to the party only laid the basis for universal subordination to the state. While Najder is no apologist for the Church, he argues that even if it opposed necessary reforms in the past, it was not "reactionary" as a whole, certainly not in comparison with Communism.[6]

Najder feels that Michnik's attitude toward the Left puts him out of touch with the Polish people and raises questions about his intentions. While Michnik spends considerable time talking about the intellectual evolution of Leszek Kołakowski, Najder says that even among intellectuals in Kołakowski's age group, those born between 1925 and 1945, only a small few have followed the trajectory that Michnik presents as a norm.[7] Moreover, those who have evolved like this constitute the elite of Communist Poland. And here we come to the point that—in one way or another—all of Michnik's critics make against him, in the past as well as today: Michnik and his supporters are somehow complicit in Communist rule; they are themselves part of the Communist elite—if not as its leaders, then as its palatable alternative. They may have been persecuted by the Party, but only because they lost out in an internal quarrel, not because they rejected the system's foundations. Those who rejected communism outright, argue the critics, were made politically irrelevant. They could not get into the schools, find important jobs, or publish their ideas in the press. Only those who in some sense accepted the system had a chance to present, and thus to suffer for, their views.

While anti-Communist critics were being beaten down by the Stalinist police, Najder says, today's ex-Communists "occupied safe

6. Zdzisław Najder, "Dialog z Michnikiem" [A Dialogue with Michnik], in *Ile jest dróg?* [How Many Roads?] (Paris: Instytut Literacki, 1982), pp. 45–46. Original published in *Kultura* (Paris), no. 9, September 1977.

7. Najder, "Dialog," p. 48.

positions in the party." Even those like Michnik who matured in the post-Stalinist period started from a privileged position "because of their early views and connections."[8] The Left is thus compromised by its origins and even Michnik—a *"presently uncompromised* freedom activist"[9]—is tainted by original sin.

Najder is by no means Michnik's most severe critic. On the contrary, his was an attempt to guide an "honest" but erring young intellectual onto morally and politically more solid ground. But Najder was the first to explicitly raise the point about complicity that shapes much of the popular, and populist, reaction to Michnik.

With the "relics of party thinking still lingering" in Michnik's thought, Najder is skeptical about Michnik's real commitment to dialogue. The notion of a Church-Left alliance is fine, says Najder, provided one keeps in mind the proper sense of proportion: the Church represents an "enormous social force" and "strong moral authority" while the Left can offer only the talents and commitments of a small group of intellectuals.[10] Michnik's Left, Najder believes, is a bit too sure of itself, leading to a condescending attitude not just toward the Church but toward the nation, and justifiably arouses suspicions that it is interested in alliance only if it can call the shots.

Where Najder is a cautious critic, the Reverend Józef Tischner develops some of the same arguments into a much harsher critique. And as an extremely prominent Catholic theologian from Kraków, Tischner's commentaries carry a great deal of weight. They are as close as one gets to an official Church response to Michnik. It is not a friendly one. Tischner begins by accusing Michnik of being as demagogic as the Stalinists by appropriating a moral high ground and placing the Church in a compromised position from the start. If the Left is defined as the defender of liberty, tolerance, fair income distribution, and an equal start for all, "what is left for me if I do not support the ideals of the Left? Nothing but 'chauvinism, national oppression, obscurantism, lawlessness' and similar atrocities. In the past, during Stalinism, we had no choice because the 'iron rule of history' did not permit one. Today also we have no option, because the lofty . . . ethics of 'democratic socialism' do not allow an option."[11]

8. Najder, "Dialog," pp. 48–49.
9. Najder, "Dialog," p. 47, my emphasis.
10. Najder, "Dialog," p. 50.
11. Józef Tischner, *Marxism and Christianity: The Quarrel and the Dialogue in Poland,* translated by Marek B. Zaleski and Benjamin Fiore, S.J. (Washington:

Tischner also charges Michnik and the liberals with being hopelessly out of touch with the people. It is "amazing," he says, that anyone "with eyes and ears" can live in Poland and *not* be convinced of the Church's good works.[12] If some leftists are beginning to have their doubts, well and good. They are starting to see the light. Now let them join us. But Tischner is not anxious to conduct the dialogue Michnik calls for. The "essential dialogue," he says, was completed long ago, when "the nation, the so-called 'ordinary people,' fill[ed] the churches and pilgrimage sites."[13] In this way, they voted against socialism with their feet and embraced Christianity with their hearts.

Tischner sees Michnik's distinction between a good Church and a dangerous Church as but one more effort by the Left to manipulate the Church and dominate Polish society. He recognizes no legitimate right for the outsider to criticize the faith. (Not sharing Michnik's emphasis on the separation of realms, he rejects Michnik's argument that any faith that impinges on the political sphere must be the object of critical inquiry.) That Michnik criticizes the Church rather tenderly, and purely from the perspective of political implications, does not mitigate the essential transgression. And so Tischner will have none of Michnik's plea for critical self-examination on the Church's part, too. For Tischner, the Church has nothing to explain and nothing for which to apologize. It is right and others are wrong.

In contrast to other defenders of Catholic fundamentalism, Tischner writes in learned, scholarly prose. In the spirit of dialogue, Michnik agreed to write the Foreword to the English edition of Tischner's book. But Michnik's comment that Tischner is "open to dialogue with the contemporary world" seems to be mere wishful thinking.[14] For Tischner makes it quite clear that he opposes not just Marxism but virtually the entire modern liberal legacy of the Enlightenment. While he did oppose Communism in the name of human rights, Tischner, like the rest of the Church hierarchy, made it quite clear that his idea of a just world did not stop with the defense of human rights. All along he maintained his hostility to Michnik's liberal vision of a secular order in which the Church would simply be free: free but irrelevant is how Tischner viewed such an arrangement.

Georgetown University Press, 1987), p. 153. The Polish original, *Polski Kształt Dialogu,* was published in 1981.

12. Tischner, *Marxism and Christianity,* p. 154.

13. Tischner, *Marxism and Christianity,* p. 154.

14. Tischner, *Marxism and Christianity,* p. viii.

He made all this quite explicit in the postcommunist era. "Following the confrontation of Christianity with communism," Tischner wrote in *Tygodnik Powszechny* in 1990, "Christianity now faces the confrontation with liberalism." [15]

Religion and Politics

Michnik is not convinced there must be a confrontation. On the contrary, he sees Catholicism, and religion in general, as playing a very beneficial role in a liberal polity. He does not want to expel the Church from public life, but to formalize its role as a moral force alone.

Michnik accepts and even welcomes the public dissemination of the moral injunctions of religion. He feels they act as valuable limitations both on the abuse of power by leaders and on the fascination with power by citizens. His point, however—and here he sides with secular moralists from Kant to Sartre—is that moral values can be derived from reason with no less certainty than they are derived from religion. This book is about how he and his co-thinkers learned such values from the socialist and liberal traditions. Michnik is well aware that more Poles learn their ideas from religion than from secular humanism, and so he sees religion, with its notion of limitations, serving a noble political purpose. But for Michnik, the Church plays a salutary political role only when it remains separate from the political realm. Any formal establishment of religious beliefs only changes them from moral imperatives to juridical ones, thus inviting a clericalization of public life that undermines the principles of freedom and responsibility that he feels religion and liberal humanism both share. For Michnik, then, the rightful role of religion in politics is to provide moral sanction for a nondenominational, democratic, pluralist state.

Even while praising the Church's commitment to democratic rights and publicizing the ideas of its liberal wing, Michnik feared the reemergence of a fundamentalist Catholicism. Though such fears were not as acute as they became in the 1980s, as we see in his essay "Troubles," they nonetheless led Michnik to an important theoretical discussion on the roots and consequences of Catholic aspirations for power. This is his discussion of the "Julianic Church." The term is borrowed from the historian Bohdan Cywiński and is derived from

15. *Tygodnik Powszechny,* 7 April 1990.

the history of the Catholic Church during the days of Julian the Apostate in Rome. The Emperor Julian had decreed the separation of church and state just after Catholicism had been finally made the state religion by his predecessor Constantine. What was special about the "Julianic" Church was not that it was without political power, but that it had just been *removed* from power and that it sought, above all, to get its power back. According to Cywiński, the Julianic Church pretends to be in solidarity with society against state oppression only because it wants to ride a wave of discontent back to power for itself. It is not averse to collaborating with a repressive political authority so long as it can partake in exercising that power. It is a church whose moral principles mask a deep-rooted cynicism, one that wants society to identify with it but "is never fully in solidarity with society," ready to abandon the people it defends today if offered a piece of the political pie tomorrow.

"No one," writes Michnik, "has expressed our fears with such clarity and precision." The passage he quotes at length reveals all the fears of a resurgent all-embracing Church that non-Catholic and left-wing Poles have harbored for so long—perhaps never as much as in the 1990s. What can be done about such an eventuality? Michnik's answer is twofold. First, he says, it really doesn't matter if the Julianic syndrome is true. The Church is so far from political domination, he wrote in 1976, that to even worry about such a thing is to help the Communists maintain power, just as anticlerical sentiment had done since 1945. His second response is to acknowledge that the threat from the Church may be real. The only way to counteract it, he argues, is to ally with the Church. A Church that longs for power is not just the result of having tasted power in the past; it is also the "result of isolation." By their hostility toward the Church, Polish liberals forced the Church to be hostile toward them. In conditions where secular elements control everything, the secular world's constant criticism of the Church have left the Church no way to fit into a modern pluralist system even if it wanted to. By treating the Church as an enemy of modernity, the secular intelligentsia forced it to remain an enemy of modernity. The wonder for Michnik was not that there remained a strong fundamentalist current within the Polish Church, but that, despite everything, certain parts of the Church showed a modern and liberal orientation anyway.

This is where Michnik enters into *mea culpas*. They understood it better than we did, he says. We fought the Party in the name of democracy and attacked the Church in the name of modernity without realizing that we were thereby hindering the realization of democracy and modernity alike. We sabotaged democracy by joining a raid on those who were defenseless, and we harmed the cause of modernity by giving Catholics good reason to mistrust our intentions. The only way to push the Church toward democratic modernity is to take away the basis for its mistrust. To encourage the progressive evolution of the Church, the Left must show an act of faith. It must be ready to unite with the Church despite all the illiberal elements still present within it. The only way to support the Catholic liberals is to help them prove to Catholic conservatives that the Church has nothing to fear from the secular world.

It was a brave argument but also a very shaky one. His left-wing critics pointed out that uniting with the Church might just as easily strengthen the fundamentalist elements as the liberal ones. Perhaps the secular intelligentsia's gesture of goodwill would be taken as a sign of weakness rather than of friendship. If that were so, an alliance would hurt the liberal cause rather than help it.

The dispute was akin to the Western debate about détente with the Soviet Union. While Western liberals argued that close relations would undermine Soviet hardliners by depriving them of their convenient enemy, conservatives argued that détente would only embolden the hardliners by sending a signal that the West was weak. Similarly, Michnik's claim that only an alliance with the Church could undermine the fundamentalist elements within it met the objection that an alliance could just as easily strengthen those elements as weaken them. Michnik had some of these fears himself. But his entire credo pushed him the other way. Hatred and fear, he believes, breed only hatred and fear. The only way to break the vicious circle is through encounter, trust, and dialogue.

Changing Views on the Church

In 1976, Michnik called on liberal intellectuals to reach out to the Church. Just over a decade later, Michnik counseled them to maintain their distance.

His essay "Troubles," written in 1987 and included here at Michnik's request as an Afterword, marks a decisive shift in Michnik's public stance toward the Church. Feeling that the pendulum had swung too far the other way, Michnik criticizes intellectuals who, one might say, had followed his old advice too closely and had embraced the Church too intimately. Borrowing a theme from Julien

Benda's influential 1927 essay *La Trahison dès clercs*,[16] in which Benda denounces intellectuals for having betrayed critical thinking in order to serve political passions, Michnik suggests that Polish intellectuals may be guilty of a "second betrayal" by abandoning critical thought and "casting [their] lot with Catholic doctrine and the Church hierarchy." He goes so far as to say that the "Iranization" of Poland is now a distinct possibility, with the country "plunged into a provincial kind of nationalism and grovel[ing] in the chaos of ignorant tribal hatreds." No longer perceiving Church values as having a salutary effect on Polish politics, Michnik saw religion intruding on politics to such an extent that the idea of a secular state itself was in jeopardy. Liberal intellectuals, he said, had a responsibility to stop this trend.

It is not the task of this Introduction to assess the validity of Michnik's new fears. But the transformation is so dramatic that we must at least ask why. Why did Michnik feel compelled to write such a piece? What prompted fears of an "Iranian syndrome" in Poland? There are two parts to the answer: changes on the part of the Polish Church, and changes in Michnik's ideological preferences. Let us look at each of them in turn.

In the 1970s, the Polish Church coexisted rather well with the Communist authorities. Anxious for political stability, Party leader Edward Gierek sought to reverse the bad relationship between Church and state that marked the late Gomułka period and made a series of moves that considerably relaxed tensions. When Karol Wojtyła was selected as pope in 1978, the state authorities responded with a graciousness that illustrated the remarkable working relationship the two sides had attained. (Countries like the Soviet Union or Czechoslovakia would not even allow bishops to be freely named by the Vatican.) So comfortable was the Church with this new relationship that when shipyard workers on the Baltic Coast went on strike in August 1980 demanding the right to form independent trade unions, Primate Cardinal Wyszyński urged them to go back to work without having won their demands. While this was not quite the alliance between "altar and throne" that liberals always feared, it demonstrated that many in the Church had come to believe that things could best be improved by working from within. Even as the secular democratic opposition grew increasingly well disposed toward the

16. Julien Benda, *The Betrayal of the Intellectuals,* translated by Richard Aldington (Boston: Beacon Press, 1959; original translation, 1928).

Church, the Church remained skeptical, until the founding of Solidarity in 1980, of what that opposition could accomplish.

The "secular Left," following Michnik's advice, did make its leap of faith and embraced the Church after 1976. Its excited pride in the Polish pope, its unswerving support for workers marching behind religious symbols in 1980, its praise for the episcopate and willingness, even eagerness, to see the Church regain a prominent public presence all testify to the intelligentsia's readiness to disown its anticlerical past. Although liberal Catholics like Turowicz and Mazowiecki worked very closely with the opposition (Mazowiecki personally traveled to the Lenin Shipyard in Gdańsk to advise the strikers in 1980 and was chosen by Lech Wałęsa to edit the national Solidarity newsweekly), the Church as a whole largely kept its distance. Although proclaiming support for Solidarity after it was founded, the Church remained wary of the radical democratic ethos that inspired the union. In December 1980, the Episcopate's press spokesman weighed in with a denunciation of Jacek Kuroń just as the Party was also warning of the nefarious influence of such "radicals." But the Church did not attack the union per se, nor did it try to substitute itself for the union in political negotiations with the state.

The declaration of martial law in December 1981 changed the situation dramatically. Instead of being the outsider to the conflict between the Party and Solidarity, the Church now found itself actively pursued by each side. The Party sought a legitimate social authority to sanction its rule, while Solidarity, now underground, wanted the Church to throw its full weight behind the struggle for its relegalization. The Church chose to pursue a line of its own. It accepted gifts from the martial law authorities, such as permission to build more churches, train more priests, and use the state media to broadcast religious services, but it did not defend the government in return. It sought and accepted the support of Solidarity, but it refused to become in any sense a spokesman for the banned union.

In the first period after the declaration of martial law, Michnik defended the Church against those who wanted to see it more actively engaged in the struggle against the government and underplayed the evidence of a new fundamentalist turn. It was an interesting approach. To underground activists who demanded an activist Church, Michnik appeared, paradoxically, as a timid defender of a conservative Church that chose not to get directly involved in politics. In fact, Michnik's point was to preserve the principle that the Church stay separate from state politics. Having the Church lead the fight for Solidarity during martial law would only give it the authority, the credentials, and, most important, the habit to intervene in public policy disputes in the democratic Poland that would follow martial law. Consequently, although he occasionally expressed reservations about Catholic nationalism during this period, Michnik felt it more important to defend than to criticize the Church. The Church had rebuffed suggestions that it form Catholic trade unions as a substitute for the banned Solidarity and refused to sanction the formation of a Church-affiliated Christian Democratic party. Its impact on political life seemed to be mostly a moral one, just where Michnik wanted it to remain.

Michnik grew more critical when it became clear that the Church was trying not so much to avoid politics as to assert a special role for itself in politics. If it was the assertiveness of Catholics like Mazowiecki and Turowicz, he would have had no problem. But the new assertiveness came from the most conservative elements of the Polish Church, which became particularly prominent when Józef Glemp became Polish primate after Cardinal Wyszyński's death in May 1981. Glemp was poorly known not just in liberal intellectual circles but even among the Polish faithful when named by Pope John Paul II as Wyszyński's successor. But he quickly became a de facto leader of Polish aspirations when martial law was declared soon after he became primate and, as so often in the Polish past, the Roman Catholic Church found itself the only significant independent social institution tolerated by the authorities.

Under Primate Glemp, the Polish Church moved persistently in a nationalist, fundamentalist direction. Liberal oppositionists like Michnik first tried to pretend otherwise. In his July 1981 afterword to this book, Michnik notes "signs of fanaticism and intolerance" in the Church, but says only that it is still not clear how the Church will respond. In 1982 and 1983, many liberals tried to excuse as "gaffes" Glemp's comments and allusions about the unfortunate influence of "Jews, Freemasons, and Trotskyists" on the internal life of Poland and, in particular, on Solidarity.[17] They also tried to ignore the Church's 1982 beatification of Maksymilian Kolbe, the Franciscan monk who sacrificed his life for another's at Auschwitz, but who had earlier edited an extremist antidemocratic, anti-Semitic newspaper.

17. Such reactions are well described by Antoni Pawlak in "Feralna Data," *PWA*, no. 208, 6 October 1989, Warsaw. This is a good, brief account of illiberal Church politics in the 1980s and of one liberal's growing opposition to it.

By 1984, when Primate Glemp wrote and signed an introduction to a new edition of Roman Dmowski's 1927 pamphlet, *Church, Nation, and State,* one could no longer have any doubts regarding Glemp's political sympathies: they lay with Dmowski's *Endecja* political tendency, the major nationalist party in the interwar period known for its illiberal and authoritarian politics, support for a strong leader, advocacy of Catholicism as a state religion, and violent anti-Semitism. The act of openly identifying himself with the program of one particular political tendency, and an illiberal one at that, was a sign that Glemp's Church was determined to involve itself directly in the struggle for determining the nature of the postcommunist political future, a struggle that, as everyone in Poland understood, was already well underway in the mid–1980s.

Glemp's political views were most plainly made clear in a leaked internal document from 1988 that was widely discussed in the secular opposition press. The primate here came out explicitly against the notions of pluralism and a secular state. State institutions, he wrote, must embody the "character and aspirations" of the nation. In a Catholic nation like Poland, "neutral" institutions are out of place because they are not "in tune with the national mood." Glemp finds even the notion of tolerance objectionable. By presenting Catholicism "as only one of many possible world-views," the idea of tolerance "treats the Church as a marginal phenomenon," a status that Glemp's Church was decidedly going to avoid. Moreover, some things simply ought not be tolerated—atheism, for example, which is "abnormal" and "based on falsehood." The Church, wrote Primate Glemp, "cannot support" the right of nonbelievers organizing their own institutions.[18]

Glemp pursued the campaign against liberal values by finding and exploiting issues in which he knew liberals would be in agreement with the Communists and thus feel unable, in conditions of united struggle against the Communists, to defend their own principles. In 1984 the Church waged a major battle with the government over the right to hang crosses in public schools and began its campaign to outlaw abortion. It has pushed strongly for the legal adoption of Church guidelines on both issues ever since. (In 1988, for example, the Church forced the withdrawal of a sex education textbook from the public schools even though a half million copies had

---

18. Prymas Polski, Józef Glemp, "Uwagi o projekcie dokumentu Prymasowskiej Rady Społecznej," 6 June 1988, published in *Aneks* (London), no. 53, 1989.

already been printed.) Michnik discussed Church involvement in education extensively in his book. While defending the Church's right to establish parochial schools for those who choose a religious education, he was adamant about the need for general public education to be free from sectarian influence. Ever sensitive to the rights of minorities, which as a nonbeliever of Jewish origin included him too, Michnik felt this was especially important in Catholic countries such as Poland. But he felt unable to press the issue in the mid–1980s when to do so would place him on the side of the Communists. It was the same with the abortion issue. The liberal Left was on the defensive, and losing ground.

The dilemma Michnik and others first faced in this dispute in the mid–1980s well illustrates the enormous obstacles to preserving liberal principles in much of postcommunist Eastern Europe. The problem is that modern secular rules, such as nondenominational education and the separation between church and state, were fully instituted in Poland only by Communism. Consequently, the Church has been able to present its campaign against liberalism as an ongoing part of the struggle against communism. The liberals' goal has been to end Communist rule without demolishing the modern principles communism happened to be the one to introduce. In his book, Michnik distinguishes between the "political atheism" of the Bolsheviks, which seeks to eradicate religion and subordinate all individuals to the state, and the "secularization" championed by liberals, which he defines as "complete separation of church from state, complete separation of state from church, and complete civil rights for all." As Glemp's campaign made clear, however, the Church did not accept the validity of this distinction.

The assassination by undercover security police of pro- Solidarity priest Jerzy Popiełuszko in October 1984 gave a further boost to the Church's campaign. Having a priest as its one martyr seemed to tie the Solidarity ethos to the Church more closely than ever. (That Glemp had previously censured Popiełuszko for his activism was conveniently ignored.) As the only space in Poland where Solidarity banners could be freely displayed, churches sometimes seemed to resemble movement headquarters—indeed, St. Brygida Church served as Lech Wałęsa's unofficial headquarters in Gdańsk. The Church was pursuing an activist policy on all fronts and was scoring success after success. By the mid–1980s, parish priests, with regular access to public school records, were checking attendance in afterschool religious education classes on the basis of public school class rosters.[19] Peer pressure on the few who did not attend is not hard to imagine.

More and more, it looked like the dialogue Michnik had proposed was in danger of becoming a rout. In 1976 he had argued that by moving toward the Church, the Church would move toward the liberals. By 1987 he saw that the movement had been mostly the other way, just as his critics had argued it would. Michnik saw few intellectuals resisting the trend. Even his two closest radical comrades from the 1960s, Jacek Kuroń and Jan Lityński, either became Catholics or tried very hard to do so.[20]

"Troubles" is Michnik's response to this new situation. It focuses on the responsibility of intellectuals, not the clergy. Michnik has no quarrel with intellectuals embracing God; more than once he has said he envies those who are able to do so. What disturbs him about recent developments, however, is that intellectuals seem to be embracing the Church for political reasons, either because they genuinely feel political life ought to be organized around Catholic standards, or because they want to use the Church to advance other political causes. For Michnik, either option constitutes a betrayal of the intellectual's ethos. Any kind of political conversion is a betrayal. What is necessary is the separation of the realms of religion and politics, not their conflation. Through a brilliant excursion into the credos of Stefan Wyszyński and Witold Gombrowicz, Michnik shows that even these two diametrically opposed thinkers hold this view. The intellectual seeking politics from the Church betrays not just the separate missions of church and politics but his own calling as an intellectual. The ethos of the intellectual is reason, skepticism, and irony, while that of the cleric is faith, conviction, and certainty. The intellectual who puts his reason at the service of the Church betrays his calling not because the Church is hostile to reason, but simply because the Church is based on principles other than reason.

Michnik's complex argument here is similar to that of the prerevolutionary Russian philosopher Nikolai Berdyaev.[21] Just as Ber-

19. Janusz Mucha, "The Status of Unbelievers as a Group in Polish Society," in *Journal of the Anthropological Society of Oxford* 20:3 (1989).

20. See the discussion by Jacek Kuroń, *Wiara i Wina* [Faith and Guilt] (Warsaw: Nowa, 1989), in the chapter titled "Lewica—Prawica. Bog" [Left—Right. God], as well as his earlier "Zło które czynię" [The Evil that I Commit], in *Krytyka* (Warsaw), no. 12, 1981; and Jan Lityński, "My z marca" [The March Generation], in *Karta* (Warsaw), no. 5, 1988.

21. Nikolai Berdyaev, "Philosophic Truth and the Moral Truth of the Intelligentsia," in *Landmarks* (New York: Karz Howard, 1977; original, 1909), pp. 3–22.

dyaev attacked the Bolsheviks not for being antireligious but for being *too* religious in their attitudes to politics—that is, for embracing faith precisely in the sphere of history and politics where it did not apply—so Michnik rebukes Polish intellectuals for failing to respect the rules of the autonomous sphere of politics. Unlike Berdyaev, Michnik sees the political realm as ultimately the more important one. And that is why he counsels intellectuals to move away from the Church. For he feels that the rational, modern, Enlightenment values of the intellectuals cannot survive in the Church since they are foreign to its very mission. Given the many enemies the nation has had to face, the Polish Church, he says, probably *"had* to be . . . somewhat parochial and somewhat obscurantist." But while such values may have helped national survival, they are not conducive to democracy or modernity. That is why Polish culture needs not just Wyszyński but Gombrowicz, not just the cleric but the intellectual, not just the priest but the jester. It needs the savvy critic who can break down all orthodoxies, and thus it needs the intellectual who will stay apart from the Church.

By the late 1980s, Michnik had changed a great deal since *The Church and the Left.* He became increasingly critical of the Roman Catholic Church and notably less enthusiastic about participatory democracy. When I asked him about these changes in the summer of 1990, he replied that he did not think he had changed much at all.

His reply makes sense, I think, only if we understand Michnik's overriding concern to be the introduction into Poland of liberal democratic values and institutions. In the 1970s he was convinced—and who in Eastern Europe was not?—that the main obstacle was Communist rule. If the Church could be an ally in the fight against the Communists, so much the better for democracy. His earlier enthusiasm for popular participation should probably be understood the same way. Decades of Party control over social life had disaccustomed people from taking responsibility for their lives. In the eyes of Michnik and other radical opposition theorists in the 1970s, Poland was living through a spiritual malaise. The political situation, they felt, could change only if people became more active themselves, on their own, apart from Party control, in any way they felt comfortable. Michnik's focus on reconstituting an autonomous civil society, an idea so central not only to KOR in the 1970s but to Solidarity in 1980, was aimed at mobilizing the citizenry that could supplant the Communists and run the country democratically when there was finally a chance to do so. Like an alliance with the Church, popular participation in politics appeared to be an important part of the struggle against the Communists for democracy.

Michnik's changes, and continuities, stem from his recent beliefs that neither the Church nor widespread popular participation in politics can any longer help the cause of liberal democracy in Poland. The basis for his change of heart on the Church has already been outlined. As for participation, Michnik revised his views, paradoxically, at the moment they seemed to come to fruition. This is one of the little-known aspects of the transformation of the 1980s: the way the old liberal leftists abandoned their uncritical support for unsupervised civic initiatives and became proponents of democracy run by elites. Tracing the evolution of this phenomenon is beyond the scope of this Introduction, but insofar as Michnik in the 1990s cannot be understood apart from this change, a few words are in order.

Jacek Kuroń was the first in Michnik's milieu to express reservations about workers' activism when he accused Solidarity activists of being uninterested in fair government and thereby jeopardizing the democratic evolution of the country.[22] In 1985 Michnik chimed in with one of the most stinging indictments of grassroots revolutionary activism ever written by an ostensible supporter. Many worker activists in 1980–81, Michnik now charges, were irrational hotheads, hostile to common sense, contemptuous of the notion of compromise, and incapable of recognizing the "limits and realities" of the real world. Modeling themselves after a "sultanic" Lech Wałęsa, they were blinded by the ambition to become local despots.[23] They are, in a word, steeped in illiberalism. The characteristics he ascribes to these workers—"new radicals," he condescendingly calls them, as opposed to veteran ones like himself—are, for Michnik, but the building blocks of a new totalitarianism.

The validity of Michnik's evaluation is not important here; a more positive assessment of rank-and-file activism is certainly possible. Indeed, Michnik himself usually speaks positively about the first Solidarity experience as a whole. The point is that Michnik's attitude toward participation changed noticeably in the 1980s, as he no longer believed that widespread participation would favor a liberal outcome. The best guarantee for such an outcome, he now felt, would be a reform process led by liberally minded elites on both sides. It is in this direction that Michnik now worked—with consid-

22. Jacek Kuroń, "Nie do druku" [Not for Print], in *Polityka i odpowiedzialność* (London: Aneks, 1984). These remarks came in a 1981 interview Kuroń considered so controversial that he allowed publication only after the declaration of martial law.

23. Adam Michnik, *Takie czasy* [Such Times] (London: Aneks, 1985), p. 43.

erable success. The Round Table negotiations of 1989, in which Michnik played a central role, produced a series of agreements between government leaders and Solidarity officials, with little rank-and-file input, that led, without bloodshed, to the ending of Communist rule.

Michnik's attitude toward capitalism also changed during the 1980s, though this of course was a regionwide phenomenon, reflecting the consensus that the old state socialist system, however reformed, could not bring about the modernization Eastern Europe desperately needed. His new economic views also dovetailed nicely with his new political views, as Michnik saw in marketization a way to institutionalize limited civic autonomy without dangerously empowering too many potentially irresponsible people. In politics and in economics, Michnik had moved from a position of liberal communitarianism to one of liberalism alone.

•   •

Despite the many changes in his views, and the many changes in the times, Michnik ends "Troubles" the same way he ends his book: with a plea for dialogue. People should maintain a healthy skepticism about their professed solutions, never believe they alone have the answer, always be ready to hear the truth expressed by the other. They must, in other words, recognize limits—precisely the Christian idea Michnik is most attached to.

These are not very popular views in contemporary Poland. Indeed, these are not easy times for liberals in Eastern Europe. With Communism overthrown, and with its opponents having always said how much better things would be when that happened, people want more than just "dialogue" as their reward. Michnik, like other liberals, does not want to promise more: for them, what is central is that people are free to articulate their preferences, not guaranteed to have them satisfied. But the postcommunist period is a democratic period, and people are more likely to vote for someone who promises them something than for someone who does not. It is hardly surprising, therefore, that Michnik's candidate, Tadeusz Mazowiecki, lost easily to Lech Wałęsa in the presidential election of December 1990. Wałęsa was ready to offer substitute satisfactions for the pain that market transition exacted. He flirted with nationalist rhetoric, proclaimed his close ties to the Church, promised greater worker participation in reform, and said that capitalism under his leadership would work better because it would not rely on the former elites he accused Mazowiecki of holding onto. In Western terms, Wałęsa's program included both "Left" and "Right" elements; in the Polish debate, which to a large extent remains mired in the liberal versus nationalist divide of the past, Wałęsa leaned clearly to the nationalist end of the spectrum. (Upon taking office, however, he adopted most of the liberal economic program.)

The Church also took advantage of the crisis of postcommunism to push through some antiliberal measures. It pressured Prime Minister Mazowiecki's first noncommunist government to concede to Church requests for reintroduction of Catholic education classes into public schools and for severe administrative restrictions on abortion rights. As the Church preferred, there was no parliamentary vote and no public discussion. (Anti-abortion legislation as a whole was put before parliament only later.) Church pressure reached a new high point in the spring of 1991. As liberal voices spoke about the need to protect minorities, the Church requested "protection" for majorities. Primate Glemp proposed that the provision on the separation of church from state be stricken from the Constitution, since the majority of the population was Catholic. A Catholic Vice-Minister of Health announced he could not sanction the use of condoms even as a protection against AIDS, since only "deviants" contracted the disease. (When the minister was dismissed, Glemp compared the disciplinary action to the Stalinist terror.) The pope, meanwhile, used his visit in June 1991 to urge Poles to resist the European path of secular, consumerist liberalism.

One way the Church has tried to justify its campaign is to argue that it was Catholicism, not the democratic opposition, that brought Communism down. Reverend Tischner has played a central role in articulating this view. Solidarity, he wrote, succeeded not because of its democratic ethos but because of its Christian ethos. Indeed, he argues that *only* Christianity could topple Communism, since it alone "knows that the human soul is a Christian soul."[24] Whereas Michnik argues that what is evil about communism is its totalitarian character, Tischner holds that communism is "something more than totalitarianism": it is "a version of European neopaganism." Catholicism must now challenge liberalism, Tischner feels, because the final victory over communism will come only when Christian faith is "substituted" for communist faith, and not, as Michnik would have it, when questions of faith are placed outside of politics altogether.

24. Reverend Józef Tischner, "Homo Sovieticus," in *Tygodnik Powszechny,* 24 June 1990. Other quotes in this paragraph are from the same article.

In these new conditions, Michnik has felt more isolated than ever. With his misgivings about nationalism and clericalism, he is again accused of being "out of touch" with the people. His old identification with the Left is used by nationalist critics to argue that he is a "crypto-communist," just at the moment, ironically, when he has abandoned his old communitarian ideas. Yet his firm defense of liberal principles keeps him on the Left in an era when political parties, contending for votes, are ready to appeal to nationalist and clerical sentiments. The dividing line between the Right and the Left in the 1990s is between nationalism and a liberal internationalism more than between capitalism and socialism. The new Right's fears are that market reform will endanger Polish sovereignty, not that it will engender inequalities. It values worker participation for its ability to nullify the influence of "aliens" (Communists, Jews, foreigners), not its capacity to teach self-government. Michnik's co-thinkers have described themselves as being not to the left of center but to the "west" of center, but in the internal debate of the 1990s, that puts them on the Left anyway. Michnik himself has the sense that his position no longer fits into any viable political tendency. "For people like me," he told an interviewer in May 1991, "the time for playing politics has passed."[25]

Besides the liberal politics, what from the book remains current for Michnik? First, there is the centrality of moral values in politics and a consequent respect for religion. When asked in 1990 what he felt were the most important principles in politics, he replied, "Same as always: the Ten Commandments, the principles of the Sermon on the Mount."[26] But perhaps most of all what remains is his commitment to dialogue. Indeed, part of the reason he is still attacked as a "leftist" is that he remains wary of any notion of absolute truth, and this relativism clashes with a perceived need for a new unifying theme in postcommunist society. For Michnik it is the search for a more just world that is still most important, and for that search dialogue remains the indispensable tool.

Michnik concludes his book with a poem by Zbigniew Herbert urging intellectuals to challenge the injustice around them: "You have little time you must give testimony." He concludes "Troubles" with a

25. "Gra w Trzy Karty," an interview with Adam Michnik conducted by Janina Paradowska, in *Polityka,* 1 June 1991, p. 3. English translation, by me, in *Telos,* no. 89 (Fall 1991): 95–101.

26. "Nie judzić" [Don't Provoke], interview with Adam Michnik conducted by Anna Wrzalińska, in *Reporter* (Warsaw), November 1990.

line from that same poem counseling restraint: ". . . attain the good you will not attain." That, Michnik told me, is an admonition that one must pursue the quest for a just world while recognizing simultaneously that the goal can never be achieved. The process always continues, the dialogue never ebbs. This lingering thought of his stands as a fitting final introduction to his book.

PART ONE

THE CHURCH IN THE POSTWAR PERIOD

TRANSLATOR'S NOTE

Writing in a context where "Left" automatically conveyed association with the policies of the communist parties ruling Eastern Europe, Michnik is careful to present his own view of what he feels the Left represents. He criticizes the standard leftist view equating religion with dangerous superstition by recounting the lives of two Polish Catholics closely allied with democratic leftist politics. He also mentions here two main opposing tendencies within postwar Polish Catholicism: PAX, created in 1945 and aligned closely with the Communist authorities, and Znak, formed in the more open atmosphere after 1956 and expressing liberal views that Michnik is most sympathetic to. Between these two tendencies stands the official Roman Catholic hierarchy represented by the episcopate and Cardinal Stefan Wyszyński, the Polish primate from 1948 until his death in 1981. Michnik treats only the hierarchy and Znak as legitimate representatives of Polish Catholicism.

THE LEFT AND THE CHURCH

In this book I will be using the concept of the "secular Left." Because of the imprecision of the term, I will explain how I understand it by referring to four dates in modern Polish history: 1936, 1946, 1956, and 1966—each date separated from the next by one decade.

It is rather easy to define the Left of 1936. Its essential features were antifascism, support for a planned economy and for agricultural reform, and the demand for the separation of church and state. The Polish Left at the time resembled its classic Western European prototype, just as did the Polish Right. Ten years later, however, the picture was significantly more complicated.

In line with official historiography, we are accustomed to identifying the Left of 1946 with support for the "new reality" and for the new government installed by the Red Army. This is also how many people at the time viewed the matter, particularly among intellectual circles inside Poland. Not only did the ideologues of the Polish Workers' Party (PPR) such as Jerzy Borejsza, Władysław Bieńkowski, and Stefan Żółkiewski always appeal to the "ideals of the Left," but so did those leaders of the "official" Polish Socialist Party (PPS) who were in favor of collaboration with the Communists, such as Julian Hochfeld, Oskar Lange, and Adam Rapacki. The majority of the prewar PPS leadership, however—people such as Kazimierz Pużak, Antoni Zdanowski, Zygmunt Zaremba, Józef Dzięgelewski, Adam Ciołkosz, and Zygmunt Żuławski—came out in opposition to the "new reality," as did several prominent intellectuals of the Left, such as Maria Dąbrowska, Jan Nepomucen Miller, and Maria and Stanisław Ossowski. There was now a real division within the traditional Left. While the journal *Kuźnica* and its editor Żółkiewski emphasized the PPR's "progressive" program of social reforms, moderate socialist leaders Maria Dąbrowska and Zygmunt Żuławski stressed the totalitarian and obscurantist methods of the reformers. This division within the Left deserves to be kept in mind, for too many writers lightheartedly equate the ruling "Progressive System" with the political programs of the entire Left. As we shall see, however, not all left-wing programs entail acquiescence to lies and tyranny.

Ten years later came 1956, the year of the Polish October. The Left now defined itself through a double negation: it opposed the conservative and reactionary forces inside the Party, in particular the so-called "Natolin faction," and also opposed the traditional Right, represented above all by the Roman Catholic Church. The left-wing weekly *Po prostu,* for example, attacked Stalinists and Catholic religious instructors alike. Leszek Kołakowski, the chief theorist of this "October Left," who was accused by the Party leadership of "oppositionism," "revisionism," and other related heresies, was in fact a close associate of *Argumenty* as well, the weekly organ of the Society of Atheists and Freethinkers that waged a continual battle against religion and the Church. The revisionists were largely made up of ex-Stalinists rebelling against Party orthodoxy. In the excitement of October, they began to establish contacts with the anti-Stalinist Left, with people like Dąbrowska and the Ossowskis. The secular Left had two enemies: the Central Committee of the PUWP (Polish United Workers' Party) and the Catholic Church. The unfortunate consequences of this state of affairs became clear only after another ten years had passed.

The year 1966 was marked by a sharp conflict between the PUWP leadership and the Roman Catholic episcopate. The revisionists, together with the group of radical youth gathered around the program of Jacek Kuroń and Karol Modzelewski, stood and watched the most serious political conflict in Poland since the dissolution of *Po prostu* in 1957—and none of them spoke out. People of unassailable honesty and courage, they nonetheless thought it both natural and appropriate to read and listen, without protest, to the barrage of lies and absurdities hurled by Party propaganda. There was Leszek Kołakowski and Włodzimierz Brus, Maria Ossowska and Antoni Słonimski, but not one of these moral leaders of the secular Left's intelligentsia spoke out publicly against the scandalous propaganda campaign directed at the bishops, who were ludicrously accused of betraying national interests. The position of these students and intellectuals toward the conflict between the Church and the Party was best summed up in the amusing *bon mot* of one of their leading representatives: "At last each side has finally found a fully worthy opponent."

At the time, Leszek Kołakowski took the same position: equal hostility to the Church and the Party. In a sermon in late 1965, Cardinal Stefan Wyszyński favorably cited Kołakowski's essay, "Jesus Christ: Prophet and Reformer." This essay, together with Wyszyński's friendly commentary, might have provided a basis for the Church and secular intelligentsia to establish some common ground. Yet that was not to be, as Kołakowski publicly distanced himself from the Cardinal's interpretation of his article. During the entire conflict over the Polish episcopate's pastoral letter to the German bishops,[1] Kołakowski maintained his silence. He broke it only in October 1966, when he delivered his celebrated lecture to the students of Warsaw University on the tenth anniversary of the Polish October. In this brilliant and perceptive talk, Kołakowski drew a balance of the last decade of Party rule. His assessment was so critical and his formulations so radical that he was expelled from the Party as a result. Yet in this entire insightful, penetrating presentation, Kołakowski said not one word about Party policy toward religion and the Church. The secular Left understood the need to fight for the extension of democratic rights, but it did not see the Church as an ally in this fight.

And so, after another decade has passed, I pose the question again: what is the Left today, in 1976? I am not able to answer this question unequivocally. In recent years, as a result of the deep crisis in Communist ideology, national-chauvinist tendencies have grown considerably, in government circles as well as within the opposition. Both sides are divided. Here, I am more interested in the divisions within the opposition. Following a distinction developed by a friend of mine, I will say that the opposition consists of two groups: those who believe in the superiority of the capitalist system and those who support the idea of democratic socialism. I am simplifying things, of course, but still, it is this second group that I identify with the Left. This Left champions the ideas of freedom and tolerance, of individual sovereignty and the emancipation of labor, of a just distribution of income and the right of everyone to an equal start in life. It fights against national-chauvinism, obscurantism, xenophobia, lawlessness, and social injustice. The program of this Left is the program of antitotalitarian socialism.

1. Discussed in chapter 4.—TRANS.

From the very beginning, relations between the Church and the socialist movement were extremely poor and marked by mutual animosity. Both sides made accusations that are difficult to evaluate clearly so many years later. For the Church, the socialist program was a violation of the principles of God's natural law, and thus a harbinger of spiritual nihilism. In hindsight it would appear that such accusations, so derided by socialist writers, were not so completely absurd. They deserve careful reconsideration even today. According to the socialists, meanwhile, the Church was hostile to social reform, maintained close ties to the earthly oligarchy, sought to dominate and control all spheres of secular life, and was intolerant of both non-Catholics and nonbelievers. As a result of their negative assessment of the political role of the Church, the socialists became hostile to religion as such and adopted atheism as their programmatic credo. Religion was understood, by Marx for example, as an ideological justification for existing conditions and was interpreted exclusively within the categories of false consciousness. "Religion," wrote Marx, "is the sigh of the oppressed creature, the heart of a heartless world, as it is the spirit of spiritless conditions. It is the opium of the people." Marx postulated the "positive abolition of religion." He wrote: "The criticism of religion ends with the doctrine that man is the highest being for man, hence with the categorical imperative to overthrow all conditions in which man is a degraded, enslaved, neglected, contemptible being." [2]

Marx's atheism and anthropocentrism were directed against the specific social functions which religion fulfilled, the functions to which it had been reduced over the course of centuries. But let me be clear: I am not saying that there is room for a God, Christian or otherwise, within the edifice of Marx's or Engels' historical philosophy. My point is that Marx's unshakable atheism stems not so much from antipathy to the very idea of transcendence as from his opposition to the conservative social doctrines of the Church of his time.

In Poland the process was similar. Forgoing erudite historical exposition, let me instead call on the testimony of Jerzy Zawieyski, who can be suspected neither of being a Communist nor of having an obsessive hatred of religion or the Church:

What did Catholicism and the Church mean for us, former socialists and believers, in the 1920s? I must painfully admit that the Church itself, in the

2. Karl Marx, "Toward the Critique of Hegel's Philosophy of Right: Introduction," in *Writings of the Young Marx on Philosophy and Society,* translated and edited by Loyd Easton and Kurt Guddat (New York: Doubleday, 1967), pp. 250, 257–58.

person of its officials and its clergy, constituted for us the greatest obstacle on the road to Catholicism and faith. Catholicism seemed to us to be identical with anti-Semitism, fascism, obscurantism, fanaticism, and all that was antiprogressive and anticultural. The priest-deputies in the Sejm [the Polish parliament] waged their battles with ugly words and ugly methods, and the vicious and odious anti-Semitic activities of Father Trzeciak outraged all of us. The program of the so-called "all-Polish youth" adopted the telltale slogan of "God and Fatherland," and its program was reactionary, aggressive, and oozing with hatred. The fighting in universities and youth organizations brought nothing but dishonor to young Catholics, for it was these circles that spawned the punks with razor blades and brass knuckles.

Some Catholics actively assisted the nationalist and even fascist movements. They saw it as part of their continual struggle against "the secular enemy," an imaginary enemy that did not want this battle and sometimes didn't even fight it.

For example, look at the attitude of the clergy to "Wici," the movement of rural youth, at the people's university near Przeworsk. As an independent, radical peasant organization, Wici refused to subordinate itself to the Church hierarchy. In response, the clergy fought Wici every way it possibly could. With very few exceptions, Wici found its cultural and educational activities sabotaged every step of the way by the hostility of the local clergy.[3]

This passage can stand as a partial answer to the question of why the secular Left was so negatively disposed toward the Roman Catholic Church. But here is another passage:

Any, even the most refined and best-intentioned defense or justification of the idea of God is a justification of reaction. . . . The idea of God *always* put to sleep and blunted the "social feelings," replacing the living by the dead, being *always* the idea of slavery (the worst, hopeless slavery).[4]

The author of these words was Lenin. Elsewhere the same author wrote the following:

Marxism has always regarded all modern religions and churches, in each and every religious organization, as instruments of bourgeois reaction that serve to defend exploitation and to befuddle the working class.[5]

3. Jerzy Zawieyski, *Droga katechumena* [A Catechist's Road] (Kraków: Biblioteka Więzi), p. 35.

4. V. I. Lenin, "Letter to Maxim Gorky" (November 1913), in vol. 35 of *The Collected Works* (Moscow: Progress Publishers, 1966), pp. 128–29.

5. V. I. Lenin, "The Attitude of the Workers' Party to Religion" (May 1909), in vol. 15 of *The Collected Works,* p. 403.

These two passages of Lenin can stand as a partial answer to the question of why the Christian churches were so negatively disposed toward secular socialism.

The conflict between the secular Left and the Roman Catholic Church in Poland was, in the interwar years, a total conflict. Perhaps no one personifies the resulting situation better than Henryk Dembiński. A prominent activist of the Catholic "Rebirth" group, from Stefan Batory University in Vilnius, Dembiński was the intellectual and political hope of his generation. Sent on a government stipend to Rome and the Holy See, Dembiński broke with the Catholic movement and soon became a leading spokesman of the Left. And yet it is clear from many of his writings that despite vehement attacks on the clergy and on the scandalous church connections of the Endek[6] paramilitary cutthroats, Dembiński never stopped being a believing Christian. Official Communist historiography somehow always misses this point. Sometimes the PAX press mentions it, suggesting that if Dembiński had survived the war he would have become a PAX activist like Bolesław Piasecki. But this is absurd, as is clear from the following passage, for no one who wrote such words could ever have ended up in PAX:

A key part of the struggle for democracy is the struggle for the political rights of the people, for the equal chance, at least formally, of everyone to rise to a position of power. When not only the legislative branches but the entire body of administrative and judicial organs of power, on all levels, will be based on direct election, *then* we can say we have the necessary prerequisites of democracy.

Democracy in its essence, however, cannot be reduced to the principle of election to all levels of government. Not even a complete packet of political rights, including the right to vote for all important positions, can guarantee that the ballot box will even partially convey the will of the people to the centers of power. Elections can truthfully convey the views . . . of even the most privileged social groups only when political thought can be formed in a climate of freedom.

It is thus necessary to guarantee the inviolability of the individual, of his privacy, correspondence, and living quarters. Freedom of association and freedom of speech must also be guaranteed, as must freedom of the press and scientific and academic freedom. Only then will the masses be in a posi-

---

6. "Endek"—pertaining to the National Democrats, the major right-wing, nationalist, anti-Semitic political party of the interwar period in Poland.—TRANS.

tion to fully understand their own interests, able to recognize the ideology and choose the representation that best meets their needs.

A democracy that gives people political rights without giving them civic rights is not a democracy at all. For if you blind, gag, and plug up someone's ears, and then have some official (uniformed or not) lead that person to the ballot box, the resulting vote will belong not to the one who cast it but to those who have usurped his power.

In order to elect the right representatives and adequately monitor their activities, the citizen must have not only basic democratic rights but also the right to look inside at the functioning of the state apparatus. . . . As far as the governed are concerned, the workings of state should be as visible as the interior of a glass house. The less information about the expenditures of public officials, the less democracy there is. When budget figures are classified, government officials shrouded in secrecy, and judicial and administrative affairs kept under wraps, democracy is in jeopardy. When secrecy grows, democracy declines.[7]

Henryk Dembiński's road illustrates not only his own drama but also the drama of Polish Catholicism and the Polish Left. This resolute antifascist, advocate of deep social reform and enemy of Endek gangs and brass knuckles, could find no support whatsoever in the Catholic circles of his time. Yet the Left, for its part, was neither willing nor able to fully accept this original and complex personality in all his richness. Dembiński was able to become a spokesman of the Left only at the cost of intellectual self-mutilation, by stripping his political thought of its religious sensibility and its religious zeal. Impoverished by the loss of such a crucial dimension of his character, namely the belief in God, Dembiński finally became an accepted man of the Left. He could still speak the truths and the values of the Scriptures, but he could no longer call them "scriptural." He could demand just social reforms, but he could not appeal explicitly to the Christian ideal of justice in interpersonal relations. The Left had thereby gained a talented political writer but lost the insights of a profound thinker concerned with the weighty problems of human existence.

Yet there was no third road for Dembiński. There was no intellectual formation at that time which could unite the social program of the Left with Christianity. At most, one could be a leftist publicly and a Catholic privately. The reverse, however, was very rare indeed.

7. Henryk Dembiński, *Wybór Pism* [Selected Writings] (Warsaw: Książka i Wiedza, 1964), p. 138.

It is against this background that there appears the "exceptional figure" of Father Jan Zieja. Let us listen again to the testimony of Jerzy Zawieyski:

This priest was an exception. I remember him at one of the Wici conferences. He spoke simply, differently than the other priests, and seemed to fundamentally grasp the situation at hand. He spoke of the Gospel, of the spirit of justice of the Sermon on the Mount. He was, I learned, a poor man from Polesia. His name was Zieja.[8]

Father François Six has said that the meeting ground for French Catholics and nonbelievers was the antifascist Resistance.[9] In Poland during the Nazi occupation, a group of young socialists tried to organize a similar meeting place. This group was gathered around the underground journal, *Płomienie* [Flames]. Its ideological leader was Jan Strzelecki. The significance of Strzelecki's writings on the need for dialogue between Christianity and the Left cannot be overestimated. Recalling the years of the Occupation, Strzelecki wrote:

If "Christian compassion is . . . an unrelenting crusade against indifference and hatred" (Mounier), then everything that was the living embodiment of that compassion, such as the Christian injunction to love thy neighbor, seemed to us during those years to be one of the heroic dimensions of humanity, one of the values which endowed even this anti-human period with an uncommon splendor. This compassion was one of the moral forces leading people to come to the assistance of others, to risk death rather than refuse to help. And every system of ethics which considered this choice to be the only right one, which dignified this choice through appeal to a specific worldview, we felt to be an ethical system that the world desperately needed. If people did what they ought to do, assisting those in need, it did not occur to us to try to shake the foundations of their faith. If they called "God" that principle which led them to believe that the fate of the oppressed is a collective responsibility, then we saw their God as a symbol of humanity, a symbol of that inner compulsion which drives one human being to help another even if it means challenging death in the process.[10]

8. Zawieyski, *Droga katechumena*, pp. 37–38.
9. X. Jean François Six, *Od "Syllabusa" do dialogu* [From Syllabus to Dialogue] (Warsaw, 1972), p. 73.
10. Jan Strzelecki, "Próby świadectwa" [Attempts at Testimony], in *Kontynuacje (2)* (Warsaw: PIW, 1974), p. 45.

Pondering the ethics of Christianity, Strzelecki wrote:

During the war, we saw Christian ethics as one of the forces that gave people the strength to resist. It helped them resist the rules and the orders of all those earthly substitutes for God, those contemporary Leviathans which, in return for obedience, offer people the consolation of feeling themselves part of a community, the consolation of jettisoning relativistic individualism. Christianity stood as a counterpoint to the self-admiration of party, state, and nation, as well as to the ethics of the militaristic collectives which presented their Ten Commandments in a language of mysticism and gunfire. Christian ethics taught responsibility for individual life. I am speaking about an ethics that places the value of salvation above all other earthly values: above group recognition, the gratitude of the Führer, the fear of death or of being disdained by others. I am speaking of an ethics that puts brotherhood in God (that is, in absolute values) above the brotherhood of the tribe or the gun.

Christian heroism was not a common occurrence. Yet it pervaded the atmosphere all the same, like a residue of bygone centuries, with force enough to draw people away from compliance with criminality, away from despondency and isolation. This was a seductive model. . . . It challenged people to reach the sublime in a humble way, giving them a power that the powers of hell could not destroy. And thus it was attractive to socialists, too. We respected its underlying foundation, considering it somewhat similar to our own. And such an attitude continues to this day. That is why we shrug our shoulders when someone mistakes our respect for religion as collusion with fideism. We are not talking about respect for "religion in general." We are saying that we share with Christianity a belief in human dignity, something we elevate high above the poisonous charm of militaristic communities.[11]

This understanding of Christianity and of Christians led Strzelecki to abandon atheism and repudiate an antireligious orientation. In his 1946 programmatic essay, "On Socialist Humanism," Strzelecki advanced a position that would cause numerous polemical attacks. He would be accused of "revisionism," "abstract humanism," "social-democratic tendencies," etc. Strzelecki wrote:

In art, the point is not to substitute one esthetic theory for another, or to bring about a situation where only one theory is the subject of university lectures and café conversation. Instead, the point is for art to be more like everyday life and for life to be more like art, for life to find in art its shape and form. In the same way, our point is not to replace Catholicism with some sort of

11. Strzelecki, "Próby świadectwa," pp. 46–47.

state cult like Robespierre's cult of reason, but rather to make it possible that religious life, too, in its various forms and communities, might attain depth and fulfillment.[12]

Unfortunately, Strzelecki's program was left hanging in the void. Neither Catholic circles nor the Left took up its proposals. Existing attitudes merely persisted, attitudes which, in a different time, Strzelecki referred to as "black" or "red" fundamentalism. Neither ideological nor philosophical dialogue was on the agenda. There was only a sharp political conflict between a rather conservative Roman Catholic Church and a totalitarian government championing radical and progressive slogans.

Although not denying the need for social reforms, the Church rigidly defended its own possessions. The episcopate consistently attacked all measures of the new government leading to the secularization of public life, repeatedly criticizing the introduction of civil weddings and the right of divorce. The anti-Church and antireligious policies of the government together with the episcopate's rejection of the separation of church and state led to the emergence of a new kind of political division: one based on religion. Of course it was not as simple and mechanical as that. Many people who were not part of the Roman Catholic Church also rejected the new government; let us mention once again the leaders of the PPS, and the circle of intellectuals grouped around Stanisław Stempowski, Maria Dąbrowska, Maria and Stanisław Ossowski. There were also Catholics who accepted the new order and Communist party power. Calling itself the "Catholic Left," this group initially gathered around the journal *Dziś i jutro* (Today and Tomorrow), and later became known as PAX. Although it appears paradoxical, the leaders of this group, such as Bolesław Piasecki, were, prior to 1945, the leaders of an extreme right-wing tendency organized along fascist lines, known as the National-Radical Camp, or Falange. Clearly, support for totalitarian statism came far more easily to Piasecki and people of his ilk than it did to the socialists, whether followers of the cooperativist ideas of Edward Abramowski or those trained in the prewar struggle for an authentic parliamentary system.

One can thus speak of a dual type of division. On the one hand, the source of the conflict was the resistance of the Church to the secularization of public life, to the separation of church and state (a

12. Strzelecki, "O socjalistycznym humaniźmie" (On Socialist Humanism), in *Kontynuacje (2)*, p. 87.

principle, of course, that had been a persistent part of the secular Left's program for decades). On the other hand, there was PAX's Catholic Left, dividing the religious front and defining itself chiefly through its approval of the policies of the new government, a government that from week to week was ever more brazenly revealing its totalitarian character.

The overwhelming majority of the leftist intelligentsia, and not only the Catholic Left, supported the ruling Communists. One need only glance at the leading journals of the time to be convinced of this. (See, for example, *Kuźnica, Odrodzenie, Twórczość* or *Myśl Współczesna.*) In fact, the very roots of the subsequent moral and theoretical collapse of the Left can be found in the intellectual and political conceptions of this first period. It was precisely then that the great trek began, leading so many decent and honest people down the road to acquiescence with Stalinist deception, criminality, and coercion.

This is an important topic that deserves very careful reflection. I do not like those people of the Left who frivolously attack their whole past (something quite fashionable of late), nor do I like those who frivolously justify it (something also quite fashionable of late). For me, there is no doubt that one of the crucial factors leading to the Left's ideological decisions of the time was the fear of the clerical Right. This was a fear conditioned by a specific view of Polish Catholicism, a fear frequently justified by the genuinely reactionary character of the Roman Catholic Church during the period of the Second Republic (1918–39). For people of the traditional Left, it was easier to defend coercion when it served such a clear, widely agreed upon matter such as the secularization of civic life.

This argument frequently reappears in discussions with people who used to be active with the PPS. They defend their ideological choice of the time by citing their fear of the power and influence of the reactionary circles. "There was no third road," they say. "We were not able to predict the future, but we remembered the past, such as the role of the Church before 1939, all too well." Meanwhile, Catholics who have been and remain in sharp opposition to communist power often say, "How can we trust those people who, after the war, took part in trampling our most basic rights? How can we collaborate with people who were once in alliance with lies and coercion and who have never had to answer for their deeds?"

Both these stereotypes have had their consequences. In 1966, the secular Left maintained a damaging silence during the official campaign against the episcopate. Two years later, in 1968, Catholic circles themselves (with the notable exception of the "Znak" group) kept painfully silent during the state-organized pogrom of the secular intelligentsia.

A significant part of the secular intelligentsia placed considerable hopes in postwar reforms. They hoped these reforms would do away with social and cultural backwardness and bring about a new Poland, progressive and just, tolerant and democratic. The essential feature of this vision was the idea of separation of church and state. All legal reforms that tended toward this goal, such as the 1945 decision to introduce civil weddings and the right of divorce, met with the firm approval of the Left's secular intelligentsia.

Against these reforms stood the episcopate. It must be emphasized that the episcopate opposed not only the right of Catholics to divorce, which would have been understandable. Rather, the bishops spoke out against the right of *any* citizen to obtain a divorce, even those unaffiliated with the Church. From the perspective of a nonbeliever, the matter seems all too clear: the Church was simply defending its privileged position. The Left's approval of the secularizing policies of the Communist government, therefore, does not seem to raise any problems.

And yet I would say that the matter is not so simple. The entire political context of those years demonstrates that the goal of these juridical reforms was not so much the separation of church and state as it was the *subordination* of Church *to* state—to a state, moreover, committed to creating an atheist nation. The attempt to subordinate the Church was only one part of an official policy aimed at subordinating all of society to the state, aimed at destroying everything in society that was independent and able to act on its own. In a word, it was an element of the politics of totalitarianism.

One may respond that the separation of church and state is always a positive good, even if carried out by a government that we find unappealing. To this I would answer that there is a fundamental difference between the attempt to secularize civic life (that is, to make religion a private affair of the citizen in which the state may not intervene) and the attempt to liquidate both Church and religion and create an atheist nation. I would add, moreover, that a necessary condition for the authentic separation of church from state is the separation of state from church, and not the transformation of the church into an obedient tool of an atheist state, such as we have, for example, in the Soviet Union. Complete religious freedom is a condition for the separation of church and state. Separation means that nonbelievers are no longer second-class citizens. It most certainly does not mean that believers now take their place. The identification of secularization with state-sponsored Marxist-Leninist ideology in its Stalinist form is absolutely and completely false. This ideology, passing itself off as science, fills all the functions of an official state religion. If one believes that the worship of God should be a matter of indifference to the state, then it follows that the state should be equally indifferent whether or not one worships the idols of Party, History, and Progress.

It would be fitting here to recall the accurate words of the French intellectual Jean-Marie Domenach. "Strictly speaking," wrote Domenach, "secularism means not allowing any single idea to monopolize the state. In this way it would appear that secularism is the best way to protect political consciousness from hypertrophy and to guard society from idolatry." Secularism, according to Domenach, is "an insurance created by believers and nonbelievers alike against the seizure of the state by totalitarian philosophies." [13]

I cannot add to Domenach's precise formulation. I might only note that people of the Left, people who have passed through Marxism, should understand that the truth is always concrete. I can easily understand the illusions of 1945, but I cannot comprehend those people who today, thirty years later, repeat those very same propositions. In other words, the validity of certain ideas depends on the context in which they are presented. An anticlerical (though not antireligious) position put forth during the interwar years was, in my opinion, an expression of democratic and progressive aspirations. Although it is not without some painful self-reflection that I read today the prewar comment of then Reverend Wyszyński to the effect that "our intelligentsia is preparing the groundwork for communism—and the scaffold for itself," still, I believe that opposition to the political role of the Church was, at that time, from the standpoint of the Left, something reasonable and understandable. This same anticlericalism, however, takes on a completely different meaning when the Church is resisting the attempts of the state to establish total control of the spiritual life of society.

That which yesterday was progressive and democratic, which seemed to lead to freedom and tolerance, in a changed situation

13. Jean-Marie Domenach, "Świadomość religijna i świadomość polityczna" [Religious and Political Consciousness], in *Więź* (Warsaw), no. 6, 1968, p. 18.

served only reaction, opening the floodgates to violence and blind fanatacism. People of the secular Left—and the author of these words places himself squarely within that camp—must never forget this. We became an unwitting tool in the hands of a totalitarian power which, with a foreign mandate and foreign assistance, acted against the interests of the Polish nation. Until we recognize this clearly and openly, we will not be able to count on the trust and understanding of those with biographies quite different from our own.

2

TRANSLATOR'S NOTE
In 1944 the Red Army expelled the Nazis from much of Polish territory and set up a government run by Polish Communists. The initial toleration of non-Communist forces came to a halt by 1948, when even the Polish Socialist Party was forced to merge into the Polish Workers' Party (the Communist party), thus creating the Polish United Workers' Party that ruled Poland until 1989. Aiming to control all independent forces, the Stalinist government began restricting the freedom of the Roman Catholic Church, as discussed in this chapter. Michnik documents the Church's resistance to state control, arguing that this resistance constituted a strong defense of human liberties in general.

THE CHURCH UNDER TOTALITARIANISM

I have before me Pope Pius XI's encyclical, "On the Church and the German Reich" [*Mit brennender Sorge*]. Published in March 1937, this encyclical presents the position of the Church vis-à- vis Nazi ideology and the policies of the rulers of the "Thousand Year Reich." In it, we find the following:

The believer in God is not he who utters the name in his speech, but he for whom this sacred word stands for a true and worthy concept of the Divinity. . . . Whoever follows that so-called pre-Christian Germanic conception of substituting a dark and impersonal destiny for the personal God, denies thereby the Wisdom and Providence of God. . . . Whoever exalts race, or the people, or the State, or a particular form of State, or the depositories of power, or any other fundamental value of the human community—however necessary and honorable be their function in worldly things—whoever raises these notions above their standard value and divinizes them to an idolatrous level, distorts and perverts an order of the world planned and created by God. . . . None but superficial minds could stumble into concepts of a national God, of a national religion; or attempt to lock within the frontiers of a single people, within the narrow limits of a single race, God, the creator of the universe, King and Legislator of all nations.[1]

In the section, "True Faith in the Church," we read the following:

In your country, Venerable Brethren, voices are swelling into a chorus urging people to leave the Church, and among the leaders there is more than one whose official position is intended to create the impression that this infidelity to Christ the King constitutes a signal and meritorious act of loyalty to the

---

1. Printed in *The Papal Encyclicals, 1903–1939,* edited by Claudia Carlen (Raleigh: Consortium, McGrath Publishing Co., 1981), pp. 526–27. (Referred to hereafter as *Papal Encyclicals.*)

modern State. Secret and open measures of intimidation, the threat of economic and civic disabilities, bear on the loyalty of certain classes of Catholic functionaries, a pressure which violates every human right and dignity. Our wholehearted paternal sympathy goes out to those who pay so dearly for their loyalty to Christ and the Church; but directly the highest interests are at stake, with the alternative of spiritual loss, there is but one alternative left, that of heroism.[2]

On "Morality and Moral Order," the encyclical reads:

It is on faith in God, preserved pure and stainless, that man's morality is based. All efforts to remove from under morality and the moral order the granite foundation of faith and to substitute for it the shifting sands of human regulations, sooner or later lead these individuals or societies to moral degradation. The fool who has said in his heart "there is no God" goes straight to moral corruption (Psalms xiii. 1), and the number of these fools who today are out to sever morality from religion, is legion. They either do not see or refuse to see that the banishment of confessional Christianity, i.e., the clear and precise notion of Christianity, from teaching and education, from the organization of social and political life, spells spiritual spoilation and degradation. No coercive power of the State, no purely human ideal, however noble and lofty it be, will ever be able to make shift of the supreme and decisive impulses generated by faith in God and Christ.[3]

On natural law:

Such is the rush of present-day life that it severs from the divine foundation of Revelation, not only morality, but also the theoretical and practical rights. We are especially referring to what is called the natural law, written by the Creator's hand on the tablet of the heart (Rom. ii. 14) and which reason, not blinded by sin or passion, can easily read. It is in the light of the commands of this natural law, that all positive law, whoever be the lawgiver, can be gauged in its moral content, and hence, in the authority it wields over conscience. Human laws in flagrant contradiction with the natural law are vitiated with a taint which no force, no power can mend. In the light of this principle one must judge the axiom, that "right is common utility." . . . Emancipated from this oral rule, the principle would in international law carry a perpetual state of war between nations; for it ignores in national life, by confusion of right and utility, the basic fact that man as a person possesses rights he holds from God, and which any collectivity must protect against

2. *Papal Encyclicals*, pp. 529–30.
3. *Papal Encyclicals*, p. 531.

denial, suppression or neglect. . . . The believer has an absolute right to profess his Faith and live according to his dictates. Laws which impede this profession and practice of Faith are against natural law. Parents . . . have a primary right to the education of the children God has given them in the spirit of their Faith, and according to its prescriptions. Laws and measures which in school questions fail to respect this freedom of the parents go against natural law, and are immoral.[4]

The encyclical addresses the following words to the youth:

If the State organizes a national youth, and makes this organization obligatory to all, then, without prejudice to rights of religious associations, it is the absolute right of youths as well as of parents to see to it that this organization is purged of all manifestations hostile to the Church and Christianity.[5]

And finally,

Religious lessons maintained for the sake of appearances, controlled by unauthorized men, within the frame of an educational system which systematically works against religion, do not justify a vote in favor of non-confessional schools.[6]

These extensive quotations from the papal encyclical are intended not only to demonstrate to the secular reader the highly complex nature of the relationship between the Holy See and the Third Reich. It is also our intention to point out the fundamental line of reasoning used by the Church in its criticism of Nazi totalitarianism. As an institution summoned to serve God and to speak the message of the Gospel, the Church focused its criticism on those parts of Nazi policy which prevented it from fulfilling its obligations. German bishops called attention to the restrictions placed on the Church and on Catholicism, and in their attacks on the regime, not surprisingly, they put these matters at the top of their list of objections. (See, for example, the pastoral letter issued in Fulda on 20 August 1935, which was read from the pulpit and then confiscated by Nazi censorship.) It is possible to see this merely as the Church's attempt to protect its own privileges. It can be treated as one more piece of evidence proving that the Church is concerned only with its own particular interests. Yet we would do well to consider what it really

4. *Papal Encyclicals*, pp. 531–32.
5. *Papal Encyclicals*, p. 532.
6. *Papal Encyclicals*, p. 534.

means, and what functions it really serves, to defend the particular privileges of the Church in conditions of totalitarian dictatorship.

Let us take one example. In 1935, the German bishops wrote the following:

The marriage laws of the Catholic Church, such as the prohibitions of marriage between relatives and of the barbarous practice of divorce, have acted as an incalculable blessing for the purity of blood and the good of the family. It would be catastrophic for human relations if, in contrast to Christian laws, marriage now began to be understood solely from the point of view of racial purity.[7]

In other political conditions, the struggle for the right of divorce was an effort to broaden the sphere of human freedom, and the defense of Christian marriage law (which as state law concerned non-Catholics as well) meant the restriction of such freedom. Under conditions of Nazi dictatorship, however, the meaning of this conflict had changed fundamentally, and the defense of the Catholic concept became a defense of human rights against the claims of totalitarian racism.

The defense of religion in Nazi Germany was something more than just the defense of religion; it was a defense of individual autonomy as well. By speaking out in defense of religion, the Church was speaking in defense of the principle which holds that the human individual is not the property of the state but has innate rights that no state may usurp.

An analysis of the Church's conflict with the Nazi authorities clearly shows it was impossible to reduce the role of the Church to purely confessional matters and that any attempt to do so lay squarely in the interests of the Nazis. In this particular context, abolishing the Church's privileges would be tantamount to abolishing perhaps the last bastion of human rights. While the abolition of parochial education in France at the beginning of this century was part and parcel of the separation of church and state, abolishing parochial schools in Hitler's Germany signified only the complete domination of education by the Nazis.

Let us repeat: identical demands, formulated in differing circumstances, may have very different meanings. One cannot compare the struggles of the Church to maintain parochial schools in a Nazi dictatorship with its struggle to maintain them in republican France.

7. "List pasterski biskupów niemickich" [Pastoral Letter of the German Bishops], in *Szkoła Chrystusowa*, no. X, 1935, p. 180.

Does it really make sense to characterize the defense of religious education in the Third Reich as the defense of reaction and obscurantism? Isn't the consolidation of a totalitarian regime, regardless of whether it utilizes right-wing or left-wing phraseology, the most "reactionary" development of all? Isn't it time that we in the secular Left finally come to grips with the fact that in the face of totalitarian dictatorship, the traditional divisions of "progressive" and "reactionary," "Right" and "Left," are less essential than that fundamental line that divides the supporters of totalitarianism from its opponents? And are we not obliged, in light of this understanding, to revise our traditional views of the nature and the role of the Roman Catholic Church in postwar Poland?

I remember a meeting of the Warsaw University branch of the Party in December 1966. The main item of discussion was the still hot topic of the expulsion from the Party of Professor Leszek Kołakowski. Professor Włodzimierz Brus, a leader of the opposition in the Warsaw University Party organization, and a man with considerable moral authority among the students, spoke in defense of Kołakowski. Brus's courageous and brilliant presentation unleashed a veritable storm, eliciting aggressive (if not very skillful) responses from Stanisław Kociołek (then First Secretary of the Warsaw PUWP) and Andrzej Werblan (then head of the Central Committee's Science and Scholarship Department). It was clear to all that Brus was locked in a bitter and open conflict with Party authorities. Criticizing the decision to expel Kołakowski, Brus sought in particular to refute the charge that Kołakowski "objectively" supported the "reactionary policies" of the episcopate and Cardinal Wyszyński. What does such an accusation really mean, Brus asked rhetorically. And he answered: Why, it can only mean that since Kołakowski stands with Wyszyński, then Wyszyński stands with Kołakowski! What praise they thereby give to this most reactionary leader of the most reactionary Church in Europe!

Włodzimierz Brus was undoubtedly speaking sincerely, and it certainly was not his intention to argue that the regime and the "revisionists" should find a common enemy in the episcopate; there could be no question of any such alliance at that time. And yet Brus was publicly presenting decidedly negative views on the episcopate just after an aggressive anticlerical campaign had been waged by the government in connection with the pastoral letter to the German bishops. Brus was only saying what many of us were thinking. We believed that, "despite everything," the main enemy of progress was located in the same place as always, on the traditional Right, and that its chief spokesman remained, as always, the hierarchy of the Roman Catholic Church. I believed this, too; today I recall this period only with shame. It is hard to believe that I could have been so surprised and angry, two years later, when this "reactionary episcopate" perceived the conflict between the regime and the leftist intelligentsia as an intra-family quarrel among communists. Did we, people of the Left, ever give the bishops any reason to think otherwise?

Let us go back a bit. And let us begin the ideological reckoning with ourselves, not with others. After 1945, did we ever do anything that might cause believers to stop identifying the Left with antireligiousness? How did we react to the increasing persecution of the Church? How did we react to the frame-up of Bishop Kaczmarek? How did we react to the liquidation of *Tygodnik Powszechny* [Universal Weekly] in 1953? How did we react to the illegal arrest of the Polish Catholic primate? Did anyone in our milieu utter a single word of protest? Did we maintain at least our silence, in the spirit that you do not kick someone who's already down? Let us answer honestly: We supported the often cruel policy of repression, for we saw it as part of the road to "a great new world." We accused the Church of being "reactionary" and a whole host of other great sins, ignoring the fact that in this atmosphere of totalitarianism, it was the Church that was defending truth, dignity, and human freedom. Of course, it was also defending its own privileges and many other things that we find quite unappealing. But let us not atone for someone else's wrongs. We ought not reckon with the sins of others before we reckon with our own.

I feel obliged to explain here, as I begin to deal with my own traditions and my own past, just what caused this fundamental reassessment of Christianity and of the Church in the eyes of people like myself, people very distant from and even hostile to the Church. I am thinking here of the monthly journal *Więź* [Links], which played a very important role in our intellectual and spiritual development. I will speak later of the genesis and ideological profile of this journal. Here it is worthwhile mentioning certain features of *Więź* editorial policy: its stubborn and persistent efforts to engage people with different views in dialogue, its unflagging commitment to healing the rifts dividing believers and nonbelievers, its constant willingness to step outside of closed religious circles.

Więź discovered a language that could speak to us. It constructed new types of intellectual links. Yet its editors did not have an easy life. They were fanatically opposed by PAX and distrusted both by secular circles and the episcopate. PAX saw *Więź* as supporters of socialism in its humanist form, while PAX had accepted totalitarian Stalinism. Church circles saw *Więź* as a Trojan horse presenting a threat of modernist infiltration. As it turned out, they had it upside down. If *Więź* brought ideological diversity anywhere, it was to the atheist and anticlerical circles. With patience and farsightedness, as seen in the articles of editor Tadeusz Mazowiecki and others, the *Więź* group managed to show us a different, far more truthful side of the Roman Catholic Church. It showed us the profound sense of dignity of the Catholic bishops. And finally, it managed to open up some of us to the mystery of the supernatural. Thanks to the intellectual experience of reading *Więź*, I see Church history quite differently than I used to. In particular, I have a different view of the role of the Church in the postwar years.

In the period of intense Stalinist terror, from 1948 through 1955, Poland was a country of lawlessness—its Constitution a worthless piece of paper and religious freedom a mere fiction. The line of the Church was essentially the one laid out in the encyclical of Pius XI. It defended its faith as well as its right to speak the teachings of the Gospel. Let us try to reconstruct the line of the Church on the basis of contemporaneous Church documents, including pastoral letters of the episcopate and letters of the Polish primate.

In the "Letter of the Episcopate to Polish Catholic Youth," dated 15 April 1948, we read the following:

The new needs of the country in its time of reconstruction, the necessary changes in social and economic life, now coincide with the shrill propaganda of the materialist worldview. . . . There is no lack of voices asserting that the time for Christian education has passed and that different ways of educating the next generations must be sought. Current slogans call for the complete "reconstruction of human consciousness," by which is meant education according to materialist principles. The new order of the world, the new attitude to the times, is to be without God and without religion, outside of the Christian traditions of the nation. . . . The Church cannot agree to Catholic youth being trained without God, with the omission of His teachings and the rejection of His commandments. . . . The Church does not hide your eyes from your earthly obligations, but it raises you in the spirit of your supreme dignity as free and reasoning children of God, connected with the fate of this world but striving toward eternal salvation. You must seek the whole truth, and therefore also the innate and the revealed truth. You must realize the whole person in yourself. . . .

Be firm about those views that abase the human as God's creation.

Stand fast against all attempts to convince you that man has nothing in common with an act of creation of an eternal God, but instead simply "came out of the trees." Resist these attacks through active faith.

Against the onslaught of the press, the propaganda, and the living apostles of materialism, you must react with particular calm. Conduct yourselves with kindness and forbearance. Remember that they, for the most part, know not what they do. Harden yourselves against their erroneous attacks. Cast aside the flood of materialist literature. But all the more eagerly and systematically, take up your schoolwork. . . . Thorough study will slowly reveal to you the many walks of life. It will show you that economic affairs occupy a lofty place but not the only place, since they cannot satisfy all the wishes of man. . . . Do not rage against the materialism of the elderly, and respect the goodwill of those within the materialists' ranks who are honestly working for a better tomorrow for the working masses. . . . Be realists, but within the bounds of God's law, and never renounce Christian ideals. Make up your mind to work not just for the prosperity of the country, but for its Christian culture and Christian soul as well. . . .

Materialism recognizes neither God's commandments, Christian ethics, nor any permanent moral norms at all. It professes a cult of immediacy, of sensual pleasure, of struggle for better living conditions, and of hatred. To you falls the honorable task of rescuing the principles and practice of Christian morality in your own lives and surroundings. . . . Be pure of heart. Respect, in your behavior, the holy Law of God and its dignity of man. Love your neighbor with the sincerity of evangelical love. . . . Guard against hatred, the scorching breath of hell. In face of the postwar collapse of civility, avoid selfishness and do nothing to harm your neighbor. . . . And love the truth. Be its advocates and its apostles. Deception depraves the soul and is contrary both to morality and to the rebirth of the nation.[8]

In the "Pastoral Letter of the Polish Episcopate on the Commemoration of Christ the King," the bishops wrote as follows:

Do not send your children to schools from which religious education has been removed. In Poland there are no legal grounds for forcing children to attend secular schools. . . . We call on everyone to engage in creative action. Each must conscientiously attend to the demands of his profession. Farmers must conscientiously sow the fields. In the steel mills, mines, workshops, bureaus, and stores, let there be decent and honest labor, such as is the calling of all humans. The rebuilding of Polish life, of the capital, the

---

8. *Listy Pasterskie Episkopatu Polski* [Pastoral Letters of the Polish Episcopate] (Paris: Editions du Dialogue, 1975), pp. 63–66. (Referred to hereafter as *Pastoral Letters.*)

cities, the farms and the churches, must continue onward. Let us preserve our spiritual confidence and inner peace. Maintain your personal, national, and Catholic dignity. Let no dark elements provoke you to irrational steps. For us, Polish life should be dear and holy. It must not be risked unnecessarily. Polish blood must not be squandered in senseless power plays. The nation must remain strong, virile, and able to bring about the greatness of tomorrow.[9]

Here, in documents from the first months of 1948, is the Church's "antimaterialist" program of resistance. The program of the bishops is a struggle for the right of religious education. The model of behavior they suggest is loyalty to Christian ethics and the cultivation of evangelical virtues. Their appeal that people resist "materialist tendencies" (that is, communist ideology) is accompanied by a firm warning against joining the armed underground. Theirs was a call not so much to political opposition as to moral or philosophical opposition. Such a program resulted from the situation of the country at the time. In 1948, one year after the falsified elections to the Sejm, the last remnants of authentic political pluralism had been liquidated. In September 1946, prior to the elections, the Church was still calling on Catholics to vote "only for those people, lists, and electoral programs that do not conflict with Catholic teachings and Catholic morality."[10] In 1948, however, there was no longer any possibility of choosing anything. Communist rule, in reality as well as in the popular consciousness, was in place and could not be overthrown. The program of the bishops became a program of self-preservation and restraint. Thus, in these pastoral letters, it is easy to detect the tone of calm, the appeal for conscientious labor, the hopes for stabilization and for a relatively peaceful existence for the Catholic community in the new conditions.

The tone of the pastoral letters of 1949 is already quite different. In the course of a year, international relations had markedly worsened. Stalin's conflict with Yugoslavia had begun. In Poland, the PPS and PPR were "united" into the PUWP, and the violent campaign against Gomułka and the so-called "right-wing nationalist deviation" within the Party was underway. The authorities announced a policy of collectivization and of increased Party vigilance, which meant increased police terror. The new situation was reflected in

9. *Pastoral Letters*, pp. 70–71.

10. "Orędzie Episkopatu Polski w sprawie wyborów do Sejmu" [Statement of the Polish Episcopate concerning the Elections to the Sejm], in *Pastoral Letters*, p. 42.

state policy toward the Church, as can be seen from government and church documents alike. In March 1949, the ministry responsible for Church-state relations sent the episcopate a long list of complaints. It charged "certain sections of the clergy" with "intensified unfriendly activity toward the government and the people's state" and warned that "the government will not tolerate any seditious actions."[11]

No wonder the episcopate's pastoral letter of March 1949, "On the Joys and Concerns of the Church," was written in a rather dramatic tone:

As . . . the position of the Church becomes ever more difficult and it becomes harder and harder to carry out our missionary work, and when, in addition to all this, the blame for the current state of affairs is placed solely on the side of the Church hierarchy, it is necessary, at last, to give testimony to the Truth.

The bishops remind us of the thousand-year "historic concordat between the Catholic Church and the Polish Nation," and ask:

Is there really nothing more urgent for Poland right now than to sever this historical connection? Is it not more important to forge unity in the struggle against the devastation wrought by the war and in the campaign to properly rebuild the Fatherland?! Does anybody in Poland really believe that the Church is a dangerous political power? In the aftermath of the moral calamity caused by the war, which will help the Fatherland more: secularization, or the sanctification of the national spirit? Which is healthier for Poland: to break it apart into struggling sects, or to strengthen it in one faith? Isn't the greatest danger for the Nation precisely this attempt to separate nation from Church?

After these questions comes the appeal: "Catholics! The great moment of Christian conscience has come! You must answer these questions for yourselves."

In sharp terms, the bishops attacked the notion that the Catholic clergy were somehow hostile to working people and to the nation:

The Catholic clergy in Poland is nothing more than the sons of our great land. They have emerged from the hard soil of the countryside, from the artisans' workshops, from the workers' districts of the cities. . . . For centuries the people have seen priests among them, through foul and fair. . . .

11. Mikołaj Rostworowski, *Słowo o PAX-ie* [On PAX] (Warsaw: Instytut Wydawniczy PAX, 1968), p. 47.

That is why it is so difficult to convince the people that the clergy are their enemies. Polish priests built the first schools. They opened people's eyes and introduced them to books. They founded libraries, hospitals, orphanages, and even the first co-operatives. . . . Yes, it is difficult to convince anyone that the Catholic clergy is somehow alien or hostile to the Nation! . . . Teaching love for God, our clergy never forgot about love for the Fatherland! In fact, one so perfectly intertwined with the other that the clergy could show, through the example of the crucifixion, that it is sometimes necessary even to die for the Fatherland. . . . Too many priests have died for Poland for us to be able to doubt whether they truly loved the Nation!

The bishops then addressed the priests directly:

Dear Brothers of God, you do not need to clarify your attitude to the Nation. You did not arrive here only yesterday! . . . Thanks to your untiring work, you have performed the greatest service to public life. Of you it can be said that you have well served the nation, that you have not taken Polish bread for free! In face of the slanders of the enemy, maintain your calm. Remain loyally at your posts. Zealously embrace the prophecies of the Gospels, for this is the best, and indeed your only "politics." As you know, you were not summoned to political work but to the salvation of human souls! Your job is aimed at bringing peace to the Fatherland, whether this means a journey to the dying in the dead of night, strengthening people in their patience, or protecting the holy faith against sectarians and blasphemers, defending the cross, the boarded-up Catholic schools, and the right of prayer in the nurseries!

You correctly believe that Poland must not be godless, if it is to be a place with justice for all! Therefore, defending the faith does not mean engaging in politics, but carrying out the duties of the priestly mission! . . .

Together with you, we painfully note that many priests have been torn away from their altars! We are concerned by the large number of priests who have been sentenced and accused. Indeed, we are not even in a position to help these people, as we are unable to learn anything about the basis of the charges or the nature of their interrogations. We call on each of you: stand fast to your holy mission! Maintain it with peace, confidence, and dignity!

Regarding the monastic orders:

It is precisely the monastic orders that first cleared the way for civilization. . . . The first hospitals, the first shelters for travelers, the elderly, and the orphans, all came about from the work of the monasteries. They created numerous foundations. They were the substitutes for nonexisting Ministries of Health and Social Welfare. . . . The Church, which has provided inspiration for this blessed monastic work, has no reason to be ashamed of it. . . . Today, when such alarm is being created about this work, when nuns are being removed from hospitals (which are sometimes also their own residences), when various religious associations of a monastic character are being dissolved, the Church is hopeful that passions will die down and that justice and reason will prevail. It is up to the Church to determine whether the organizations it has created live up to the demands of society or have become obsolete. . . . Brothers and Sisters of the orders, you are not taking Polish bread for free. You have earned it honestly by your hard work. You have a natural right to retain your monasteries, a right to spend your old age there, you who have given and suffered so much in your social efforts. It would be a grave injustice to throw out on the streets precisely those people who have worn themselves out in service to their neighbors. As your hospitals and clinics are today being socialized, we know that through your self-sacrificing labor you have long ago socialized them yourselves. . . . For the good of society, we firmly hope that the rights of the Catholic institutions, monastic orders, boarding schools, hospitals, and nursing homes, as well as the rights of their owners, will be fully respected.

And once again, the bishops took up the issue of religious education in the schools:

The cause of justice and social peace demands that Catholic youth be able to associate freely within the schools as well as in religious organizations on the outside. Justice demands that Catholic schools not be kept in a state of permanent, tormenting uncertainty regarding their own existence. Nationalizing the Catholic schools or stripping them of their rights, expelling nuns from schools, closing Catholic nurseries and boarding schools, expropriating school property—we would consider any of these activities to constitute a grave injustice.

At the end of their pastoral letter, the bishops addressed the entire Catholic population:

We appreciate your contributions to economic growth, and we rejoice with every healthy achievement. We only wish that you do not forget that the road to a just Poland lies through justice toward God. Therefore we ask you, Brothers and Sisters, to stay strong in your faith, courageously resisting all temptations to turn away from God. . . . Accept God and Church openly! Defend the holy cross! A Catholic neither removes crosses from the walls nor participates in blasphemous meetings. A Catholic assists neither in taking religion out of the public schools nor in closing down Catholic schools. . . . Catholic youth! . . . Defend against the betrayal of your heavenly Father and your Mother-Church! Do not take part in atheistic gatherings! Do not speak out against your Creator! Do not renounce Him, Who loved you till death on the cross!

As to the assault on your conscience by atheist youth, by godless journals and unions—you must bear this with courage and dignity. Do not go among the blasphemers. Do not sit on their councils. Do not read their godless press. Do not sing their blasphemous and hate-filled songs and hymns, alien to the Christian spirit. . . . Be aware that by betraying God, you cannot build a better Poland! These are our requests, and these are our warnings.[12]

Official Church documents can very often constitute rather deceptive evidence and, in any case, can never be sufficient proof for a historian. Episcopal letters or papal encyclicals on national socialism can in no way answer the difficult questions concerning relations between the Roman Catholic Church and the Third Reich. There were various phases in this relationship. Times of heated conflict were followed by periods of compromise. Different bishops coexisted with the Hitler regime in different ways. All the same, it is precisely the official documents which show the Church's main line of criticism of Nazism.

It was the same in Poland. Here, too, the practice of the postwar period was both richer and more complex than the episcopal letters. In these letters, one can find only a bare hint of the tremendous tensions and drama of the day-to-day reality of the times. The remark that priests are "not summoned to political work but to the salvation of human souls," is an allusion to the group of "patriot-priests" organized by the pro-regime Committee of Priests. The creation of this committee was one of many attempts to split the Church from within. Let us look at the documents, beginning with the keynote parliamentary address of Premier Józef Cyrankiewicz in January 1949:

The government stands firmly by the principle of freedom of conscience and of religious belief. . . . At the same time, however, the government will not tolerate the aggressive attitudes of certain representatives of the clergy, and particularly of the Church hierarchy, nor will it tolerate their attempts to interfere in affairs of state. . . . All attempts to utilize the pulpit or the frock in order to arouse hostility to the people's state . . . will be beaten back with the full firmness and severity of the law. The government will, however, support those clergy who have given and continue to give proof of their patriotism, . . . those who do not let themselves be used for antigovernment political games.

12. Pastoral letter of the Polish episcopate, "On the Joys and Concerns of the Church," in *Pastoral Letters*, pp. 75–82.

In light of such declarations, there appears to be no doubt that state authorities really did seek to divide the clergy.

Similarly, the bishops' remarks concerning the clergy's many social activities over the centuries were a reply to the persistent accusation that the Church was a "reactionary" organization. And the patriotic declarations in these letters must be read in the context of recurring charges that the episcopate supported the Vatican's pro-German position with regard to the Western lands. ("These priests," we read in one propaganda pamphlet of the times, "subordinate the interests of the Polish nation to the interests of the Vatican and stand in the service of imperialism. If the Pope tells them to wage battle against their own nation, then they wage battle against their own nation.") From the standpoint of a professional historian, one can accuse the Polish episcopate of grossly simplifying the past, as well as a tendency to exculpate itself of all sin. The point, however, is that this was no simple academic exchange of opinion aimed solely at arriving at historical truth. Instead, it was a sharp ideological conflict in which one of the sides, with a monopoly of the mass media, resorted to lies, calumny, and police repression.

The bishops' program was, without doubt, a program of defending the Church. More than one of its points may strike us as reactionary and unacceptable. We should be careful, however, before passing judgment on their reactionary character, since this can easily lead to absurdities. Let me cite just one example here, albeit one that seems rather common in secular left-wing intellectual circles. In 1964, one journalist discussed Church policies in the following way:

In one of its meetings in May 1946, Church authorities took a stand with regard to a series of antisocialist events in our country, including a number of anti-Semitic incidents organized by right-wing groups. When the League for Struggle with Racism asked the episcopate to condemn these occurrences, the episcopate decided that the primate would give their reply, and the primate then stated that Jews were being killed not because of anti-Semitism in Poland, but because they were leading Communist activists. The episcopate did not consider it appropriate to make any appeals regarding the problem of anti-Semitism, since an appeal would have a political character.[13]

13. Stenographic report of discussion on "Cooperation between Believers and Nonbelievers in People's Poland," in *Dialog i Współdziałanie* [Dialogue and Interaction] (Warsaw: Instytut Wydawniczy PAX, 1970), p. 63.

The problem of anti-Semitic disturbances after the war, the most notorious of which was the 1945 pogrom in Kielce, is too complex to discuss here. It is difficult to polemicize with a position of the episcopate known only from an unfriendly synopsis. And yet it is also difficult to forget that Catholic intellectuals close to *Tygodnik Powszechny* published a declaration unequivocally condemning the anti-Semitic excesses. And we must also note the charge, frequently repeated (for example, by Stefan Korboński), that these excesses were provoked by the secret police, something which muddles the picture even more. I mention this last point in light of the fact that the author of the article quoted above was none other than the editor of the journal *Wychowanie* [Upbringing], Wojciech Pomykało, a man well known for his Black Hundred-type declarations,[14] particularly in 1968. A charge of anti-Semitism coming from the likes of Pomykało is so grotesque that it doesn't even call for a reply. The context in which the Church is accused of being reactionary must always be kept in mind. Defending religion in the schools may seem rather offensive to us today, but let us remember that the bishops, thinking of the tragic fate of religion and the church in the USSR, correctly understood that abolishing religious education in the schools was only a first step to the complete prohibition on the religious training of youth. Similarly, calling on people to "not read atheist books" may sound rather shocking to us today. At the time, however, this was a clear way of saying that Christian ethics meant refusing to participate in the official public life of the totalitarian state, and refusing to support totalitarian political ideologies. Indeed, it is difficult to deny that the bishops were right.

It turned out that the fears and prognoses of the episcopate were fully justified. Repression against the Church grew increasingly harsh, as became clear with the "Caritas Affair." Caritas was a charitable Church organization that ran 900 nurseries and day-care centers as well as 230 community centers, in addition to boarding schools, crèches, medical clinics, shelters, summer camps, etc. Funds for these activities came largely from the American Polonia Council and from the Emergency Committee of the American Episcopate. On 23 January 1950, state authorities locked up the existing parish offices and established a commissariat to supervise Caritas. "On 30 January 1950," writes Mikołaj Rostworowski, "approximately two thousand

14. The Black Hundreds were a nationalist organization frequently responsible for anti-Semitic pogroms in tsarist Russia.—TRANS.

priests were brought together in the Warsaw Polyechnic, in the most diverse of circumstances, to hear the official explanation for the state's actions in the 'Caritas Affair.'"[15] "Diverse circumstances," however, is just a bit too euphemistic a label for what in reality amounted to bribery, blackmail, and even open coercion.

On this same January 30, the episcopate issued its own letter on the Caritas Affair. The bishops protested the matter to President Bolesław Bierut, while simultaneously notifying the faithful that "when the state arbitrarily chose its own leadership for Caritas, that organization ceased being an expression of the charitable social work of the Church. The Church cannot take responsibility for organizations with arbitrary, state-appointed leaderships."[16]

On 14 April 1950, an accord was signed between the Polish People's Republic and the episcopate. This followed the decision by the government to expropriate unused Church property. Whatever one may think about such a measure today, at the time it was one more sign of heightening totalitarian terror. In light of these developments, the signing of a concordat represented, for the episcopate, a desperate attempt to find a *modus vivendi* with the state. The accord read in part:

In the interest of guaranteeing the most advantageous conditions of development to the Nation, People's Poland and its citizens, . . . the Government of the Republic, which stands for full freedom of religion, and the Polish Episcopate, taking into account the good of the Church as well as the interests of the Polish state, agree to regulate their relations in the following way:

1) The Episcopate will call on the clergy to instruct the faithful, in accordance with the teachings of the Church, on the need to respect the law and the state authorities.

2) The Episcopate will call on the clergy . . . to exhort the faithful to work harder to rebuild the country and to increase the well-being of the Nation.

3) The Polish Episcopate states that for economic, historical, cultural and religious reasons, as well as for the cause of justice, the Recovered Lands in the West must remain permanently part of Poland. Because the Recovered Lands are an essential part of the Republic, the Episcopate will ask the Holy See to change the church administrations in these areas into permanent bishoprics.

15. Rostworowski, *Słowo o PAX-ie*, p. 51.
16. "On the Joys and Concerns of the Church," in *Pastoral Letters*, p. 89.

4) The Episcopate will work against anti-Polish activity in those areas where it can, and particularly against the anti-Polish and revisionist declarations of part of the German clergy.

5) The principle that the Pope is the highest and ultimate authority of the Church refers to matters of faith, morality, and church jurisdiction. In all other areas the Episcopate is guided by the interests of the Polish state.

6) Assuming that the Church's mission may be realized in various socio-economic systems established by secular authorities, the Episcopate will explain to the clergy that it should not work against the construction of cooperative farms, since all cooperatives are in essence based on an ethical principle which strives for voluntary social solidarity and seeks the good of all.

7) In keeping with its principles, the Church, by condemning all anti-state activities, will especially oppose the misuse of religious feelings for anti-state goals.

8) In keeping with its teachings, the Church, in condemning crime, will also struggle against the criminal activities of the underground gangs and will renounce and administer church punishment to those guilty of participating in any underground or anti-state actions.

In return for these obvious concessions from the Church hierarchy, it was agreed that,

the State guarantees the right of religious education in the schools, the right of religious practice for school youth, rights for the remaining Catholic schools, and the right to pastoral care in the army, hospitals, and prisons. The Catholic University of Lublin is assured of its right to carry on its work. The State recognizes the right of the Church to conduct philanthropic and catechistic work, to run publishing houses, and issue Catholic journals. Seminary students may continue their theological studies without obstacles. The monastic orders and the monasteries may continue their work freely and are guaranteed the right to the material goods necessary for a modest upkeep.[17]

After the Concordat, the tone of the episcopate's pastoral letters grew considerably more careful. In official Church documents we no longer find anything concerning violations of law, illegal arrests, torturing of prisoners, or judicial frame-ups. The one point that the bishops did consistently defend, however, was the unity of the clergy,

17. "Communique of the Episcopate of Poland to the Faithful, On the Concordat . . . ," in *Pastoral Letters,* pp. 91–92, 96.

and their renewed appeals for priests to refrain from political activity must be understood in this light. In November 1950, just a few months after the signing of the accord, Cardinal Wyszyński addressed the clergy in the following way:

It has been our lot to partake not only in the difficult missionary efforts of the postwar period, but to be compelled to do our work in times of great disarray and intensifying religious persecution. . . . We can already name many nations and states where hundreds of priests and virtually all of the bishops are in jail, where members of religious orders have been thrown into forced labor camps, where convents, seminaries, Catholic schools, bishops' residences and offices alike have been ransacked. The most painful of these attacks have been the attempts of the secular authorities to interfere in Church administration and to provoke schisms within the ranks of the Catholic nations. In many countries, people entirely apart from the Church have been named to take the place of imprisoned bishops and priests. They usurp episcopal powers for themselves . . . and try to exercise at the altar a spiritual authority that they do not possess. . . . They often try to separate service at the altar from service to God, as they turn the altar into a place for agitators to speak out against the Church, against the authority of the Holy Father and of the bishops.

It is with great concern that we behold these gross violations, which have despoiled the most sacred things, mocked God and the Holy Church, and transformed service to God into some unwitting tool in a political game. . . .

There is no authority in the Church except that which comes from the Highest Authority, Christ. All others are not pastors but wolves. There is no priestly authority in the Church except that which derives from the See of Peter, and which flows down from the Catholic bishops to the priests below. Thus you must obey only those priests who have been sent by Catholic bishops living in harmony and unity with the Holy Father.

Our words are hard, Dear Children, but the times are hard, too.[18]

The meaning of the primate's appeal was twofold and directed to two different audiences. On the one hand, the primate was urging people to break with the anti-Communist underground, which after 1950 had lost even marginal significance. On the other hand, he was seeking to discourage the participation of priests in the political actions sponsored by PAX or by the "patriot-priests." Connections with the underground made it easier to attack the Church from the outside, while connections with PAX weakened the Church from the inside.

18. Quoted in *Pastoral Letters*, pp. 183–84.

Consequently, the concern for internal unity and solidarity is not hard to understand: at the time it was the number-one problem of the day. Any attempt to interfere in the internal matters of the Church, therefore, was bound to provoke the resistance of the episcopate.

On 9 February 1953, the Council of State issued a decree on the "creation, staffing, and elimination of church positions." On 5 May, Premier Bierut signed the executive order. Article Two of the decree reads as follows: "The creation, modification, and elimination of church positions, as well as any change in their spheres of activity, require prior approval of the appropriate state organs." Article Six states that "any person fulfilling a ministerial position in the Church who carries out, supports, or defends activities that conflict with law and public order will be removed from his position by a superior Church authority, acting alone or on the insistence of the state." [19]

This decree marks the beginning of the end of the independence of the Church. On 8 May, the bishops gathered together at a plenary session of the episcopate in Kraków and issued a protest letter to the government, in which they explicitly state that further concessions were impossible. On 4 June, in a mass delivered to the Corpus Christi procession in Warsaw, Cardinal Wyszyński clearly and unambiguously referred to these recent decisions of the government:

Between the Eternal Minister Jesus Christ and His Pupils, there was no intermediary. There was no need whatsoever to pass the ministries through the hands of someone alien. . . . The Holy Church . . . firmly defends the Ministry of Christ . . . because the freedom of Christ's Ministry is the most visible sign of man's freedom of conscience. When the priesthood is free, God's children are guaranteed freedom of conscience. Thus it is difficult to speak of any freedom of conscience when a priest is no longer free, when he is transformed, against the will of the Church, into a bureaucrat. Good people understand . . . that between us, the ministry, and you, God's beloved children, whose consciences we guide, no one may stand in between. And if someone does try to stand in the way, this would be an attack on the structure of the Church, an attack on freedom of conscience, on the essence of the ministry, on God's ministry, on Christ's Ministry.

Therefore, in our Fatherland today, the Church must do as it did centuries ago. It must—and it will—defend Christ's ministry through its own bishops—even if we pay with our own blood. The defense of Christ's ministry is a defense of everyone's freedom of conscience, for it is simultaneously a defense of the full culture of spirit. The entire Church understands

19. Cited in Rostworowski, *Słowo o PAX-ie,* pp. 74–75.

this. People outside of the Church understand this, too, even those most progressive and non-Catholic. The Polish nation thus defends its religion and its priesthood against bureaucratization. It has always considered the subordination of clergy to the state as the gravest injustice, a violation of one of the most basic rights of man. We have evidence for this even in the words of the most radical revolutionaries, for they too realized that it would be impermissible to try to take over the priesthood even if all other spheres of life had been nationalized, for that would constitute the greatest barbarity. It is impermissible to reach for the altar, impermissible to stand between Christ and His minister, impermissible to violate the conscience of the priest, impermissible to stand between the bishop and the priest. We teach that one must give to Caesar what is Caesar's and to God what is God's. And if Caesar sits down at the altar, we must say simply: *That is not allowed!* . . . We recognize only one authority for our ministry—the authority of Jesus Christ our Lord.[20]

If the decree of the Council of State constituted the invitation to battle, the sermon of Cardinal Wyszyński was the affirmative reply. The Polish Primate told Caesar, *"Non possumus!"*

The trial of Bishop Czesław Kaczmarek got underway on 14 September 1953. Cardinal Wyszyński had protested the trial in a special letter to the state authorities. On 25 September, at a commemoration for blessed Ładysław of Gielniow, the primate delivered another sermon at Warsaw's Church of St. Anne. One more time, he very precisely presented the views of the Polish Catholic Church:

St. Ładysław was not satisfied with the times in which he lived. No person can ever be fully satisfied—not with history, with the times, with ideas, with people, or even with oneself. I would be the first to be unsatisfied even were all the problems of the day to be resolved, for the solution of one set of problems is the beginning of a new set, and the solution of this next set only brings to the fore yet another series of problems. It is wrong, therefore, to tell someone that you have created something perfect, or that some idea, or some economic, social, or political system is the best of all. There cannot be stagnation. . . . Even the most perfect system . . . needs to be revised; progress depends upon it. Progress can exist only when there is dissatisfaction with the existing state of affairs. . . .

What is sainthood based upon? Upon love of truth and freedom. . . . Freedom is closely intertwined with truth. . . . We must be free from everything that constrains our minds, we must be free even from ourselves. "If

20. "Sermon of the Primate of Poland during the Corpus Christi procession," at the Church of St. Anne, Warsaw, 4 June 1953. (Typewritten manuscript in author's possession.)

thou wilt be perfect, go and sell that thou hast" (Matthew 19:21). Only when we are truly free from everything that binds us will we be able to go forward to God. Only then will we hear the voice of God. . . . And so truth and freedom are the fundamental values. Only when they exist, like sparkling dew, will mercy flow forth, flooding us with supernatural love. . . .

The Church shall forever demand truth and freedom. Perhaps this is why the Church has so many enemies, for Christianity will always summon people to resist and do battle with falsehood. The Church will always call out, "If thou wilt be perfect, go and sell that thou hast." Break with everything that binds you, and strive freely toward God. Stand in truth, which only God knows.[21]

The state's reply to the primate came quickly. On that very same evening of 25 September 1953, Cardinal Wyszyński was arrested and taken away from Warsaw.

My friends in the secular Left are largely unaware of these texts and these facts. By citing them above, and by quoting generously from the documents of the time, my aim has been to show my left-wing friends just what the Church really faced during the Stalinist period and to show them the real position of the Catholic bishops. If my friends will compare the *actual* demands of the episcopate with all that they have read in the official press *about* those demands, they will perhaps begin to realize the magnitude of their ignorance. And if they compare those demands with the practice of the Stalinist state authorities, they will better understand the question I now put to them: where, in those times, lay the main enemy of progress and justice? Was it in the Catholic churches? Or did it lie in Party committee headquarters and in the offices of the secret police?

Many of the specific formulations of the episcopate's pastoral letters may be offensive to us today; others may seem anachronistic. But the fundamental question is this: did the Church, in the Stalinist period, defend human rights? Did it defend freedom and human dignity? I answer these questions in the affirmative. I stand in full agreement here with Czesław Miłosz, who wrote that in the Stalinist period, "churches were the only places that could not be penetrated by official lies, and church Latin allowed one to believe in the value of human speech, which elsewhere was being degraded and used for the basest tasks."

21. "Sermon of the Primate of Poland at the commemoration of St. Ładysław," at the Church of St. Anne, Warsaw, 25 September 1953. (Typewritten manuscript in author's possession.)

3

TRANSLATOR'S NOTE:

Although Stalin's death in March 1953 brought no immediate improvement in the situation in Poland (repression actually intensified for the first few months), the Stalinist system had in fact suffered a blow from which it would not recover. In February 1956, Soviet leader Nikita Khrushchev denounced Stalin at the 20th Congress of the Soviet Communist Party. Within months, huge opposition movements emerged in both Poland and Hungary, led for the most part by so-called "revisionist Marxists" who sought to recapture the humanist and democratic ideals of the original socialist project. In October these movements culminated in a popular uprising in Hungary (suppressed by Soviet tanks) and the return to power in Poland of Władysław Gomułka, the Communist leader who had been purged in 1949. Gomułka quickly established good ties with the Church, giving it representation in the Sejm (through the "Znak" group of deputies) and even permitting the reintroduction of religious education in the public schools. Yet Gomułka turned hard against the revisionist intellectuals, who did not care much about concessions to the Church and who tried to push the system in the direction of a Western social democracy. In the following two chapters Michnik discusses how the Gomułka regime turned first against the secular Left and then against the Church. The common enemy, he suggests, demonstrates that these two groups share something essential: the desire to defend basic liberties against violation by an all-powerful state.

CHURCH-STATE RELATIONS IN THE POST-OCTOBER PERIOD

The VIII Plenum of the Party, which elected Władysław Gomułka to the post of First Secretary, began on 19 October 1956. Exactly one week later, two of Gomułka's close associates, Władysław Bieńkowski and Zenon Kliszko, visited the imprisoned Cardinal Wyszyński. As a result of their discussions, the Polish primate returned to Warsaw and, after a three-year hiatus, resumed his official duties.

The primate took no part in the ensuing political infighting. The one area where the Church applied pressure was on the question of religious education in the schools. "A verbal agreement between the government and the episcopate was worked out on 8 December [1956]," writes Mikołaj Rostworowski. "It stipulated that religion would be taught as an optional class for those students whose parents requested it in writing. On 31 December, the Council of State issued a new decree on the organization and staffing of Church positions, thereby annulling . . . a decree from 9 February 1953."[1] These concessions to the Church were to have serious political consequences.

Immediately upon taking power in the Party, Gomułka began a campaign aimed at quelling the spontaneous political mobilization of the populace. In his very first speeches he was already attacking the "revisionists," denouncing their demands for power to the workers' councils, trade unions independent of the Party, abolition of censorship, and pluralism within the youth movement. In an effort to neutralize Catholic circles during this battle with the revisionists, the new Party leadership, in addition to the concessions already mentioned, permitted the reactivation of *Tygodnik Powszechny* under the old leadership of Jerzy Turowicz. (The paper had been closed in March 1953 and then reopened under the control of PAX.) Such tactical measures paid off handsomely.

1. Mikołaj Rostworowski, *Słowo o PAX-ie* (Warsaw, 1968), pp. 115–16.

Soon after religious education was reintroduced into the schools, the revisionist press, including *Po prostu* [Simply Speaking], the organ of the so-called "Angry Ones," began to run articles on the intolerance of the religion instructors and discriminatory practices against children not attending religion classes. It was easy to detect here an opposition to the very principle of religious education in the schools. Given the revisionists' ideological foundations, with atheism and anticlericalism as key components, such opposition was understandable. In fact, for all of their criticisms of Stalinism, none of the revisionists, not even the most vituperative, ever included religious persecution on their list of Stalinist crimes. At most, they saw such persecution as a mere tactical error, which, by pushing the Church to extremes, would only strengthen "religious superstition." Many revisionists actually considered the dramatic decline in the influence of Catholicism and the Church as one of the very few merits of the Stalinist period of "errors and deviations."

Interestingly, in their criticisms of the Party and of party orthodoxy, the revisionists frequently made unflattering analogies to the Roman Catholic Church. The more they felt the Party resembled the Church, the more negative their attitude to the Party. In condemning the fideism and irrationalism of the muddled constructs of Stalinist "diamat" (dialectical materialism), the revisionists appeared as the heirs of the rationalists, counterposing "reason" and "tolerance" to the "fanatical faith" of the Stalinists.

Surely there was a good deal of truth in the revisionists' remarks on the bad atmosphere in the schools following the reintroduction of religious education. Indeed, it is difficult to quarrel with their call for the separation of church and state along the French model. The point, however, is that all these arguments must have sounded dubious and even hypocritical to Catholic ears. "How is this?" Catholics no doubt were asking. "All of a sudden, *now* they've become great defenders of tolerance? Where was their cherished tolerance when the government was persecuting the Church and suppressing religious instruction? Or when *Tygodnik Powszechny* was dissolved and priests were being thrown into jail?" From the point of view of the bishop who only yesterday had been harassed, the "Angry Revisionists" must have seemed a particularly noxious tendency. For this was a group of people that only yesterday had denounced religion and the clergy. These people had been ideological activists for the Party, champions of the regime at its very cruelest. And now, still without accepting any personal guilt, continuing to attribute responsibility to "objective conditions" and agreeing to repent only for the sins of others, these people, ever the moralists, were accusing *others* of intolerance—and precisely those "others" who were yesterday being hounded!

The revisionists' objections to the new Party leadership must also have seemed suspect to the Catholics. "These are people who used to write apologies for the policies of Bierut. Why such moral rigor precisely now? Why such inflexibility against the relatively liberal policies of Gomułka, a man who has declared his willingness to defend the nation from Soviet intervention and avert a repeat of the Hungarian tragedy?" This was the basis of the acrimonious debate between Stefan Kisielewski and Wiktor Woroszylski, in which the former defended and the latter opposed the government's refusal to ally itself with the revolutionary events in Hungary. That Woroszylski was completely in the right, both morally and politically, is not the point. The point is that with its concessions to the Church, the government had torpedoed the chances for any possible agreement between the revisionists on the one hand and the Church hierarchy and traditional Catholic circles on the other.

The public statements of the episcopate in the first years after October were marked by moderation, a tendency toward the apolitical, and even a certain goodwill toward the regime. Its statements frequently consisted of appeals to believers on the need for Catholic education of the youth or of broadsides against abortion. Yet none of the statements had an antigovernmental character. On the contrary, in its pastoral letter on the new school year, delivered on 3 September 1959, the Church referred to the fifteenth anniversary of the PKWN Manifesto[2] as "fifteen years since the recovery of independence." The letter called on people to cultivate such virtues as family life, sobriety, modesty, cleanliness, diligence, and economy, and said that the reintroduction of religious education into the schools was "great proof of the wisdom" of the state authorities.[3] In the bishops' 17 March 1960 letter to the clergy, "On Pastoral Work," we find similar language. There, the bishops called for honest work and sound commitment, condemning

2. July 1944 Manifesto of the pro-Communist Polish Committee for National Liberation, establishing a new government in Poland and declaring the London-based Polish government-in-exile a nonentity.—TRANS.

3. *Listy Pasterskie Episkopatu Polski* [Pastoral Letters of the Polish Episcopate] (Paris: Editions du Dialogue, 1975), pp. 184–88. (Referred to hereafter as *Pastoral Letters.)*

negligence, laziness, drunkenness, and theft of public property. . . . We Poles work a great deal, but we do not always do so conscientiously. We are able to respect our own goods, but we do not respect the collective goods of the Nation. We tend to forget that shoddy work, theft, and the destruction of social property hurts all of us and postpones economic progress.[4]

This concern for the social and economic situation of the country, along with a complete lack of oppositional or polemical elements, stood in perfect harmony with the Party's push for material prosperity and its propagandistic appeals for "a good day's work." All conflicts between the government and the Church hierarchy were kept safely from public view.

This does not, of course, mean that there were no conflicts. Let us look at the testimony of one competent witness to these events, Gomułka's close associate Władysław Bieńkowski:

One part of the post-October political line, and one that was bitterly attacked by conservative elements of the apparatus, was the attempt to regularize relations with religion and the Church. The government's tactic here was to avoid the need for a legal regularization of those issues which directly concerned the majority of the population, such as the question of religious education in the schools. Instead of dealing with such issues in a new law, the government chose a method of "political interaction," that is, the idea of removing religion from the schools gradually, in concert with the alleged "maturing" of society. The duplicity of this policy was obvious. In effect, it meant turning over this very sensitive problem to the arbitrary will of local despots and sectarians, who naturally tried to "accelerate the maturing process" through various kinds of abuses and provocations. Religion was removed from the schools under various pretexts, not infrequently because of the alleged "will of the people." . . .

The Party conservatives focused their attacks on the new educational policy aimed at purging the school system of the distortions of the Stalinist period. Within weeks after the VIII Plenum, the "anti-October" elements in the Party had formed an organization to fight the new educational policy. Few people know that the founders of this "Association of Secular Schools" consisted almost entirely of secret police and Party functionaries who had been removed during the October upheavals. Only later did they recruit a large number of teachers and educational activists. This association gradually became a kind of second "party" ministry of education, supported by local Party committees against the school authorities. With the help of the

4. *Pastoral Letters*, pp. 197–98.

local committees, the association organized various kinds of provocations. . . . The chief motive in all this was to maintain the "ideological activism" of the Party. Education was a wide and particularly convenient field for doing so.[5]

Barely a few months later, in this same year of 1960, the episcopate decided to go public with the conflict. During summer vacation, state authorities had decided to abolish religious education in the schools. The episcopate replied with letters (4 September) to the priesthood and to the faithful. The letter to the priesthood was an appeal for unity:

During this year, we have seen a growing tendency aimed at sowing mistrust and disharmony between priests, bishops, and the curia administration. In certain cases, there have been attempts to portray bishops as the persecutors of priests. Subtly, the view has been spread that it is the bishops who are responsible for priests going to jail, for the elimination of religion from the schools, for the exorbitant taxes levied against the clergy, etc. . . . This offensive against the Church has several aims: to undermine the trust of the faithful in their ministers, to divide priests into those "more" and those "less" loyal to the state, and to strike at our material assets.

The guiding principles of the priesthood, according to the episcopate, should be "unity, trust and love." "We will not be divided into 'patriots' and 'non-patriots,' into 'progressives' and 'reactionaries.'" And on the question of the relationship between the clergy and politics, the bishops wrote:

As citizens we owe the state our loyalty, and we have an obligation to carry out just orders. We are also obliged to love the Nation and to care for its interests, to enrich all those values we have in mind when we speak of the Fatherland. . . . Yet it is impermissible to bind the clergy to any political system, to the policies of any state, and especially to any party struggling for power. This has never been in line with the spirit of the Gospels of Jesus Christ or with the will of the Church. History, after all, teaches us only too painfully that when the Church acts as a support for any crown or government, this has ended badly not only for the clergy, but for God's cause in general.

The bishops called the elimination of religious education from the schools a "cynical" step carried out contrary to the Concordat and

5. Władysław Bieńkowski, *Socjologia klęski* [The Sociology of Defeat] (Paris: Instytut Literacki, 1971).

against the will of the parents. They spoke of the "rise of secularization and demoralization," the "intrusive shallowness and barbarity of
official propaganda," and the "ever-expanding lawlessness and violence" of contemporary life. "Following the reasonable and humanitarian post-October period in the schools, there has now come a wave
of militant, fanatical atheism." And yet due to all this, "religion is
becoming increasingly appealing, precisely because it is forbidden
fruit."

In its pastoral letter "On the Present Dangers," addressed "to
God's Children of the Church of Christ," the episcopate spoke firmly
and even radically:

Today, faith in Christ is threatened . . . by the attacks of the atheists. Intensifying their activities every month, they fight the Church with outright in-
human fanaticism. In this battle the atheists possess all the modern means.
Moreover, they have put on a mask of tolerance, humanitarianism, and progress. Yet when Catholics try to defend themselves, they are charged with
being "anti-state," hostile to the system and God knows what else.

In response to such accusations, the bishops wrote:

How many times have we heard the outrageous charge that the holy Catholic
faith, "our life and our hope," is nothing but "reactionary, obscurantist, and
backward." Yet this is the faith that has unified Nation and state, that has
nourished virtually all Polish generations, including thousands of the very
best sons of the Nation—from Mieszko and Bolesław to the saints and the
blessed, from scientists like Copernicus and great writers like Skarga, Mickiewicz and Sienkiewicz, to the clerical and lay martyrs of the concentration
camps and the Warsaw uprising. . . . Can anyone be surprised that we Catholics are so outraged when that which is most holy to us is so inhumanly
reviled and desecrated? . . . One must respect what we call religious sanc-
tity, and not insult our deepest religious feelings, which are so deeply connected with our patriotic feelings.

We most solemnly declare that we will not allow our Catholicism to be
called "religious fanaticism." . . . We would be fanatics only if, in our
churches and on our pilgrimages, one could hear talk of hatred, of incitement
to violence and vengeance. But no one has yet heard these things—neither at
Jasna Góra nor any place else. On the contrary, at every confessional and
from every pulpit, the Catholic hears not only words of compassion but also
the admonition to devoutly meet various injunctions: those concerning the
worship of God as well as those which, through love, regulate our attitudes
to family, marriage, the state, and to personal and social property. . . .

The charge that we are somehow "backward" is one we reject just as decisively. We do not at all desire a return to those long gone and not always fortuitous ways of the Middle Ages. . . . The charge that the Polish Church is "capitalist" must finally be put to rest. One by one, all our most important means of subsistence have been taken from us. If our parishes, dioceses, and convents possess anything anymore, it is just some piddling remnants for which surely no one can envy us. Our hospitals, social and educational establishments . . . have been taken over by the state. And everything which has been left to the Church is burdened with a tax so high that we are simply unable, despite the best of intentions, to pay it. Priests, monks, and nuns survive literally from their own labor, in addition to the Christian generosity of the faithful. And those sums that we allegedly "extract from society" stay in the country and serve the cause of general economic revitalization, returning to society in the form of upkeep and reconstruction of churches and in a thousand other forms of social service.

We are not "anti-state." Indeed, as believing Christians, we cannot be. In the words of Christ, we say, "Render unto Caesar the things which be Caesar's," and "unto God the things which be God's" (Luke 20:25). We defend ourselves legally against any possible excesses by the government. This is our human and civic right, and presumably no one will deny it to us Catholics. . . . It is certainly more "anti-state" for the atheists to *violate* the laws of the state than it is for us to insist on *adherence* to these laws.[6]

After 1960, the Church's conflict with the state authorities grew steadily. In June 1962, the episcopate published a document titled "Contemporary Secularization." In this document, filled with reasoned and insightful reflections, the Church differentiated between secularization as an objective process characteristic of our times and secularization as "organized activity seeking to accelerate and administer this process." The movement in Poland for secularization in the second sense is, according to the authors:

a *political* movement insofar as it is part of a political plan, led by the political authorities, and supported and executed by administrative methods, . . . and a *totalitarian* movement insofar as it seeks to subjugate all manifestations of social, family, and personal life and to eliminate all opinions and judgments based on religious conviction. It is a movement that eliminates the possibility of choice, since every child can attend only a school that systematically aims at secularization.[7]

6. *Pastoral Letters*, pp. 209–12.
7. *Pastoral Letters*, p. 263.

On the question of secularization I will speak later. Here it is only important to stress the firm and uncompromising tone of the document, itself ample testimony to the intensifying conflict. One sees this same tone in the Church's March 1963 declaration, "On Religious Upbringing," where the bishops sharply criticized official policies aimed at restricting and sometimes even preventing religious instruction. Among those forbidden to teach religion were monks, nuns, and even lay people, precisely those who "could not abide by such a ban, so contrary to their conscience, since their very mission in life obliges them to proclaim the truth of Christ." When they continued to do so they were fined. Religious education was then forbidden in private apartments, parish halls, etc., allegedly because of safety regulations. According to the bishops, however, "such a ban was also unacceptable, for it was contrary to confessional freedom and signified the effective elimination of all religious education in certain areas." And so came a new wave of fines. Parish priests were required to submit full reports of their religion classes to the local branch of the Ministry of Education. "But pastors cannot submit such reports to the authorities, for religious education . . . is a normal part of the missionary work of the Church, and not subject to control by education officials." The refusal to submit reports became one more occasion to impose fines on religious instructors. "Moreover," wrote the bishops,

besides the various prohibitions and the fines meted out to instructors, there are many other ways to impede or prevent young people from participating in catechism. There have even been cases where youth who do attend religious education have been threatened and repressed along with their parents. It is a known fact that certain social groups have received explicit orders prohibiting them from sending their children to religion classes. . . . What is our position concerning such impediments? We will continue to provide religious instruction to our youth. . . . We will faithfully carry out our obligations, with the conviction that we are acting in accordance with the most binding Polish legal resolutions.

The bishops found confirmation of their "conviction" in the texts of the Constitution of the Polish People's Republic and in United Nations documents signed by the Polish government:

Voluntary religious education is a question of conscience for every citizen. To subordinate this decision to the control of the Ministry of Education—which in fact often prohibits religious instruction, demands reports that include the roster of all those attending such classes, and administers fines for teaching religion—is to threaten freedom of conscience, religion, and up-bringing. And this can in no way be reconciled with Polish and international legal principles.[8]

We see a certain evolution in the texts cited above. As a result of the intensifying conflict between Church and state, the language becomes increasingly strident with time. It appears that the Gomułka regime never thought seriously about a lasting coexistence with Catholicism. The declarations and compromises from the period of October 1956 were but tactical measures caused by a difficult political situation and the weakness of the new administration. Repression against the Church increased as the political situation stabilized, and the episcopate, realizing the illusory nature of its post-October hopes for an honest compromise, began to formulate its views in more drastic language. A most dramatic tone appeared in the pastoral letter of 28 August 1963, titled "Polish Bishops to Polish Priests." The letter was preceded by a verse from the Gospel of St. John, which lent the document a special significance:

And when he had thus spoken, one of the officers which stood by struck Jesus with the palm of his hand, saying, Answerest thou the high priest so? Jesus answered him, If I have spoken evil, bear witness of the evil: but if well, why smitest thou me? (John 18:22–24)

In this letter, the bishops sought to explain to the priests "why we cannot 'compromise' any further, since such 'compromise' can only be a betrayal of truth, justice, Christ, and of our ministry in Poland." (They are speaking, of course, of concessions to the increasing demands of the state authorities.)

The bishops opened their letter by recalling the great hopes they had attached to the favorable attitudes of Party and state officials to Pope John XXIII: "We felt a breath of fresh air when we read . . . a series of relatively objective and serious articles. . . . There seemed to be hope that the ghosts of falsification, discrimination, and spitefulness had at last been overcome." The bishops said they had honestly thought "that in the attitude of the governing atheists to the masses of the governed believers, the rusty chains of prejudice and stereotype had been broken at last." Yet, "such hopes were without foundation." The official declarations and gestures had proved to be

8. *Pastoral Letters*, p. 290.

mere maneuvers, "one more attempt to break up the unity of the Polish Church." The episcopate was denounced by the Party for its alleged hostility to the new ideas of Vatican II and was presented as "one of the backward episcopates in the world," unfavorably counterposed to "the French and even the German episcopate," even though these two were condemned as "imperialist." The repressive measures taken against the clergy were said to be due to the obstinacy and inflexibility of the "backward" Polish episcopate. Repression was thereby presented as "a defense of tolerance and of freedom of conscience." The bishops wrote: "Even the seizure of property—of cars, cycles, typewriters, watches, and sometimes even personal linen—is presented as a result of 'the bishops' unwillingness to compromise.'"

The episcopate therefore deemed it necessary, once again, to recount the true situation and to articulate its own point of view:

We do this, Brother Priests, in an internal form, in a letter to you, people who are mature in a spiritual as well as civic sense. Although many voices have urged us to go public with a list of anticlerical harassment, abuse, and discrimination in our country, we have decided not to do so at this time so as not to elicit a wave of outrage and indignation against government representatives. In spite of everything, we continue to hope that responsible elements will prevail, that the government will abandon this false and enormously dangerous path, and acknowledge, at last, that the vast majority of the nation also possesses human rights.

The bishops then discussed some of the realities facing the Church:

The repressive apparatus has remained untouched. The Church is still being ruled by Party functionaries of the Bureau of Religious Affairs and its local affiliates, together with the secret police. They rule utterly and irrevocably. Yet they try to do so most discreetly and anonymously. But these people, without exposing themselves on the outside, are carrying out a policy of the gradual annihilation of the Church in Poland.

The bishops cited a long list of facts to support this general thesis. They noted that the "lower-level seminaries for boys of high school age who want to devote themselves to theological studies in the future have quietly been eliminated." Even the higher-level seminaries were being systematically harassed:

In Kraków there has been an attempt to confiscate the building of the Seminary of Silesia, which was originally constructed from the contributions of coal miners. In another city, government administrators claim that the seminary has too many rooms and that outsiders must be housed there in order to rectify the situation. Why is it that we have not yet heard of outsiders being housed in *university* rooms? Or of scaling down the reading rooms, laboratories, and lecture halls of *state* schools?

Contrary to the assurances of the authorities, candidates for theological training were still being drafted into the army. And nuns were systematically removed from hospitals, losing both the right and the opportunity to practice nursing:

Why? Only because they are dressed in the habit, an external sign of an ideology different from the official one. . . . Does this not resemble the star that Jews once had to wear, signifying "the lowest category of human"? Is persecution called by its name only when it appears on distant, alien turf?

The bishops spoke of the ban on church weddings and child baptism applicable to military officers on active duty, police officials, and "members of certain political organizations." They also spoke of the difficulties of religious instruction, the ban on Catholics using the media to propagate their faith, the brutal censorship of Catholic publications, and the persistent harassment and relentless material burdens that they faced. They accused the state authorities of insincerity, hypocrisy, and of falsifying reality:

We consider lying to society to be a great injustice done to our Nation. . . . And the sordid suggestions put forth by certain officials that the Church use its authority in order to cover up or sanction the pernicious climate of lies prevailing in the country—such suggestions are a great danger to society at large.

To substantiate this claim, the bishops quoted the following section of Pope John XXIII's encyclical, *Pacem in terris* (Paragraph 48):

Hence, a regime which governs solely or mainly by means of threats and intimidation or promises of reward provides men with no effective incentive to work for the common good. And even if it did, it would certainly be offensive to the dignity of free and rational human beings.[9]

This is why, the bishops stated:

all attempts to destroy the Church are simultaneously attacks upon human integrity, honesty, dignity, and mutual trust, values that Christianity contin-

9. *Papal Encyclicals, 1958–81,* edited by Claudia Carlen (Raleigh: McGrath Publishing Co., 1981), p. 112.

ually urges on its followers. It is possible to undermine these spiritual quali-
ties, it is possible to fill people with lies and deceive them with frauds, but
by doing so you are at the same time destroying all civic virtue, without
which there can be neither professional satisfaction nor social goodwill.

The law of the state cannot be in contradiction with natural law,

whose principles, written within all of us, may be read by any thinking,
reasoning person. These principles are present in our very human existence,
in our collective nature, as the guiding principles of God our Creator. No one
is free from them, not even the person who thinks or knows himself to be a
nonbeliever. The power mandating these rights, etched deep within the human soul, is universal. These rights require you to do good, without regard
for any possible material advantages; and to avoid evil, without consideration of any short-term benefits that may accrue. This implies a moral imperative for mutual human respect, even though this may be contrary to the
advice of those motivated by particular interests or those who exercise
power.

In this context the bishops quoted another section of *Pacem in
terris* (Paragraph 51):

Governmental authority, therefore, is a postulate of the moral order, and derives from God. Consequently, laws and decrees passed in contravention of
the moral order, and hence of the divine will, can have no binding force in
conscience, since "it is right to obey God rather than man" (Acts 5:29). Indeed, the passing of such laws undermines the very nature of authority and
results in shameful abuse.

"We have no intention," wrote the bishops, "of using the words
of John XXIII against the present government in Poland. We warn,
however, of the calamitous effects of irresponsible government." The
bishops then drew a comparison to the Nuremberg Trials:

The accused criminals at Nuremburg were convicted not on the basis of some
written legal code. Rather, they were judged guilty of crimes against humanity, crimes against human conscience. For the constitution they had violated
was the universal one, ingrained by the Creator in human thought, human
aspirations, and human sensibility.

The crimes of Hitlerism, according to the Polish bishops, had
their origins chiefly in the Nazis' "scorn and contempt for natural law
and for the personal dignity of all human beings which this law protects." The Polish state authorities, whose struggle with the Church

the bishops called "blind fanaticism," were said to be following a similar course. "Illegal restrictions on the basic right to full human development," the bishops wrote, "belong to the same category of crimes for which Hitlerite criminals stand trial even today."

But this letter was not limited to purely Church matters:

Together with you, Brother Ministers, we want to explore the troubling economic situation of our country. We truly want to understand it. Yet we cannot comprehend why it is that some Party activists, the supposed representatives of the working class, do not really look out for the interests of the workers and peasants. Without caring about the wages of the worker or the standard of living of his family, these activists are themselves always trying to take care of their own incomes, which far exceed the real wages of some industrial workers, not to mention the income of farmers and farm workers. From the standpoint of economic democracy, the rise of this new class, numbering several thousand people at most, with a standard of living far higher than that of the average manual laborer, is a very troubling development. It is not the individual example that is so troubling, but rather the fact that these types of people, with utter disregard for the average living conditions of the average worker, are beginning to consider a luxurious life-style to be their lawful due. . . . Of you, Dear Brother Priests, we ask that you not put your material needs above what is reasonably necessary, always taking into account the general standard of living in Poland. . . . We have not sought, and we do not intend to seek, a Church that is triumphant on earth. . . . We have heard enough of the charge that in old times the Catholic hierarchy and clergy used to support earthly kings and bask in their glory. Perhaps that sometimes did happen. As a result of such past experiences, therefore, let us now keep as far as possible from the kings and the mighty of this world. . . .

Because we have been victimized by unfair laws and decrees . . . , we are forced every day to recommence the struggle: the struggle to preserve religion and the Church of Christ, . . . the struggle for truth and for those human and heavenly rights given to us by God. In this struggle we may not, however, resort to that primeval principle, condemned by Christ our Lord, of "an eye for an eye, a tooth for a tooth," or "whatever you do to me, I will do to you." We may not resort to methods contrary to the Gospels, nor can we accept hatred and anger in ourselves. . . . Let us learn not only to be just in this struggle but also to be generous. Let us learn to forgive, especially where we see but a spark of goodwill or a touch of sincere shame. [Clergy and faithful should emerge from this struggle] spiritually enriched and internally purified. Only then will it be our complete victory.

On prospects for the future:

Looking at current developments, we are deeply convinced that the age of militant atheism has passed, together with its false systems and tendencies. A new age is coming, an age of the brotherhood of nations and of races. John XXIII's idea of universalism will take hold of all of humanity. . . . We must act with all means at our disposal so that within our nation there is no hatred of other religions and other nations: not of Germans . . . , not of Russians, and not of anybody else. We have every right to defend our way of life and our own national development; we have a right and a duty to love our Fatherland. But we must do so without hating our neighbors, even those who yesterday did us harm. . . . We are, and we most certainly want to stay, the guardians and the sponsors of true, authentic national culture—not parochial or narrow-minded culture, but a culture with a broad, ecumenical sweep, appealing to the entire world and to all people of goodwill.

On relations with the state, the bishops spoke firmly and unambiguously:

Do not allow yourselves to be divided. Do not accept the divisions into those less or more "devoted to Caesar," into "positive" and "negative," into "patriots" and "non-patriots." We well know that . . . the priest who walks away from Our Lord begins to serve an idol. And here we have the origin of the personality cult in its various forms. . . . You must remember the principle from the Acts of the Apostles: that whenever the powerholders give unethical orders, transcending human possibilities, "one must serve God more than man." Orders contrary to human nature, contrary to the Gospels, the Rights of Man, the Constitution—such orders one may not carry out.[10]

This appeal to "civil disobedience" was no mere rhetorical flourish. In response to a government order prohibiting nuns, monks, and catechists from teaching religion, the episcopate issued a simple appeal to the clergy: "We ask you, dear Brothers, Sisters, and Catechists, to continue to carry out your noble mission, which in every society is so highly valued."[11]

The episcopate did not retreat from this position so expressed. But neither was the state very amenable to compromise. The conflict grew unremittingly, until it became an open conflict in December 1965.

10. *Pastoral Letters*, pp. 296–313.
11. *Pastoral Letters*, p. 314.

4

TRANSLATOR'S NOTE:
In a pastoral letter addressed to German Catholics in December 1965, the Polish episcopate offered forgiveness to the Germans for the latter's actions in Poland and asked for forgiveness from the Germans for wrongdoings committed by Poles against them. The letter sparked an uproar, with Party and revisionist circles both condemning the stance of the Church. Coming at a time when the Soviet bloc still lacked formal relations with West Germany, the letter became the basis of a major propaganda campaign against the Church. Michnik argues that the willingness of the left-wing intelligentsia to go along with the campaign only made it easier for the Party to turn against the intelligentsia in 1968.

THE CONFLICT OVER THE PASTORAL LETTER

The sharpening of the conflict between the Church and state was part and parcel of the overall governmental policy aimed at restricting democratic liberties. But before trying this policy out on the Church, the government had already turned against the "revisionist" circles, that is, against the secular intelligentsia.

The retreat from the slogans and practices of the Polish October began soon after the assumption of power by Władysław Gomułka. First came press attacks on the revisionists; then came administrative measures. *Po prostu,* the highly popular weekly of the young intelligentsia, was shut down by the government exactly one year to the day after the Party Plenum that had brought Gomułka back to power. When students held protest meetings against the decision, special militia units broke them up with force, often quite brutally. At the same time, the government closed down one literary journal, *Europa,* before even the first issue had appeared! This provoked the resignation from the Party of several prominent writers, including Jerzy Andrzejewski, Mieczyław Jastrun, Paweł Hertz, Juliusz Żuławski, Jan Kott, and Stanisław Dygat. At the beginning of 1958, the weekly *Nowa Kultura* [New Culture] was virtually liquidated as well. Attempts to force the journal to adopt a new ideological line (led by Andrzej Werblan, the Party representative in *Nowa Kultura)* caused a mass resignation from the editorial board: Wiktor Woroszylski, Tadeusz Konwicki, Wilhelm Mach, Marian Brandys, Leszek Kołakowski, Witold Wirpsza, and Jerzy Piórkowski all handed in their resignations.

Meanwhile, by 1961, those politicians representing the more liberal wing of the Party had all lost their leadership positions. Władysław Bieńkowski was no longer Minister of Education, Stefan Żółkiewski lost his post as Minister of Higher Education, and Julian

Hochfeld was replaced as Director of the Institute for International Affairs. Antoni Słonimski, meanwhile, lost his position as head of the Writers' Union. At the same time, the political police and the prosecutor's office became more active—witness the trials of Rewska, Kornacki, and Rudzińska, or the Henryk Holland affair.[1] In early 1962, on the basis of a police provocation, the government dissolved the Club of the Crooked Circle, one of the last relics of October, and one of the last places in Poland where truly free speech was still possible. *Przegląd Kulturalny* [Cultural Review], a weekly which had kept a certain independence from the increasingly restrictive and nationalistic tendencies within the Party apparatus, was closed down in 1963. At the XIII Plenum of the Party in July 1963, the Party declared war on "hostile tendencies" in science and culture. A discussion club at Warsaw University was dissolved, as was the "Club of the Seekers of Contradiction," a political discussion group for high school youth.[2] Ever more restrictive censorship policies led to a sharp clash between intellectuals and the Party leadership, of which the "Letter of 34"[3] was only the most prominent example. Then there were a series of trials: of Melchior Wańkowicz in the fall of 1964 and of Jan Nepomucen Miller in the summer of 1965. Autumn 1964 also saw the beginning of the well-known Kuroń and Modzelewski affair,[4] and in July 1965 these two were sentenced to prison terms of three and three and one-half years, respectively. Soon afterwards, Warsaw University students who had been involved with them were sent before a special university disciplining commission.

All of these repressive acts elicited protests from intellectual circles. Many prominent figures, including Maria Dąbrowska, Antoni Słonimski, Maria Ossowska, Tadeusz Kotarbiński, Edward Lipiński, Leopold Infeld, Leszek Kołakowski, and Włodzimierz Brus, spoke out publicly in various ways. The year 1966 found intellectual

---

1. Between 1958 and 1962, Hanna Rewska, Jerzy Kornacki, and Hanna Rudzińska were put on trial for distributing the émigré journal *Kultura* in Poland, charged with distributing texts "detrimental to the interests of the Polish state." In 1962, dissident writer Henryk Holland fell out of a window to his death—apparently, a staged suicide.—TRANS.

2. Michnik was one of the founders and main activists of this group.—TRANS.

3. An open letter to the Party leadership, signed by thirty-four prominent intellectuals, demanding greater democratic liberties.—TRANS.

4. The then-radical Left activists Jack Kuroń and Karol Modzelewski wrote and distributed a long "Open Letter" to the Party rank-and-file, offering a Marxist critique of the system and calling for a "genuine" workers' revolution to bring "real socialism" to Poland. Published in English as *Revolutionary Marxist Students in Poland Speak Out* (New York: Merit, 1968).—TRANS.

circles of the secular Left sharply at odds with the political authorities. In this conflict, the Party leadership showed no inclination to compromise. The official policies of the government suggested that there could be no hope for reconciliation.

As the Vatican Council and 1965 were both nearing an end, the Polish episcopate sent a letter to the Catholic bishops of Germany which was to become the subject of considerable controversy for quite some time. That was over ten years ago. It took me ten years before I actually read a copy of the letter. But now that I have read it, carefully, the truth is that I can find in it nothing, absolutely nothing, that could justify the surprisingly hostile reaction it elicited in otherwise quite civil people. Nor can I find anything that might explain the unexpected susceptibility of these critics to the demagogic arguments of officialdom. And I am not speaking of your average journalistic lackeys. On the contrary, I'm talking of respected people such as Konstanty Grzybowski and Bogusław Leśnodorski, Michał Radgowski and Tadeusz Mrowczyński, Andrzej Gwiżdż and Marian Małowist. But then, why talk about others? For I myself participated in this ignominious spectacle, though the very thought of it makes me blush with shame. I am embarrassed by my own stupidity, though, of course, stupidity is no justification.

Why did I do this? Why did I decide to run that interview with Professor Grzybowski in *Argumenty,* the journal I was working for at the time? In response to my questions, and in the context of a general propaganda assault on the Church, Grzybowski gave a very critical assessment of the past and present of the Church. I myself felt fully irreproachable. After all, no one had forced me to do this piece, or even tried to talk me into doing it. What guided my hand was not weakness of character but rather the absurd conviction that I was speaking out in a just cause. It was one thing, I thought, to have conflicts with the Party, conflicts that I had already had. My disagreements with the Church I saw as something entirely different. That my contribution was not part of a debate but an assault, that I spoke not in my own voice but, *nolens volens,* in the voice of a propagandist in an unjust cause—of all this I was unaware. Even though I knew the episcopate's position only from the biased accounts and the out-of-context quotations I saw in the official press, I considered its position to be nothing more than a defense of the "trenches of the Holy Trinity."[5] Unable to see anything more, I mindlessly repeated the jokes

5. A phrase from *The Un-Divine Comedy,* the most prominent work of the great nineteenth-century Polish writer Zygmunt Krasiński.—Trans.

about how Gomułka and Wyszyński deserved each other. And it's not as if I didn't have enough information to know otherwise! After all, it wasn't the bishops who had signed my earlier arrest warrant, nor was it they who insisted on my expulsion from the university. But their language was something foreign to me, something impenetrable, and it only solidified my altogether twisted conception of the Church. I make no attempt to justify my actions, for nothing can justify participation in organized lies. It is not the motives but the consequences of our actions that are most important. And yet without this personal digression I would not be able to write about relations between the Church and the secular intelligentsia.

Various aspects of Church documents from that period did offend me; indeed, they offend me even now. Yet in the letter to the German bishops I can find virtually none of those elements of Polish Catholic ideology which I feel are so difficult to accept (and which I will talk more about later). On the contrary, there are many good and refreshing parts in this letter. For example, rarely does one find in Church documents such open recognition of the drawbacks implicit in the notion of the "Polish Catholic":

There has always been a certain Christian symbiosis of Church and state in Poland. It has existed from the very beginning, and in fact has never really been broken. In time, this led to the virtually universal belief among Poles that that which is "Polish" is also "Catholic." It also gave rise to a particularly Polish religious style, in which the religious element is intrinsically bound up with the national element, with all of the positive as well as the negative aspects of such a situation.

A little further on, writing about the relations of medieval Poland with the West, the bishops emphasize the participation of foreigners in the creation of Polish culture. They write of German merchants, architects, and artists, "of whom many were Polonized, with only their German family names remaining." They write about Wit Stwosz from Nuremburg, who built an artistic school in Kraków that became so important for Polish culture.

Poles have deeply respected their Christian brothers of the West, who came to them as emissaries of genuine culture. And we have not overlooked their non-Polish origins. With regard to Western culture, including German culture, we truly have much to be thankful for.

Such a vision of the nation and of national culture, free from chauvinism and xenophobia, is one secular intellectuals ought to feel par-

ticularly close to. It is completely different from the nationalist Endek conception of Polishness frequently encountered in Catholic
circles. Not accidently, the bishops emphasized the free and tolerant
traditions of Polish culture and stressed that the true motto of Poland
was the war-time slogan, "For our freedom—and yours."

Adopting the more tolerant and freedom-oriented tendencies of
the Polish tradition, the bishops were courageous enough to draw the
proper conclusions of their position. In particular, they sought to dis-
tinguish between Nazism and the German people. First, they spoke
of the black spots of Polish-German relations, such as the policies of
Frederick the Great, Bismarck, and above all the savagery of Hitler.
Then they took up current matters. Although they were firm in their
position that Poland's western borders must be considered final, they
did try to understand the German point of view: "For the Germans,
as we can well understand, the Polish border on the Oder and Nysa
rivers is part of the bitter fruit of this last war of mass destruction,
just as is the suffering of the millions of German refugees and reset-
tled people."

As the last quotation illustrates, the Polish bishops understood
the magnitude of the injustice done to Germans who were expelled
from their lands. Not all of these Germans were Nazis, yet all of
them were stripped of their homes and property. One can, I think,
argue that this massive resettlement was an unavoidable consequence
of the Nazis' genocidal war, but one cannot, without nationalistic
blindness, say that such events are morally insignificant: an injustice
is always an injustice. The letter did not spare the German bishops a
long list of injustices done to the Poles, but neither did it neglect the
sufferings of Germans:

> We know very well that a large proportion of the German people found
> itself under inhuman Nazi pressure. We are aware of the terrible internal
> anguish undergone by many honorable German bishops; it is sufficient to
> mention the names of Cardinal Faulhaber, von Galen, or Preysing. We know
> of the martyrs of the "White Rose," of the fighters from the resistance move-
> ment of July 20, and we know that many priests and lay persons alike gave
> their lives in sacrifice (Lichtenberg, Metzger, Klausener and many others).
> Thousands of Germans, both Christians and Communists, shared, in concen-
> tration camps, the fate of our Polish brothers. . . .

And it is precisely for these reasons that we must try to forget. Today
we need not polemics, not cold war, but the beginning of a dialogue, which
the Vatican Council and Pope Paul VI are now trying to introduce every-

where. If there is goodwill on both sides, . . . a serious dialogue must surely come about, and will in time bring good results. . . . We feel it is imperative that we commence this dialogue now, during the Vatican Council, . . . so that we can get to know each other better, learn each other's national customs, religious devotions, and styles of life, which are rooted in and conditioned by our pasts. . . .

Catholic ministers of the German people: we ask that you celebrate, together with us, our Christian millennium. Do this in your own way, whether by your prayers or by setting aside a special day for this purpose. For every gesture of this kind we will be grateful to you. . . . In the most Christian and the most human spirit, we extend to you . . . our hand. We offer our forgiveness and we ask for your forgiveness. And if you . . . take this hand so fraternally extended, we will then be able to celebrate our Millennium with a clear conscience, in the most Christian of ways.[6]

In the ten years that have passed, the deeply humanistic meaning of this letter, as well as its political wisdom, have now become clear. Events have only confirmed the correctness of the episcopate's position: for Poles, there can be no other road than that of dialogue with democratic German opinion. We must jointly overcome the effects of the Nazi apocalypse. Fanning the fires of national hatred is a sure road to nowhere. No rational person can accuse the Church of questioning the permanence of Poland's borders or of "forgiving" Nazi criminals. Today it is with shame and disgust that we read the servile and hypocritical words of government apologist Zbigniew Załuski, who spoke of the "repentance of innocents and the absolution of the unrepentant." At the time, the regime questioned the very right of the bishops to issue such a letter. "Who authorized the Polish episcopate to make such a declaration?" asked the Party daily *Trybuna Ludu*. And in the Warsaw daily *Życie Warszawy*, one could read that the bishops had

arbitrarily entered the field of foreign policy, which has nothing to do with the religious mission of the Church. Who authorized the bishops to speak out on issues of foreign policy . . . without prior consultation and coordination with the Polish government? In whose name are the bishops speaking out, with a position contrary to the opinions of all of society and against the interests of our country?

6. *Listy Pasterskie Episkopatu Polski* [Pastoral Letters of the Polish Episcopate] (Paris: Editions du Dialogue, 1975), pp. 830–36. (Referred to hereafter as *Pastoral Letters.*)

Following these rhetorical questions came the warning: "One thing is certain: in our people's republic . . . there is no room and there will be no room for such ostentatious arrogance." On 19 December 1965, soon after his return from the Vatican Council, Cardinal Wyszyński responded in a sermon delivered at the Warsaw parish of the Immaculate Heart of Mary:

When I returned to Poland, I was greeted with a great deal of clamor, shouting, and noise. . . . The Polish bishops have been reproached for not sending their letters to the people in charge. Is it customary for letters addressed to specific persons to be disseminated on all sides? A letter is intended for its addressee, and in this case the addressee was the German episcopate. . . . Yet let us suppose that we had wanted to publish our letter. What would the censorship have done? . . . Would the letter have thereby been more authentic? In the face of such conditions, I would prefer to remain silent. . . . I do not intend to engage in polemics, and I will not engage in polemics on such a low level. . . . Still, I am convinced that I do not deserve the treatment that I am presently receiving in my own country. But so it is, and so in the name of God, all I can say to my slanderers (for I cannot call them anything else) is that I forgive you!

Soon after, the episcopate as a whole spoke out in a new document read in church on 10 February 1966. The bishops replied to the charges with considerable calm and wisdom:

We were not speaking in the name of society, nor were we speaking in the name of the Nation, in its secular or political sense. Although the overwhelming majority of the Polish Nation is Catholic and expresses an allegiance to the Church, we bishops do not consider ourselves thereby to be the political leaders of the Nation. Our mission is something else. . . . We spoke as the representatives of the Catholic circles of the Polish Nation, and our right to speak out in such a way we derive from Christ, and from the ministries we fulfill in His Church. We derive our right to speak out also from the faith and loyalty of all of you, that is, from those whom we want to serve not with political wisdom, and not by building this or that political system, but by showing the way to Christ. . . . Those people who do not feel a vital connection with the Catholic community should not think that we have spoken in their names.

We have no intention of instructing those who measure everything by human dimensions alone. We address ourselves to those who believe that Jesus Christ, Who lived on earth . . . , is our God and Supreme Lawgiver. We address ourselves to those who believe Christ's words. And Christ declares that He will bring unto people a new law. His law is difficult: "A new commandment I give unto you, That ye love one another" (John 13:34). Within this law there is one most difficult element, something lacking in every other religion, something to which it seems particularly difficult for human beings to adhere: the injunction to love one's enemies. "Love your enemies, bless them that curse you" (Matthew 5:44). For many this seems to conflict with common sense, which tends to revolve solely around worldly matters, and which rules out the help of grace in the realization of every good, particularly the most difficult good. And yet this law is the condition of hope. It is the catalyst of all efforts aimed at social progress and at the resolution of apparently irresolvable contradictions. . . .

We can see how a crisis of inflexible, formal, human standards is present in the world today. These standards have proven to be inadequate for the resolution of social problems, and even more inadequate for resolving international conflicts. But when the formal codes break down, when official representatives are powerless, unable to come to agreement, then people of goodwill seek to come to agreement on their own, outside the bounds of official politics. They feel themselves part of that great community of the family of man, something above the divisions of borders, languages, and political systems. . . . We were thinking of this when we wrote to the bishops and Catholics of Germany. We wanted to tell them that if we are to live in peace as neighbors, after a thousand difficult and mostly painful years for us, this can come about only on the basis of mutual understanding. And this must be an understanding not just in treaties, but above all in the souls and consciences of our two nations. . . . We offered words of forgiveness for those people who understand their own guilt and who sincerely desire to peacefully coexist with us. . . . We offered forgiveness like Christ on the cross offered forgiveness. Through the mystery of the Cross Christ forgave everyone, including us who are speaking to you, and you who are listening to us. . . .

Does the Polish Nation have reason to ask our neighbors for forgiveness? Certainly not! We believe that as a nation over the centuries we have done the German nation no wrong. . . . But we also accept the Christian principle, lately so emphasized in literature as well, that "no one is truly innocent" (Albert Camus). We believe that . . . if over the course of history only one Pole had committed a vile act, we would already have reason to apologize. If we seek to be a nation of noble and kindhearted people, a nation of a better future, there is no other choice.[7]

This reply of the episcopate, firmly defending its point of view in a tone of dignity and humanism, only provoked a new series of

7. *Pastoral Letters*, pp. 435–37.

attacks by state authorities. Relentless criticism of the Church in the mass media was accompanied by administrative repression. The state obstructed, and sometimes even prevented, religious processions from taking place. Police used clubs to break up the Corpus Christi procession in Warsaw. Then there was the notorious harassment of the holy portrait of the Black Madonna of Częstochowa. In one case, on 2 September 1966, while the portrait was being moved from Warsaw to Katowice so it could make the rounds of churches and local parishes in the latter area, it was seized and brought back to Częstochowa. The authorities refused to allow it off the premises of the Church of Jasna Góra. During celebrations of the Millennium, the authorities organized anti-Wyszyński street demonstrations in several cities. In Warsaw, a crowd of Party members specially rounded up for the occasion, led by plainclothes officers of the security police, "spontaneously" started chanting, "Send the Cardinal back to Rome!" Despite such requests, the Cardinal was denied a passport to visit Rome, and the pope was prevented from visiting Poland, as were representatives of the German episcopate. Meanwhile, numerous employees around the country were losing their jobs for trying to defend the bishops and their letter.

The tone of government propaganda together with the actions of local authorities raised analogies to the persecution of the Church during the period of the Kulturkampf. The state's polemics recalled the worst Stalinist models.

And in this situation, the Left—at best!—reacted passively. It kept silent when the Church was being slandered and defamed, and it kept silent during the street demonstrations and the vicious calumnies in the press. Someone may ask, "But what could the Left have done? Wasn't silence itself a form of protest?" No. In 1966, unlike in Stalinist times, silence was not a form of protest. In the Stalinist years, the silence of Maria and Stanisław Ossowski had a definite oppositional content, and only out of ignorance or bad faith can one charge the Ossowskis with complicity in the persecution of religion. In those times the silence of the Ossowskis was deafening. But during the year of the Millennium the situation was completely different. On a number of occasions secular intellectuals had already raised their voices against aspects of Party policy—for example, in the "Letter of 34." No, the source of their silence must be located elsewhere. The problem, it seems to me, was that too few people understood the true meaning of those events. Few were able to grasp the real reason for the unleashing of nationalist emotions or the brutal attacks on the only independent institution in the country.

What then was the conflict all about? The government authorities wanted to terrorize society, to instill a sense of xenophobia, to unify the nation around chauvinistic slogans. They hoped to create a link, in popular perceptions, between Christian humanist values and the notion of treason. Whatever was antitotalitarian was henceforth to be considered antipatriotic. In a word, their goal was the "totalitarianization" of the public and private lives of the Polish people. The next phase of this process, this time at the expense of the secular intelligentsia, came with the "March Events" of 1968.

5

TRANSLATOR'S NOTE:

In January 1968 government authorities closed down the Warsaw production of *Dziady* [Forefathers' Eve], the play by the great nineteenth-century national bard Adam Mickiewicz, when its appeals for democratic rights against the Russian tsarist authorities were applauded a bit too energetically by the largely student audiences. The students responded with strikes and large protest rallies, and the government responded to this by arresting key leaders (including Adam Michnik) and sending police and goon squads to brutally disperse student protesters on 8 March 1968. Thus began the "March events." Perceiving an opportunity to settle accounts with their growing number of intellectual critics, the authorities expelled and dismissed hundreds of students and professors. Entire university departments were dissolved and then reconstituted under strict Party control. This assault on the intelligentsia was presented to the public as an attack on "aliens" and Jews trying to sabotage Poland from within. The mass media focused on those of its opponents with Jewish-sounding names (Michnik, for example, was frequently referred to by his father's name, Szechter) as the government tried to present the conflict as one between good Polish patriots and bad Jewish radicals and ex-Communists. The consequences of the March events were a severance of ties between the Party and the revisionist intelligentsia, the exodus of most of the Jewish population in Poland, and the constitution of a new democratic Left—the group to whom Michnik addresses this book—that would play a key role in the opposition movement up through Solidarity and into the postcommunist governments after 1989.

THE CHURCH IN 1968

There is no room here for a detailed historical account of the "March Events," or of the "pogrom" of the leftist intelligentsia carried out under anti-Semitic cover. What interests us here is the popular conception of the episcopate's attitude to these events, which argues that the episcopate viewed the movement of intellectuals and student youth as part of an internal quarrel among Communists, and that it saw the subsequent anti-intellectual pogrom and anti-Semitic demagoguery as but one more "settling of accounts" within the Party.

I am convinced that this is a gross simplification. It is worth citing a few facts and documents. Let us begin with one document, titled "A Statement of the Polish Episcopate on the Distressing Events," dated 21 March 1968. "In recent weeks, a series of troubling and disturbing events has shaken many Polish cities, particularly within university communities. Wishing to remain faithful to the mission of the Church in the contemporary world, we Polish bishops feel obliged to speak out on this matter." Referring to the teachings of Vatican II, the bishops note that "the Church see its mission in the propagation and preservation of true peace among people." The goal of this effort is:

a social arrangement in which the basic rights of the individual and society are respected. These are the right to truth, freedom, justice, and love. All the problems that divide people in today's world ought to be resolved not by force but by frank dialogue. Only such a method can bring about an end to discrimination and lead to truth and justice in interhuman relations. Only this method reflects the dignity of man; indeed, man's moral strength is expressed precisely in this way. The use of physical force does not lead to the genuine resolution of human or group conflict. On the contrary, the brutal use of force is an outrage to human dignity. Instead of acting to preserve social peace it only exacerbates the painful wounds. The Polish bishops have sent a special message about this matter to the government.

Addressing students, the bishops wrote:

We are trying to understand and to comprehend the sources of the unrest that you feel, the unrest it seems all young people in the world feel today. It is an unrest whose roots reach to the very depths of human affairs. It is an unrest concerning the meaning of human existence, and it is connected with the search for truth and freedom, which is the natural right of every human being in his personal as well as social life. . . . And so we bishops, together with the entire Polish Church, will continue to pray with young people and for young people. . . . We commend to God all those for whom these last days have brought so much suffering.[1]

In his 30 March sermon in Warsaw for teachers and instructors, Cardinal Wyszyński referred to the current events:

Our young, well aware of the difficult conditions in which we live, have but modest demands. They seek respect for their humanity, complete honesty, and at least a modicum of love and justice. . . . We must speak to young people with our hearts. For the heart they understand, not the whip! . . . We must not forget that the future of Poland belongs to its young! . . . Anyone isolating himself from the youth is suicidal, whoever he may be. For it is impossible to speak of the future of the Church, the state, or the nation without speaking of our youth. And that is why one must not shut oneself off from it. It is wrong to offer only repression; we must also offer our hearts, our love, our confidence, our respect, and our understanding.[2]

At the sermon for Holy Thursday delivered at Warsaw's Cathedral of St. John, Cardinal Wyszyński took up the question of anti-Semitism. There were strong words in this sermon about "spectacles of hatred," people being "reviled," and about the need for "honestly recognizing the right of *all* people in our Fatherland to be loved."

Such disturbing things we are witnessing in our country. Our hearts ache with pain. It would seem that for a certain category of people there is neither love nor a right to compassion. There are things taking place which we can hardly even imagine! . . . Perhaps I am responsible, as Bishop of Warsaw, for not speaking enough about the right and duty of all human beings to love one another, regardless of accent, language, or race. Perhaps I am respon-

1. *Listy Pasterskie Episkopatu Polski* [Pastoral Letters of the Polish Episcopate] (Paris: Editions du Dialogue, 1975), p. 518. (Referred to hereafter as *Pastoral Letters.)*
2. Stefan Cardinal Wyszyński, *Idzie nowych ludzi plemię* [And Comes the Tribe of New People] (Poznan, 1973), p. 287.

sible for not warning you so you could avoid the monstrous ghost of a revived racism, for it is in the name of race that we are supposedly defending
our culture. *But that is not the way to defend culture!* Not through hatred!
. . . We can defend our culture *only* through love.[3]

In the 3 May "Statement of the Polish Episcopate," the bishops
returned once again to the March events, saying that they were compelled to do so by "the continuing turn of events." Let us look at one
long excerpt:

Clearly the issue at hand concerns the very foundations of social and public
morality, and in this sphere Christ's Church will never cease to fulfill its
mission. . . . The Church's mission is to propagate peace, and the conditions of peace are justice and social love. Each constituent of the nation and
every citizen of the state must be free to help shape the common good according to his own legitimate convictions and conscience. No one should be
called an enemy simply because he holds different views. . . . This is especially important for the proper functioning of political representation, which
should be a place for the free exchange of ideas, motivated by concern for
the good of society, and sensitive to all the problems that pervade society.
Subordinating government to one social group only stifles an exchange of
views and robs this institution of its true sense, while it deprives society of
the ability to express its opinions or to shape its collective life according to
the wishes of its citizens. If they take this road, the authorities risk losing
contact with society. Similarly, the press and other means of mass communication can function properly only when everybody has the right to present
their reasonable views and to defend them. If the legitimate right of free
speech is suppressed, the role of the press becomes destructive. . . .

The principle of freedom of belief has particular significance for national culture, which is made up of various branches of artistic and scientific
creativity. In the sphere of arts and sciences, freedom to research and to
disseminate the results of research is essential. Without this, there is no possibility to deepen and develop culture. The scholar's mission is to strive for
truth in his chosen field. This is true for all areas of scholarly research, including philosophy, which from its inception has searched for answers to the
most basic questions of human existence. . . . The history of culture, science, and especially of philosophy teaches us that these fields can flourish
only under two conditions: full scientific freedom, and a guaranteed right for
representatives of different viewpoints to carry on a dialogue. . . . The Cath-

3. Cited from *Na Antenie,* 24 November 1968; also, see Stefan Cardinal Wyszyński, *W sercu stolicy* [In the Heart of the Capital] (Rome, 1972), pp. 93–95. The two
printed versions of this sermon differ slightly.

olic Church . . . attaches great importance to dialogue between representatives of different viewpoints, including dialogue between believers and nonbelievers. Such dialogue truly serves the cause of progress. It teaches respect for the truth as well as for the human individual, whose dignity is expressed by his approach to freedom and truth. To those who have put their life's effort into the search for scientific truth, we express our due respect. We also express our firm hope that the principle of tolerance befitting the noble traditions of our nation will be reflected in the social and political life of our country. Indeed, it is because of our concern for these noble traditions that we are so saddened by the defamation of the good name of our nation in certain foreign circles. We are speaking here of those attempts to charge the Polish people with responsibility for the extermination of the Jews, which was carried out in Nazi death camps. This is a terrible moral injustice, especially when we consider that millions of Poles died in these very same camps. In memory of these our compatriots, and in light of all the evidence of compassionate assistance rendered by Poles to persecuted Jews during the Occupation, we demand an end to this false and pernicious propaganda and an end to all attempts to provoke it. Vatican II clearly articulated the nature of our relationship to non-Christian religions, including the Jews. The Polish bishops commend all of these principles with regard to their deep humanitarian content. And all of this . . . we pass on to the clergy and the faithful, who share these same concerns . . . . Our thoughts go out chiefly to students and working people. We entrust to Mary, Queen of Poland, all of our youth's noble desires for a better society and a better humanity, for now and forever.[4]

This is what the documents say. They demonstrate conclusively that the bishops openly spoke out on the side of the persecuted and their values, and against the persecutors; that they came to the defense of oppositionist intellectuals and student protesters; that they condemned the violence and slander. One cannot in good faith interpret these sermons and pastoral letters in any other way. At most, one may complain of a certain vagueness or overgenerality. On other occasions, the episcopate certainly did speak out in an incomparably more elaborate fashion, making the point far more bluntly than here. But let those of us left-wing and secular critics remember our own reactions from two years earlier, during the campaign against the Church. And let us compare our own actions of the time with the bishops' attitude during the "March Events." This should enable us to see our objections in their proper proportions. Before we behold the mote in our brother's eye, let us remember the beam in our own.

4. *Pastoral Letters*, pp. 525–26.

In light of these criticisms of my own past views, as well as the views of my ideological friends and co-thinkers, I believe honesty demands that I also address some sincere, critical remarks at the episcopate. Let me say one thing straight out: what is lacking in the bishops' statements, in my opinion, is a clear and unequivocal denunciation of official anti-Semitism. In the given situation, mere allusion could not suffice. But let me be clear: I am not saying that the Jewish question was the main and most important issue of the time. That is simply impossible in a country with hardly any Jews. But the point of the massive anti-Semitic campaign was not so much to strike out at those Jews who had managed to survive the Nazi inferno. Rather, the point was to fan the flames of national chauvinism, encourage xenophobia, cover up the real reasons for the social crisis, and disaccustom the populace from rational thought. It was an attempt to turn people into accomplices to the crimes of the state. This is why anti-Semitism was such a key issue.

Let us try to understand the sources of the Church's moderation. First, there was lack of trust. The bishops, after all, had no reason to sympathize with intellectuals who had fought against the Church and Christianity prior to 1956, spent a good part of their lives within the ruling PUWP, and who had made no secret of their dislike for the Church even in the period just prior to the March events. These intellectuals had not only refrained from condemning repression directed against the Church but continued to write in antireligious periodicals. Moreover, the bishops had no reason at all to sympathize with the widely publicized student group gathered around Kuroń and Modzelewski, whose programmatic statement, the "Open Letter to the Party," possessed all the elements of anti-Catholic leftist obscurantism. (For not only is there Catholic obscurantism, there is also anti-Catholic obscurantism!) This student group (the so-called "Commandos") together with the left-wing secular intellectuals represented much that was alien and hostile to the traditional model of the "Polish Catholic." They evinced a critical, mocking attitude to tradition; a reluctance to glorify the past, often leading to an exaggerated condemnation of Polish history; a tendency to belittle if not entirely neglect the role of Catholicism in Polish national culture; and a tendency to completely disregard the role of the Church in social life. Such tendencies, it is true, were only minor aspects of the ideology of this group. But the secular intellectuals issued no programmatic documents. Indeed, they did nothing whatsoever to make Catholic circles aware of their real position, which was antitotalitarian rather than antireligious.

I suspect that the Church really did see the clash between the leftist intellectuals and the regime as part of some sharp, intra-Communist struggle for power. No doubt they saw the officially sponsored anti-Semitism in the same way, for anti-Semitism had long been used in intra-Party struggles. If we assume that this was their assessment of the situation, it is not surprising that the Church's response to 1968 was so moderate. Nor should we be surprised that the episcopate would not want to link the long-term interests of the Church to the confusing games of intra-Party struggles. Probably this explains the episcopate's refusal to speak in concrete political and ideological terms and its decision to restrict itself to a rather general statement on the students' elementary right to protest and the intellectuals' equally elementary right to scientific and cultural freedom.

And yet even with all of this in mind, I still tend to think that this restraint was a serious error on the part of the episcopate. Because, after all, apart from any internal factional struggles, there were real people suffering from this racist demagoguery—both those who were persecuted and those who, having been drawn into the anti-Semitic persecution, became depraved co-persecutors themselves. An explicit statement by the episcopate about anti-Semitism was extremely necessary for both of these groups.

Let me explain what I have in mind by citing Tadeusz Mazowiecki's reflections on the Christian churches during the Nazi period:

The experience of Christianity in Germany contains lessons that reach far beyond those particular times and conditions. But let us understand this well: we cannot say that it is wrong for the Church, in that or any other situation, to be concerned for its own fate. Nor can we expect churches to suddenly give up everything else when it is necessary to protest or struggle for the most basic human matters. Nevertheless, the considerable disappointment with Christianity during this period teaches us something, something that must provoke Christian awareness. For we see how morally defeated the Church can become if it makes itself the supreme value and ignores the need for human solidarity, which the poor and oppressed have always expected Christianity to promote. The reason that German churches did not live up to their responsibilities is not that they were weak institutionally, but that they too often put the defense of their own freedom of action above the defense of principles. They let people down not because they were rooted in the life and traditions of their own nation, but because they failed to recognize that Christianity does not mean uncritical adherence to national traditions—indeed, it may even require opposing these traditions when their rotten elements come knocking.[5]

The rotten elements in the Polish tradition came knocking in 1968, and they knocked loud and aggressively. Armed with anti-intellectual and racist demagoguery, Communist obscurantism struck hard at the Polish adherents of democratic socialism. Striking at democratic socialism, the ruling philistines trampled those values that are also quite close to Christianity: truth, freedom, solidarity. Progressive Christian intellectuals understood this perfectly. Ignoring old quarrels, they spoke out clearly and unequivocally. I am thinking here of the parliamentary deputies from the "Znak" group. The statements of Jerzy Zawieyski and Stanisław Stomma during the parliamentary debate on the March events had enormous moral and political significance. Of even greater significance would have been the voice of the episcopate.

Of course, for the Party-state leadership that voice was already quite audible. According to the government's assessment, it was precisely the episcopate and Cardinal Wyszyński who were the instigators behind the "Znak" deputies' interpellation[6] of 11 March 1968. On 16 March, Radio Free Europe broadcast the text of this interpellation, which was directed to Premier Józef Cyrankiewicz:

Deeply disturbed by the events at Warsaw University and the Warsaw Polytechnic of 8 and 9 March, concerned for the peace of our country in the complicated international situation, and concerned for the existence of a proper atmosphere for raising and teaching our youth; and on the basis of Article 22 of the Constitution of the Polish People's Republic as well as Articles 70 and 71 of the Rules of the Sejm, we pose the following questions to the Premier: (1) What does the government intend to do in order to restrain the brutal actions of the police and the ORMO reserve police against the student youth, and to determine who is responsible for this brutality? (2) What does the government intend to do in order to provide a substantive reply to the burning questions asked by the youth, questions also being asked by broad public opinion, concerning the democratic rights of citizens and the cultural policies of the government?

5. Tadeusz Mazowiecki, "Nauczył się wierzyć wśród tęgich razów" [He Learned to Believe amidst the Mighty Blows], *Więź*, no. 12 (1971).
6. An interpellation, common to the European parliamentary process, is a formal request for an explanation of policy made by a member of parliament to a government minister, to which the minister is obliged to respond.—TRANS.

Substantiation: The Warsaw student protests came about as a result of certain clear errors committed by government representatives responsible for cultural policy. The removal of *Dziady* from the stage was felt by the youth to constitute a grievous and dramatic interference that threatened cultural freedom and insulted our national traditions.

It was possible, we believe, to have prevented the March 8 disturbances at Warsaw University. Sending ORMO vehicles onto campus precisely during the student rally only inflamed matters.

On 8 and 9 March, young protesters were beaten with extreme brutality, often endangering their lives. There were many cases of outright police brutality, even against women. Society was enraged by these actions.

We appeal to the Premier for the government to take measures to ease the political situation. This requires a cessation of the brutal actions of the police. Those who protest when faced with this brutality should not be treated as enemies of the system. Neither the youth nor society at large has expressed hostility toward socialism in these events. Those irresponsible slogans that have appeared were provoked by the behavior of the police and of ORMO, and cannot be taken as the basis for judging the attitudes of the young generation.

We also wish to express our concern about articles in the press that only exacerbate the tense situation. Neither crushing demonstrations nor forsaking communication with society will provide a way out of the situation. We appeal for your consideration.

Konstanty Łubieński, Tadeusz Mazowiecki, Stanisław Stomma, Janusz Zabłocki, Jerzy Zawieyski

Premier Józef Cyrankiewicz responded to the interpellation during parliamentary discussion on 10 June. It was he who suggested the existence of a close link between the position of the primate and the statement of the Znak group. He called attention to the student riots in Italy, which had been sharply criticized by Cardinal Colombo and Pope Paul VI. Although the premier mentioned neither that this criticism had been sparked by student vandalism nor that the Italian press had published the demands of the protesters, the statements of Italian church dignitaries nevertheless helped him construct a rhetorical straw man. "I understand," said Cyrankiewicz,

the spiritual confusion of the deputies who signed this interpellation, and I understand their choice in this conflict between the universal authority and the local authorities. And yet this is a choice in which the authors of the interpellation stand hand in hand with the instigators of these incidents. . . .

It has been widely acknowledged, by domestic and international opinion alike, that our cultural policy expresses the genuine—not merely formal—freedom of culture in People's Poland. The only ones who do not want to recognize this are those who, ostensibly defending cultural freedom, only seek to attack our country's social order and carry on an irresponsible political struggle. The greatest damage to cultural freedom in Poland has been done by those who have used this smoke screen for their hostile political ends to delude and deceive a portion of our student youth and to wage a struggle against people's power. They have shown that they place their own petty political ambitions above the interests of art and literature, above the true interests of our nation. . . . The deputies of the Znak Parliamentary Group have now joined this club by their interpellation, which, even before it reached us, had encouraged the leaders and troublemakers behind these disturbances.

Polemicizing with Cyrankiewicz would have been a completely useless enterprise. Those same "correct and proper" policies so praised by the premier would lead, two years later, to a bloody massacre of workers on the Baltic Coast, causing the ouster of Cyrankiewicz himself. It must be said, however, that compared to the ensuing parliamentary debate, Cyrankiewicz's comments were a model of civility, an honorable display of liberalism and good will. For directly after Cyrankiewicz came Józef Ozga-Michalski, a name which should not be forgotten. Ozga-Michalski delivered a speech which should someday be included in an anthology of shame. In fact, most of the speeches in this debate could be published in such a volume. They all said more or less the same thing: First, "We love the Party in general and First Secretary Gomułka in particular." Then they cursed the "enemies who look for any possible way to promote reactionary aims." Finally, each duly noted that the interpellation had been read by Radio Free Europe.

And so, Ozga-Michalski accused the Znak deputies of joining forces "with Zionism, which is in alliance with American imperialism and the revanchist forces of West Germany." He linked the interpellation to a speech at a recent West Berlin rally "in which [Willy] Brandt's son, standing before a giant portrait of Trotsky, declared solidarity with Michnik and Dojczgewant."[7] And he considered it appropriate to mention that he had seen in a West German newspaper a photograph of Christian Democratic leader Franz Joseph Strauss

7. Józef Dojczgewant was another prominent student radical of Jewish origin.—
TRANS.

"sounding a church bell in the city of Nazareth, recently captured in the blitzkrieg war of Mr. Dayan." Then, with his own twisted logic, he posed the rhetorical question, "Do the Znak deputies favor the Balkanization of our country?" He accused Stefan Kisielewski of glorifying the Sanacja and its prison camps at Brześć and Bereza and of being in alliance with General Anders and the Paris journal *Kultura*.[8] The government's present policies, Ozga-Michalski said, have nothing to do with anti-Semitism, adding that Moshe Dayan and his lieutenants cannot dictate anything to the Polish people. He also spoke at length about Ionesco and Kołakowski, the war in Vietnam, the memoirs of worker and peasant youth, about Gomułka ("the tried and trusted leader of our nation"), and the Western European existentialist philosophers ("whose goal is to paralyze our healthy social activism and thus prevent People's Poland from accomplishing its goals")

Let me quote one more of Ozga-Michalski's gems, this time concerning the position of the episcopate:

The episcopate's message to the perpetrators of these disturbances, calling on them to work for "truth, freedom and justice," amounts to moral support for anti-Polish forces. We are for discussion and candid dialogue with young people. We want the students to be not only the object of teaching but also its subject. . . . But this is not what the episcopate wants! The episcopate appeals to seekers of truth and freedom, saying that such things cannot be found in People's Poland but only in its opposite. Such prayers will not bring about the social peace that the episcopate allegedly so desires.

Zenon Kliszko, Politburo member and Vice-Marshal of the Sejm, exploded with the following words:

The Znak deputies are surely now well aware that by the position they have taken, they have found themselves in complete political isolation. Along with those whom they really wanted to support, they have placed themselves in conflict with the universal opinion of the people. . . . To whom did the Znak deputies address their interpellation? To the government? No! It was addressed to the streets! It was addressed abroad! The text was immediately

---

8. Sanacja is the name generally used for the authoritarian Polish governments of the 1930s. Brześć and Bereza were the locations of two camps in which Marshal Józef Piłsudski interned political opponents in 1931. General Władysław Anders led an anti-Communist Polish army contingent in Soviet territory during World War II. *Kultura* is an émigré political and literary monthly that has been published in Paris since the end of World War II.—Trans.

distributed throughout Warsaw. Then it was handed to Radio Free Europe, which broadcast it repeatedly. . . . The Znak deputies . . . took advantage of the situation in order to promote their own reactionary projects. . . . The Znak group, as is well known, has already defended the Episcopate's Letter to the German Bishops. Now the group has strayed even further from the interests of Poland, as it stands on the same side as the Zionists and Revisionists who have instigated and organized this entire provocation, which is aimed at disrupting the peace and threatening the vital interests of the fatherland.

Jerzy Zawieyski and Stanisław Stomma rose to defend the interpellation. First Zawieyski:

I do not appear on this platform very often. Today, I appear with great sadness. . . . I must protest, and state with all my soul, as strongly as I am able, that our action was dictated solely by our hearts, minds, and consciences. It was not directed to any foreign or international organization. . . .

Of all of the speeches here, . . . I was most disturbed by the presentation of Zenon Kliszko. He said, among other things, that our action places us outside of the Polish nation and isolates us from the people. There can of course be various criteria concerning who is part of the nation or who embodies national aspirations. But it seems to me that the most spurious criteria are those based on political beliefs. One may not look at someone's political views and only then say whether he is part of the nation or not.

It is not in my nature to be unkind, but I ask Mr. Speaker Kliszko to recall that in this very hall there have been other charges concerning who was allegedly not part of the nation, about who was isolated from the people, and that those charges concerned people who are today very prominent.

In a personal appeal to Władysław Gomułka, Zawieyski called for restraint, arguing that the Party

is itself part of life, and so is not infallible, despite its imaginative, interesting, suggestive, and even, in a historical sense, its great social concepts. Its errors may be understood. The government will not suffer any loss of authority if it admits these errors.

Zawieyski spoke out in defense of the writers who were under attack. He discussed the particularly difficult and complex situation of Polish literature, its aesthetic collapse in the Stalinist period, and the moral shock it experienced after the Twentieth Congress of the Soviet Communist Party:

That was a drama worthy of respect. . . . It was followed, however, by the imposition of new controls similar to the old administrative pressures. The dejection and false hopes of the writers only intensified their aversion to censorship, prohibitions, and all forms of restrictions. A climate of distrust was born, and from distrust came fear and suspicion. . . . The censor's red pen made many reckless errors. . . .

I was unable to attend the recent special session of the Writers' Union since I was in the hospital at the time, but my conscience demands that I say one thing. If the atmosphere at that congress was heated and impassioned, it is only because many matters were bothering its participants, because the dramatic situation caused by the official errors had alarmed them both as writers and as citizens concerned for the fate of Polish culture. . . .

Mr. Ozga-Michalski attacked the episcopate's letter on the March events. In my judgment this letter is a historic document, a beautiful letter full of civic pride.

In contrast to the methods proposed by most of these parliamentarians for dealing with people who have other points of view, Zawieyski counterposed the notion of dialogue:

The basis for dialogue, besides the goodwill of both sides, is respect for the other, the desire to understand the other's point of view. It entails a kind of transformation into the other person, a person whom one does not wish to dominate, absorb or transform, but with whom one would like to engage in a common search. This means one has to suspend and even to question one's own point of view, so that one can fully grasp the rationale of the other side. It means we must understand that right is not only within us but also outside of us.

Dialogue does not always mean talking about what divides us. It may also be an invitation to consider what we, people of the modern age, have in common. The starting point of every dialogue is not just solidarity but the spirit of brotherhood. This last word is neither too grand nor too strong. It arouses in us the desire, not always fully conscious, that we walk down the same road together. . . . This is the kind of dialogue the young people have been calling for. It is also the kind of dialogue called for by those "other reactionaries," that is, by the Znak Parliamentary Group of the Polish People's Republic. . . .

The accusations made against me, that in signing the interpellation I had one eye on the streets, on Radio Free Europe, or on the Zionists—these are very painful blows. Is this ill will? An insult? An attempt to discredit me? I do not wish to attribute such intentions to anyone. Perhaps these words were spoken carelessly, in the heat and passion of the moment. But let me just state that over the past eleven years, I have, in good faith, devoted a great deal of time, energy, and thought to People's Poland, socialist Poland. I believe in its future. But this does not mean that I am not deeply pained by the mistakes which its government often commits.

Following this magnificent and dramatic presentation, Stanisław Stomma took the floor to answer the charges of Cyrankiewicz and Kliszko:

As to the matter of dissemination, it is our view that an interpellation is neither a classified nor a secret document, and that it may therefore be made accessible to the people as well. ['Commotion in the hall,' according to the official stenographic report—A.M.] I do not know when or on what day Radio Free Europe broadcast our statement. . . . I do know, however, that news of many governmental matters are immediately broadcast on Radio Free Europe. How they get this information I do not know. And so this charge does not concern us at all.

We have called for a political assessment of the facts and have asked that the students' demands be given a hearing. . . . What we are asking for is a different approach, an understanding that a movement of enormous proportions is underway here, wrestling and searching for some way to express itself, with a series of demands stemming from deep-seated problems of society. We are speaking of *enormous social problems*. The youth are aware of it and so is the older generation. There is a great yearning for a system of socialist democracy. Young people feel this deeply, and they are showing their impatience.

In further discussion, or rather in further monologues, there was the same slander, lies, and abuse as before. Let me quote, just for the record, from a few of these speeches. Władysław Piłatowski, first secretary of the Wrocław Party organization, went so far as to accuse Jerzy Zawieyski of giving moral support to Polish Stalinists:

Certain facts have been recalled here about the tragedy of the years 1948 to 1956. This tragedy, . . . the historian will say, was a tragedy of the Party and of the nation, one which affected even you, Mr. Deputy Zawieyski. But don't you understand, Sir, that by your attitude, regardless of intention, you rendered objective support to precisely those forces which created that situation?

From the speech of Antoni Walaszek, first secretary of the Party in Szczecin, we learn that the revanchist West German Chancellor Kiesinger had been depending on support for his Polish policies not only from the authors of the notorious Letter of forgiveness and conciliation with the West Germans, [but also from] the discredited leaders of the recent disturbances, the Revisionists and Zionists who are trying to weaken socialism, and those who are preparing the transition to the so-called second stage. And let me add, gentlemen of Znak, that whether you like it or not, he is also relying on your own expressions of support.

Next came Jan Szydlak, first secretary in Poznań:

I do not hesitate to say it: Bottomless is the ocean of lies and deception presented by the authors of this interpellation. Concern for social peace . . . means . . . appealing for order, not pouring oil onto the flames. . . . People such as these—the political wrecks dreaming of a return to power, those whose main concern is to help the interests of their international bosses, . . . those who by pouring their dubious oil onto these flames only hoped to promote their own reactionary aims—such people do not want peace.

Responding to Zawieyski, Kraków Party leader Czesław Domagała announced that

not every writer can be the conscience of the nation. And certainly people like Grzędziński, Słonimski, Bejnar-Jasienica, or Kisielewski are not, never have been, and never will be the conscience of the nation. Nor will those corrupt, cosmopolitan, revisionist, and Zionist literary hacks, or the bards of anarchy and national chauvinism, or the admirers of the world of violence, human injustice, and exploitation. No, the *real* conscience of the nation is none other than the Polish United Workers' Party.

Stanisław Kociołek, first secretary of the Party in Gdańsk, attacked Stomma for his idea of a "democratizing plan," and once again referred to the position of the episcopate:

If we look at matters concretely . . . , it becomes clear that your democratic demands and aspirations would only create a field of activity for the so-called free play of political forces—that is to say, for the forces of reaction and counterrevolution. For example, when in September of last year the episcopate drew up the document *Pro memoria,* instructing priests to violate the laws and rules of the state, you stood here from this same tribunal and told us about the need for a flexible policy toward the Church. Not a word did you utter . . . against the anti-state, anti-socialist stance of the episcopate. When now, once again, . . . the forces of reaction have rushed to the attack, you say that these are but genuine questions pervading the youth and society at large. Meanwhile, the episcopate's new letter, which is both provocative and politically hostile, Deputy Zawieyski calls "a beautiful letter full of civic pride," a formulation that the deputies here understandably found amusing.

Returning to Cyrankiewicz's juxtaposition of the Polish and Italian bishops, Kociołek said that

the basic similarity in the two positions is that both hierarchies spoke out, as they have always spoken out, in the name of their old class interests. Your cardinal speaks out in the name of that struggle which he has carried on for years: the struggle against People's Poland.

In the end, what is the significance of the actions of the Znak deputies? Above all, there is the moral significance. Their statement itself was a defense of the persecuted, a defense of those who needed defense. By standing hand in hand with those who had been beaten and derided, defending their honor and the purity of their intentions, the Znak deputies demonstrated their belief in the priority of ethical values over tactical-political ones. In this treacherous world of politics, they did not try to "promote their own reactionary aims," as Messrs. Kliszko and Szydlak would have it, but rather gave first place to fundamental moral values. Of particular importance was Jerzy Zawieyski's defense of the moral and intellectual integrity of the writers under attack. I am not referring here to his calling Antoni Słonimski a "distinguished Polish poet," although in the atmosphere of the time this was a remarkable act of courage and solidarity. Nor do I have in mind Zawieyski's remarks concerning Stefan Kisielewski, where he said:

I know Kisielewski, and I know that under that mask of scorn and mockery is a man who is certainly no cynic. On the contrary, he is a man deeply involved in the life of People's Poland, an honest, honorable, and courageous man. . . . Stefan Kisielewski, who in the heat of the moment used a very inappropriate term,[9] has always defended important and good principles in his own way and according to his own conscience.

In the context of the time, such a defense of Kisielewski demanded exceptional fortitude and determination. Yet that which had the greatest moral significance, I believe, was Zawieyski's defense of those writers who had been active in the socialist realist movement years before. For here was Zawieyski, himself a writer—although one who had paid heavily, with years of silence and poverty, for his disagreement with this superficial literary program and his commitment to a religious worldview—defending other writers who had once been part of the Stalinist literary world and had then broken with it completely. For this solidarity he was denounced in the Sejm!

9. *Ciemniaki*, a disparaging word meaning ignoramuses or dimwits—TRANS.

Public opinion was able to witness the bizarre spectacle where people who had fully broken with Stalinism were accused of being Stalinists by those (such as Jerzy Putrament or Bohdan Czeszko) who had never broken with Stalinism at all!

Zawieyski's gesture also had a political dimension. It discredited the view, as did the entire interpellation and the subsequent behavior of the Znak group, that the "March opposition" consisted solely of Jews, cosmopolitans and ex-Stalinists, a view that the official propaganda was trying so hard to inculcate. Not even the most outrageous and mendacious propaganda could classify Zawieyski or Stomma in these categories.

The conduct of the Znak group had an enormous, long-term significance. It proved that political divisions were not identical with religious divisions and that the traditional lines of demarcation were completely obsolete. This was demonstrated again by Tadeusz Mazowiecki. During a March 1968 session of the parliamentary commission on science and education, Mazowiecki once again defended the students and intellectuals, thereby incurring the wrath of Party stalwart Andrzej Werblan.

On one side, then, there were the leaders of the PUWP and the Catholics of PAX and ChSS (Peasant Self-Help Society). On the other side were members of the secular Left and the Catholics of Znak. In this sense, the interpellation marked the realization in practice of the numerous articles that had appeared in *Tygodnik Powszechny* or, even more often, in *Więź*. Znak's interpellation opened a new chapter in modern Polish history. And yet it should be remembered that the interpellation owed most of its significance to the fact that it was perceived by the public to reflect the views of the episcopate and of Primate Cardinal Wyszyński.

PART TWO

THE POLITICS
OF THE CHURCH

6

TRANSLATOR'S NOTE:
In these next chapters, Michnik discusses the
ideas of the Roman Catholic Church that bear
upon politics and the organization of social
life. He tries to show connections between
Catholic views and the values dear to liberal
intellectuals of the Left.

THE ETHOS OF THE CHURCH IN TOTALITARIANISM

To understand the political views of Primate Stefan Wyszyński, let us look at his 1974 "Sermons of the Holy Cross."[1] Stressing his full solidarity with the 1963 papal encyclical *Pacem in terris,* Cardinal Wyszyński began his sermons with one of the encyclical's central ideas (from paragraph 9):

Each individual man is truly a person. His is a nature, that is, endowed with intelligence and free will. As such he has rights and duties, which together flow as a direct consequence from his nature. These rights and duties are universal and inviolable, and therefore altogether inalienable.[2]

The primate then expands these ideas of Pope John XXIII:

These rights are given to man not by society but by our Heavenly Father. It is up to us to respect these rights, care for them, develop them, protect them, and create conditions conducive to their growth. Today, chiefly in totalitarian countries, we see a revival of the so-called omnipotent state, which seeks to govern people in every aspect of their lives. Yet rights that are not dependent upon any political community exist nonetheless. Such rights depend only upon the Creator. . . . And no community, not even the mightiest, can violate these rights without inviting conflict with citizens, with man, and with his essential nature. . . . I will enumerate these rights. First, there is the right to life, or the right to a dignified standard of living. This is connected with the right to freedom, or to a certain style of life. Next, there is

1. Stefan Cardinal Wyszyński, *Kazanie Świętokrzyskie* [Sermons of the Holy Cross] (Rome: Rycerza Niepokolanej, 1974). This is a compilation of sermons delivered in January 1974 at the Church of the Holy Cross in Warsaw. Quotations in the next few pages, unless otherwise noted, are from this source.
2. *Papal Encyclicals, 1958–81,* edited by Claudia Carlen (Raleigh: Consortium McGrath Publishing Co., 1981), p. 108.

the right to enjoy moral and cultural values. These rights cannot be given; they are an essential part of man as a rational being. There is also the right to worship God according to the demands of one's own conscience. Connected with this is freedom of religion. What this means is that the believer must not be forced to create a catacomb for himself but must be able to embrace the Heavenly Father boldly and openly, to worship Him not only privately but publicly as well.

Cardinal Wyszyński then mentions "the right to free elections and to freedom of family life," as well as "the right to association," which is necessary "so that there not be a vacuum between the citizen and the state." "Freedom of assembly," he continued,

was guaranteed in the Universal Declaration of Human Rights proclaimed in 1948, and it was guaranteed so that man would truly be able to utilize that which is essential to the development of his individuality. But individuality is formed not by imposed institutions but by voluntary associations. The development of human individuality . . . depends on the guaranteed right . . . to participate in public life. Man, as a free and rational being, cannot be supplanted by compulsory institutions. Man creates institutions according to his own needs. The richness of these institutions . . . depends solely on the level of the spiritual culture of the nation. The greater the spiritual culture, the greater the need to form associations. . . . And there is one more right—the right to defend one's rights. This is a matter of inner freedom. It means that man will produce an atmosphere of such inner freedom that the citizen will not be afraid to defend his rights when they are violated. And he will know, moreover, that in the end he will find justice.

Concerning social and economic problems, Cardinal Wyszyński notes that people have a right "to demand appropriate employment in their own native land. . . . This includes the freedom to choose one's employment, which cannot be a matter of forced labor." Wyszyński mentions the right to decent working conditions, so that "man does not emerge morally and physically debilitated." He also raises "the question of just pay" and denounces the violation, by means of "voluntary obligations," of the right to rest on Sunday. In this context he criticizes the "danger of a revival of the capitalist spirit" stemming from "a deification of material production":

I greatly fear that we might experience a revival of the capitalist spirit, or that a democratic system might be controlled by a capitalist spirit, for then man would be demoted to the position of a robot and would be judged only from the standpoint of his productive capacity.

The primate sharply denounced the government's politics of atheism:

The people holding power should [understand that] power cannot be used against God. . . . If it is, it loses the basis by which it may command or obligate its citizens. . . . Therefore, state atheism or political atheism is anachronistic, [as is] assembling an apparatus to encourage an atheistic society, or state financing of atheist education.

It would be a great achievement to guarantee equal rights, an equal chance for social and professional advancement, and the right of all people to be treated equally. The faithful, grateful to God for the gift of faith, will then be less likely to take an attitude of superiority, less likely to say things that might insult nonbelievers. Standing for full respect of human conscience—even of an errant one—believers have the right to expect full respect for their own convictions, their own faith, their own Church. . . . They have a right to a peaceful religious life on all levels, in the family as well as in the professional, cultural, and political communities. . . . The climate of fear should finally pass on, so that the state authorities can gain the love of citizens by fully respecting their rights. As civil rights are respected—particularly the rights to individual freedom; to truth, charity, and justice; to social, professional, and cultural equality; to freedom of religion—the climate of fear will become increasingly superfluous. It will then be possible to reduce the fantastically overdeveloped security apparatus, which for many citizens poses the real danger.

On the question of the normalization of relations between Church and state, Cardinal Wyszyński saw as "the most important point" the need for the state "to recognize the permanence of the Church in Polish society." The basic conditions for normalization are "civic freedom, freedom to exercise one's rights, freedom of religion and freedom of conscience—in a word, freedom for Catholic society":

What is important to us is the possibility to build Catholic culture in our own country—not only material culture, but spiritual, moral, and ethical culture, an entire culture based on our own worldview. In a Catholic society there must be room for Catholic culture. Normalization is impossible without the freedom to educate Polish citizens . . . in the spirit of Christian morals. We cannot combat the destructive amoral forces harming our young generation without the right to organize our own Catholic social milieu. Only when these matters are considered, recognized, and respected will it be possible to talk about a fundamental . . . normalization of relations.

The primate concluded his reflections as follows:

A wise social structure does not consist in applying the same narrow format to all aspects of life. Rather, it consists in guaranteeing various social groups the right to freely carry on their work. . . . Finally, freedom of association, or the right of people to join together for specific purposes, must be guaranteed along with freedom of the press, freedom of speech, freedom of research, and a free public opinion. These elements make for the richness of social, cultural, national, and political life.

In light of these words, one point would appear to be beyond dispute. The widespread view, propagated by official propaganda (and quite common in leftist intellectual circles too), that the episcopate and the primate are fighting for the "restoration of capitalism"— this view is simply not true. On the contrary, the basic framework of the political and social demands contained in the "Sermons of the Holy Cross" as well as in the episcopal letters cited earlier, is actually in full accord, or at any rate not in conflict, with the Left's program of democratic transformation. Supporters of antitotalitarian socialism will feel particularly close to the ideas concerning the rights of working people and the need for genuine social and political equality.

A clearer vision of the role of the Church in Poland now begins to emerge. This is a Church that is not a political force but a religious and moral community that refuses to renounce its ethical principles even when these are violated and desecrated by the state. The Polish primate's *modus operandi,* as carried out in everyday practice, seems to be close to the German theologian Johannes B. Metz's concept of "political theology," with its idea of a critical, antitotalitarian role for the Church in today's world. The actions of the episcopate and of the primate bear witness to their devotion to antitotalitarian principles. In these same "Sermons of the Holy Cross," Cardinal Wyszyński noted that

the Polish bishops have watched with distress the recent attempts to bring all Polish youth into one monolithic organization, and we have expressed our position publicly. These attempts invariably impoverish the young generation, particularly students, reducing their opportunities to become socially cultivated human beings. Such acts will undoubtedly prove damaging to the national culture, and even to our social and political culture.

Those Warsaw University students who so vehemently protested the government's proposals to merge existing student organizations were surely feeling the same way. They were protesting attempts to turn Polish youth organizations into copies of the Soviet Komsomol. And thanks to this group of protesters (made up for the most part of nonbelievers), the "unification congress" of the Association of Polish Students and the Union of Socialist Youth proceeded without the usual unanimity, which in Polish conditions is a rather uncommon occurrence. Amidst shouts and insults, a declaration of protest against "unification" was read from the conference floor by four honest delegates from Warsaw University (Irena Halak, Konrad Bieliński, Jacek Santorski, and Tadeusz Szawiel) seeking only to bear witness to the truth.

In this context we should mention the episcopal document criticizing the proposed school reform bill, whose hidden goal was to prevent Catholic education outside of school. In its "Declaration on the Education of Catholic Youth in Poland," the episcopate put forth the following position:

At the foundation of every truly humanist system of education is the recognition of the dignity of man, the dignity of every human individual without exception. In an epoch which has experienced too many terrifying examples of human degradation and discrimination, we can protect the younger generation from demoralization only by revealing to them the greatness and inviolability of every human being. If this truth can be attained only through the teaching of various philosophical and sociological arguments, then it is necessary to say that in the Christian community this fundamental truth is most deeply rooted in the assertion that man is created in God's image, redeemed by the love of the Son of God, Jesus Christ, and summoned by God to interact with Him in governing the world, and to participate in the life of God for all of eternity.[3]

We find here a union of Christian principles with the secular principle of the rights of man. The Polish bishops spoke out not only in defense of the particular institutional interests of the Church, not only in defense of the religious rights of the Catholic community, but in defense of the civil rights of all people, regardless of religious affiliation. Indeed, they were also defending the rights of nonbelievers.

The primate and the episcopate also spoke out on the question of civic obligations. What particularly interests us here is their view on the responsibilities of intellectuals. In that memorable month of

3. *Listy Pasterskie Episkopatu Polski* [Pastoral Letters of the Polish Episcopate] (Paris: Editions du Dialogue, 1975), p. 758. (Referred to hereafter as *Pastoral Letters.*)

March 1968, in a sermon at the Church of the Sisters of the Visitation, Cardinal Wyszyński spoke as follows:

In every society there are people who have an obligation to speak the truth. They are prepared for this by their knowledge, their studies, their experiences, their familiarity with life. These people must speak the truth! It is their moral and social obligation! If they keep silent, cheap demagogues will speak out, poisoning society with illusions of suicidal solutions. *Somebody must speak the truth!* If there is a group of people who are capable of speaking the truth, both the Nation and its governors will benefit. Those who speak the truth can protect us from errors. And someone must do so.

You are responsible for the truth. You must not remain silent in fear. When you speak the truth, you manifest your love for country, nation, and state. When you keep silent, you manifest your lack of love. Your silence can only act against the interests of all.[4]

In a letter of 1 October 1969, the episcopate as a whole spoke out on this subject:

Lying is one of the scourges of social life. . . . It degrades man, insults human dignity, and undermines authority. . . . Resorting to lies not only harms the collective good but shakes the very foundations of social life. Searching for the truth and speaking the truth are ways to prevent being reduced to bondage. We are often flooded with false information. News of current events are provided tendentiously or erroneously. If we want to preserve our dignity, we must have courage enough to speak the truth. Writers, journalists, persons of letters! We appeal to you: *write the truth, defend the truth,* in all aspects of life and science. Bear witness in this way to your love for your neighbors.[5]

Aleksandr Solzhenitsyn ("Do not live in lies!") and Leszek Kołakowski ("Live in dignity!") say the very same thing.

•   •

It is no accident that the names of Solzhenitsyn and Kołakowski come up in a discussion of the programmatical comments of the episcopate and the Polish primate. For despite the radically different traditions and perspectives, there is a crucial similarity here. This similarity, beyond nations or creeds, lies in an antitotalitarian view of the

4. Stefan Cardinal Wyszyński, *Idzie nowych ludzi plemię* [And Comes the Tribe of New People] (Poznań, 1973), p. 277.
5. *Pastoral Letters,* p. 577.

unity of human rights and human duties. The idea here is that living in truth, and in the search for truth, is both the right of man as well as his duty. Perceiving such similarities is no great discovery; these ideas and values are deeply rooted in Christian and secular traditions alike. It is not difficult to find in Christian doctrine a basis for protest against the omnipotence of the state. And similar ideas can easily be found in the secular tradition as well (such as in John Stuart Mill, the classic liberal thinker, or in Karl Marx, author of many wise and insightful words against press censorship). And yet in spite of these objective similarities, Christians and leftists have never really felt united on these issues. They have never jointly defended these values nor have they ever considered themselves allies. Today there is a growing awareness on both sides that solidarity is necessary.

In recent years, leftist intellectuals have begun to change their attitudes toward the Church. They have stopped being concerned with fighting the Church and have ceased being the mouthpieces of official atheism. Many of them have discussed their new attitudes in public. In response to a *Tygodnik Powszechny* questionnaire, Antoni Słonimski, a moral authority for these secular circles, wrote as follows:

In my youth, the dispute between the Catholic Church and the progressive intelligentsia often took the form of open conflict. The Church was considered a pillar of capitalism. I myself expressed such secular views quite frequently. The Vatican was a bastion of stagnation that sealed itself off completely from a changing world. . . . And it would not open its impenetrable gates until virtually the middle of the twentieth century.

Słonimski drew attention to some fundamental similarities between the ideas expressed in the papal encyclical *Populorum progressio* and the secular principles expressed in the Declaration of the Rights of Man. Then he pointed to a convergence of postconciliar Catholicism with modern progressive secular thought, which had abandoned the "arrogance so typical of the beginning of the century." And this convergence, he concluded, is "not due to a similarity of worldviews, but to a growing feeling of responsibility for a humanity whose very existence is now threatened."[6]

Słonimski elaborated on these views in an interview for a Western journal. Asked why he, a rationalist, freethinking liberal, would

---

6. Antoni Słonimski, *Obecność* [Presence] (Warsaw: Czytelnik, 1973), pp. 9–11.

write regularly for a Catholic weekly when there were so many others to choose from, Słonimski replied, "Before the war, the Church was reactionary and communism proclaimed the progressive ideas. Today the situation is reversed."

Further evidence of this dramatic shift in attitudes can be found in the essays of the man whom the secular Left has treated as its chief theorist, Leszek Kołakowski.

There is other evidence as well. For example, in the "Letter of 15" (December 1974) concerning the situation of ethnic Poles in the USSR, as well as in the "Letter of 59" (December 1975) concerning amendment of the Constitution, religious freedom was cited as a fundamental right. Both of these letters were signed by people connected with the secular Left intelligentsia. And in a sign of the times, both letters also carried the signatures of Catholic priests. This I consider one of the most momentous transformations in Polish intellectual life.

In 1940, a German Lutheran pastor, one of the most renowned philosophers of the twentieth century, wrote about some of the "remarkable experiences" from his recent past. These were difficult years, wrote Dietrich Bonhoeffer,

when everything connected with Christianity was severely repressed. Against the worship of irrationality, blood, and the bestial instinct in man, it was necessary to counterpose reason, against arbitrary law—the written law, against barbarism—culture and humanism, against coercion—freedom, tolerance and the rights of man, against the politicization of art and science— the autonomy of these different spheres of life. And so it happened that among the defenders of these maligned values as well as among Christians, there grew a sense of a certain kind of alliance. It turned out that all of these values—reason, scholarship, humanism, tolerance, autonomy—which had until recently served as battle cries in the struggle against Christianity and the Church, were in fact extremely close to the Church. This was a time of the most unprecedented attacks on Christianity, a time when its most fundamental truths were harshly denounced in the most uncompromising manner, contrary to all norms of reason, culture, humanism, and tolerance. And the more Christianity was persecuted and oppressed, the stronger became its alliance with these values, which unexpectedly widened Christianity's horizons. The Church did not initiate this alliance in its own defense. On the contrary, it was these very values, having become in a sense homeless, that now sought refuge in the framework of Christianity, in the shadow of the Church. Yet it would be wrong to see this merely as a temporary alliance for the duration of the struggle. There was something more important here: a return to the original sources. The children of the Church, having grown up and departed, were returning to the mother in the hour of danger. And although during their absence they had changed quite a bit, having taken on a new appearance and picked up a new language, in this critical moment mother and children once again recognized each other. Reason, justice, culture, humanism had searched for and found their roots, and discovered therein a new meaning and new strength. The source they discovered is Jesus Christ.[7]

In Christian language this means that Christ, God embodied as a man, died a martyr's death on the cross for all people. He repented for their sins and thus created an inviolable law of truth and love. Surely this is the meaning of the allegory from the Gospel according to St. Matthew, when Christ, addressing the just, says, "Verily I say unto you, Inasmuch as ye have done it unto one of the least of these my brethren, ye have done it unto me" (Matthew 25:40), and then, a moment later, addressing "them on the left hand," says: "Inasmuch as ye did it not to one of the least of these, ye did it not to me" (Matthew 25:44). This allegory tells us that any injustice done to anyone is an injustice done to Christ himself.

Bonhoeffer's reference to Jesus Christ as the "source" also has a profound meaning for nonbelievers: it means that one cannot reject the Christian tradition with impunity. For by rejecting Christ's teachings of love for one's neighbor, one rejects the canonical foundation of European culture. By rejecting these teachings, we lose the foundation of our belief in the autonomous value of truth and human solidarity. Belief in the divinity of Christ is a matter of Grace, and in this sense is given only to a few. But belief in the hallowed nature of Christ's commandments is the duty of all, because it is the light that protects human freedom and dignity against violence and debasement, against nihilism and the hell of solitude.

Leszek Kołakowski has put it beautifully:

Any attempt at "invalidating Jesus," at removing him from our culture under the pretext or premise that we do not believe in the God that he believed in, is both hollow and absurd. Only people with shallow minds can attempt such

---

7. This is my retranslation from the Polish. The excerpt is from Bonhoeffer's essay "The Church and the World." An existing English version is in Dietrich Bonhoeffer, *Ethics*, edited by Eberhard Bethge, translated by Neville Horton Smith (New York: Macmillan, 1955), pp. 177–84.—TRANS.

things—people who imagine that primitive atheism is a sufficient worldview authorizing one to mutilate an entire cultural tradition according to one's own doctrinaire desires, draining that tradition of all its most precious juices.[8]

Approaching this problem from a somewhat different angle, Jan Strzelecki noted that the Nazi ordeal

made the traditional clash between the Church and the liberal intelligentsia seem like an irrelevant scene from a bygone world, for in the real world of Hitlerism our common humanist legacy was under attack. The most precious values of world civilization suddenly found themselves, together with the Church, in mortal danger, and those who defended such values were at the same time defending the basic values of Christianity, such as being-for-others, solidarity, and brotherhood.[9]

These perceptive remarks of Strzelecki may seem to belabor the obvious. And yet I and my "commando" friends[10] had to experience March '68 before we fully understood that we were dealing with a totalitarian power devoid of all scruples. It took March '68 before we realized, and saw with our own eyes, that the regime was ready to trample the most basic human values—values as dear to Christians as they are to the secular Left. It was this new awareness that has created a basis for rapprochement. We hope that the encounter with Christianity can take place in authenticity and good faith, and that is possible only on the basis of sincerity and mutual respect. Sincerity demands that we discuss not only what unites us but also what divides us—our doubts, worries, and reservations. But I do not intend to quarrel over the existence of a supernatural world. Belief in such matters, as I've already said, is entirely a question of Grace. One may admire or one may envy those endowed with Grace, but one cannot quarrel with them. At least to this writer such a quarrel seems pointless. In what follows, however, I would like to say a few words about the political ideology of the Roman Catholic Church in Poland. More than one of my concerns, I am sure, will be shared by a large number of secular intellectuals.

8. Leszek Kołakowski, "Jezuz Chrystus—prorok i reformator" [Jesus Christ—Prophet and Reformer], *Argumenty* (Warsaw), 19–26 December 1965.

9. Jan Strzelecki, *Kontynuacje (2)* (Warsaw: PIW, 1974), p. 188.

10. Polish radical student activists in 1968 were known as the "commandos."—TRANS.

7

MUTUAL SUSPICIONS

Catholic Worries

Jerzy Turowicz, the chief editor of *Tygodnik Powszechny,* once wrote that even if a given nonbeliever

is the most liberal thinker in the world, proclaiming that everyone is free to believe in anything and that all convictions are equally valid, still, in the nonbeliever's worldview, there is no place for the Church. If the earth and its people constitute a closed unit; if there is neither a nonmaterial dimension nor a dimension outside of time; if human beings can, through reason, understand, transform, and manage this world; and if, through our tragic meanderings in history, persistent progress may be made—then the Church, a phenomenon of magnificent spatial and historical breadth, is for the man of reason and progress just an enormous obstacle standing in the way of history. Acording to the rationalist, materialist perspective, the Church is necessarily just a throng of people lost at an irrationalist dead-end. Church leaders and priests become so many charlatans, consciously leading the people astray so as to reap the benefits of power, benefits derived from the governing of souls. And thus, even if the nonbeliever has the greatest respect for the convictions of others, disbelief in God makes it difficult to guard against the wish (or to guard against *acting* on the wish) that all those false convictions, all that mystification so inseparably bound up with the Church, should finally get out of the path of reason and progress once and for all.[1]

Turowicz is absolutely right. I would put it even more bluntly: secular leftists, frequently raised in an atmosphere of antireligious obscurantism, for many years were convinced (and some are still convinced) that anyone who believes in God—and certainly any

1. Jerzy Turowicz, "Ecclesia," in *Chrześcijanin w dzisiejszym świecie* [A Christian in Today's World] (Kraków: Znak, 1963), p. 25.

priest—must have some sort of personal defect. Religious belief it-self, and even more so the priesthood, was considered a sign of spiritual disability. And with premises such as these, it is no surprise that we saw the Church as an obstacle to reason and progress. It never entered our minds that there was any need to defend the civil rights of Church supporters. How could we defend religious freedom if, to us, this simply meant freedom to propagate magic and superstition? How could we defend religion if we considered religion a mere relic of backwardness? "I speak out of sadness, and because I too am racked with guilt."

Yet the dam has been broken; something is beginning to change for the better. By signing the open letters mentioned above about Poles in the USSR and the proposed changes in the Constitution, secular leftists were proclaiming their complete rejection of that obtuse, primitive atheism. And yet I do not think that is enough. Our intellectual search must go deeper. It must touch the very roots of that oh-so-haughty conviction that it is we, in the end, who really do know the true path of progress and reason. The truth, of course, is that we do not know this path. Neither we nor anyone else in the world knows the road along which history will travel. Yet it is precisely we, more than anyone else, who should understand that such pseudoknowledge about the secrets of the *Weltgeist* can have the most criminal consequences. For it is this purported knowledge of the imaginary laws of history that convinces some people that they must "lead onto the road of reason and progress" thousands of others who are not in the least aware of the need or inevitability of the New Order. Moreover, the *implementation* of such plans for the New Order and the Kingdom of Progress necessarily leads to contempt for people, to the use of force, and to moral self-destruction.

It seems to me that equally sinister consequences may stem from the presumptuous conviction that there is no supernatural order. I say "presumptuous" since the only thing we know with absolute certainty is that death will not pass us by. All the rest is groping. Our lot is the toil of existence, the stubborn search for truth. As we undertake our laborious search, let us respect those who believe that a supernatural world has been revealed to them. Let us judge them by their deeds, not by words that are twisted and distorted by others. Only then can we rightfully insist on being treated the same way by them.

Only then will we be able to insist that our own philosophical convictions, our *lack* of belief, not turn us into spiritual cripples, into people less worthy, in the eyes of the Church. We will be able to insist on being judged according to our everyday actions and not according to our nonreligious practices. By respecting others' beliefs, we can demand respect for our own disbelief. And only then will we be able to insist on the distinction between a secular worldview and the political practices of the Communist government, between secularization and political atheism, between the notion of democratic socialism and the totalitarian reality of our country.

Secular Worries

Simone Weil, a Frenchwoman of Jewish origin, a Christian who was never baptized, and the author of some of the most provocative reflections on the moral condition of our times, wrote the following words in 1942 to her friend J. M. Perrin, the Dominican priest:

The Church today defends the cause of the [inalienable] rights of the individual against collective oppression, of liberty of thought against tyranny. But these are causes readily embraced by those who find themselves momentarily to be the least strong. It is their only way of perhaps one day becoming the strongest. . . . In order that the present attitude of the Church should be effective and that she should really penetrate like a wedge into social existence, she would have to say openly that she had changed or wished to change. Otherwise who could take her seriously when they remembered the Inquisition? My friendship for you, which I extend through you to all your Order, makes it very painful for me to bring this up. But it existed. After the fall of the Roman Empire, which had been totalitarian, it was the Church that was the first to establish a rough sort of totalitarianism in Europe in the thirteenth century, after the war with the Albigenses. This tree bore much fruit. And the motive power of this totalitarianism was the use of those two little words: *anathema sit*. It was moreover by a judicious transposition of this use that all the parties which in our own day have founded totalitarian regimes were shaped.[2]

It will be no revelation to say that many people in Poland share Weil's diagnosis, as well as her fears. Yet to people who forever hark back to the specter of the inquisitorial stakes, we must say: The Church *has* changed. It stopped burning heretics at the stake long ago. No more does one hear those ominous words, *anathema sit*. The

---

2. Simone Weil, *Waiting for God,* translated by Emma Craufurd (New York: Putnam's Sons, 1951), pp. 81–82.

index of forbidden books is no longer functioning. One must either be ignorant or steeped in bad faith to fail to understand the meaning of recent papal encyclicals or the declarations of Vatican II.

Of course, one often hears the response that these changes have not affected the *Polish* Church. Such comments are truly amazing. I fully understand and admire those journalists of *Więź* or *Tygodnik Powszechny* (although not those from PAX) who call for internal reforms within the Church, but I simply cannot understand similar arguments from the mouths of nonbelievers. To those who counterpose the enlightened and progressive bishops of the Vatican to the reactionary bishops of Poland, I say this: I match you in ignorance, but you surpass me in audacity. It is not for us to engage in arguments over whether the Polish episcopate is or is not a conservative one. Because what is it that we're really talking about? About liturgical reform? The cult of Mary? The position on celibacy? Collegiality in internal decision making? Objections to the Dutch catechism? I just don't get it! Why *Catholics* worry about all this—that I understand, just as we all know why official journalist hacks such as Ignacy Krasicki or Wiesław Mysłek are so worried about the reactionary nature of the Polish bishops. But do my friends on the secular Left really have nothing greater to worry about? Perhaps the politics of Vatican envoy Cardinal Casaroli is more to their liking? This model of "progressivism" is said to have urged Cardinal Wyszyński to adopt a more "elastic" (that is, capitulationist) attitude toward the Polish government. Indeed, this is the same man who also urged a more "elastic" policy on the Spanish episcopate when it criticized the policies of General Franco.

Perhaps a critique of the internal structure of Polish Catholicism *is* desirable and in order. But it is not for me to say. It is a question for the Catholic community to decide. For nonbelievers to publicly criticize the Church on its internal conservatism is, in our conditions—we don't live in parliamentary England, after all—both hollow and ambiguous.

Many of my friends may say that *today* the Church is for freedom of conscience and of religion, freedom of the press and of research, freedom of speech and of association—but only because it is today *deprived* of these freedoms. Did the bishops so ardently defend such freedoms during the interwar period of Catholic domination? And will they defend them just as ardently when Catholicism is again recognized as a privileged religion by the state, when the altar is again allied to the throne? My answer is that only a blind person could fail to see the changes taking place in Polish Catholicism. It is enough to compare the style and level of the prewar Catholic press with that of *Tygodnik Powszechny, Znak,* or *Więź,* to be aware of the magnitude of the transformation. One need only read carefully the pastoral letters of the episcopate in order to find aspects that are new and provide the greatest hopes for the future.

Yet it is not this that is most important. Nor is it the rather banal fact that the attitude of the Church toward the Left depends closely on the attitude of the Left toward the Church. What I have in mind is something more fundamental. The point is that our affection for civil liberties would be rather suspect were we to desire them only for ourselves. Our morality would then be the morality of Kali: "When Kali steals, that is good, but when Kali is robbed, that is bad." Therefore, it is the *political responsibility* of those of us in the secular Left to defend the freedom of the Church and the civil rights of Christians, regardless of what we think of the role of the Church forty years ago, or the role it may play forty years from now. Human rights must exist for everybody—or they do not exist for anybody. That much is indisputable.

Fears of a "Julianic" Church

But this does not settle the matter. It is one thing for leftists to proclaim the indivisibility and universality of the rights of man and to defend those who are persecuted. This is their political and civic duty, part of their very creed: they either proclaim this or risk spiritual self-destruction. Their fears regarding the conduct of the Church and the Church hierarchy, however, are something else entirely. Like Simone Weil, these people often say that the Church once again wants to be the "mightiest," that it desires a return to the Constantinian model of exercising spiritual power. Let me explain this through the words of Bohdan Cywiński, who counterposed the concept of the "Julianic Church" to that of the "Constantinian Church." In his book, *Genealogies of the Indomitable,* Cywiński wrote the following:

The concept of Constantinism derives . . . from the name of the Emperor Constantine, under whose reign there first appeared the theory of dual power: spiritual and temporal. As a political model, Julianism[3] is the opposite of Constantinism. In place of the cooperation of the spiritual and tempo-

3. From Emperor Julian the Apostate, 361–363 A.D., who, according to Cywiński, "renounced Christianity and tried to destroy the Church."

ral powers, Julianism is marked by their conflict. The Church finds itself in opposition. Deprived of political power, it possesses only moral authority— and in this lies its strength. One can perhaps detect here a general rule regarding the situation of the Church in the state: its moral authority is inversely proportional to its participation in political power. . . . Moral authority is the fundamental feature of the Julianic Church, just as political authority is the mark of the Constantinian Church. The Julianic Church is morally purer, for persecution eliminates opportunists and endows the Church with an aura all its own. It is a tradition that is at once beautiful and durable. Yet Julianism is in a sense connected with Constantinism. They share common characteristics, especially where the mentality of the clergy is concerned. In an obvious way, there is a temporal connection between the two. . . . Julianism does not develop by itself; rather it is a contested form of Constantinism, arising where the state has departed from a previously accepted notion of collaboration with the Church. It would be wrong to say that the Julianic Church has nothing in common with political power: this is a Church that has been forcibly deprived of its participation in power. And that is important, because it affects the mentality of the Church. During the reign of Julian the Apostate, Church leaders looked back to the Constantinian period as the model of the correct social order. They awaited the moment when it would be possible to return to that model. Not for a moment did they recognize the legality of the system introduced by the renegade emperor. Their aim was to survive the difficult times so that, afterwards, the Church could regain its old place in the social system. The Julianic Church did not renounce for all times the notion of an alliance with the state. It only awaited the appearance of a state that would be suitable to such an alliance. Meanwhile, lacking political power, the Church was content to be a moral authority, the spiritual leader of the opposition. Such authority was something like the power of a king in exile, but it was power nonetheless. . . .

Constantinism means participation in state power. Julianism is marked by bitterness and resentment over losing that power, and not by voluntary acquiescence to the loss. This is why the Julianic Church, with all of its spiritual power, is never fully in solidarity with society, and never fully identifies with it. It does of course want society to identify itself with the Church, but this is not the same thing. Deprived of its political strength, it fights to preserve its spiritual leadership over the nation. It refuses to accept that there is any way other than the Church to bring about the spiritual or ideological integration of society, and it refuses to acknowledge the existence of any form of opposition other than those that it itself promotes and controls. If the existence of another form of opposition becomes quite obvious—one that offers society some kind of ideological alternative, allowing it to come together apart from the Church—then the Julianic Church condemns this opposition, or at least tries to disavow and devalue it in the eyes of public opinion. Never will the Julianic Church be anxious to engage in any form of collaboration against the state with any independent center of oppositionist thought. In its conflict with the secular rulers the Julianic Church prefers to act alone, without partners, toward whom it feels no sense of solidarity.[4]

No one in the secular Left has expressed our fears with such clarity and precision. What we fear is a Julianic Church politics, as well as its possible consequences.

This is a serious matter. None of us means to deny the enormous contribution of Julianism, difficult for us even to comprehend, in the Church's resistance to official lies and coercion. Yet it is necessary to remember that the negative consequences of Julianism, so excellently described by Cywiński, may be realized in our own times as well. For Julianism is not only a result of Constantinism; it is also a result of isolation. As long as the Polish bishops stood alone against the nihilism of "progressive ideology," defending not only religion and the Church but also elementary human rights and fundamental humanitarian values, Julianism was the Church's only possible recourse. As long as the secular Left proclaimed its hostile attitude toward religion and the Church, Julianism was practically unavoidable. Now this state of affairs seems to be changing. Slowly, a new kind of opposition is crystallizing, one that embraces the traditional values of the Left (Freedom, Equality, Independence[5]) while unequivocally—and hopefully for good—rejecting the political atheism of the past.

This is something genuinely new. In this situation, the Roman Catholic Church will have to decide whether, in this world, its mission is to defend the Church or to defend human beings. Does the Church genuinely seek freedom for every human being, including believers in other religions as well as nonbelievers? Or does it only seek "freedom for itself, its own faith, its own schools, its own press?"[6] Does the Church consider it possible to separate freedom for Catholics from a broader sphere of basic freedoms applicable to

4. Bohdan Cywiński, *Rodowody Niepokornych* (Warsaw: Biblioteka Więzi, 1971), pp. 262–64.
5. "Freedom, Equality, Independence" was the name of the moderate wing of the Polish Socialist Party during World War II.—TRANS.
6. Jean-Marie Domenach, "Świadomość religijna i świadomość polityczna" [Religious and Political Consciousness], in *Więź*, no. 6, 1968, p. 18.

all citizens? Further, does the Church desire—and I repeat, in this world, the human world—to be the defender of all the oppressed and downtrodden, the suffering and the persecuted, or does it intend to work for the steady expansion of its own institutional rights until the complete recovery of its privileged position in the state? Does it wish to carry on its missionary work in conditions of separation of church and state, or does it want to join with the state authorities in exercising power over the people? Finally, does it want to sponsor religious political parties, or, separating "God's from Caesar's," will it limit itself politically to the issuing of general guidelines, such as those contained in the encyclicals of Pope Paul VI?

It is not for me to answer these questions. I must, however, emphasize that for those of us in the secular Left—and perhaps for genuinely leftist Catholics as well—these are not theoretical questions but extremely concrete ones, as concrete as the nature of the Poland for which we are fighting.

It is impossible to imagine a Poland of the future without the Roman Catholic Church and its enormous influence on society. Thus it is not surprising that secular leftists are interested in the programmatical statements of the Catholic bishops. Let us take, for example, their position on the schools. For many years, the Church firmly defended the demand for religious education in public schools. This issue, as I discussed above, had specific nuances in Polish conditions, and for that reason the conflict surrounding it was particularly complicated. As long as the schools are a transmitter of the "progressive worldview" and a tool for atheistic upbringing, these "particular complications" will remain in effect. The secular intelligentsia is not attracted to this model of education; no enlightened person could be. But in what, then, does the desired model consist? For the secular leftist, the matter is simple: removing religion from the schools is part of the separation of church and state. But one consequence of the separation of the state from the Church—and such a separation is an essential condition for genuine democratization—should be the abolition of atheistic education as the obligatory ideology of the schools. Ironically, the position of the secular Left has been most precisely formulated by a Catholic deputy to the Sejm. In a 1961 speech on the reform of the educational system, Tadeusz Mazowiecki proposed a pluralist school system, and that seems to be the best solution, provided that the Church has a guaranteed right to teach religion outside of the schools. Some Church circles have been saying the same things. "Moving religious education out of the classroom has actually improved this education," some catechists are saying. "Without wanting to do so, the government actually did the Church a favor. Voluntary classes promote catechization by increasing its attractiveness."

It is difficult to say how typical or authoritative this position really is. But one thing is certain: secular circles greet this position with happiness and hope. Nothing aids the government in its anti-Church demagoguery more than the specter of Catholic intolerance toward non-Catholic children. The regrettable events of the post–1956 period, the discrimination against those children who chose not to attend religion classes, were not inventions of official atheistic propaganda. Those who experienced this know it is something to remember and to fear. An unequivocal declaration by the episcopate on this matter could play a very important role.

Jerzy Turowicz once wrote the following:

It is often said . . . that the Church, "the alleged defender of freedom," is extremely intolerant to its own adherents. It imposes its views on them, demands orthodoxy, limits their lives and behavior through thousands of rules and prohibitions, and threatens them with sanctions both worldly and eternal. Where is there any place for freedom? . . . What a colossal misunderstanding! The Church tells the individual only this, "Here is the truth about you, about your life, about the meaning and purpose of your existence. If you believe, act in accordance. If you reject this truth, you are not a Catholic. If you accept the truth but do not act in accordance with it, you are a bad Catholic, though you will not be alone." Worldly sanctions? What sanctions? We impose neither fines nor prison terms . . . . Exclusion from the sacraments and from the community of the faithful? Yes, but such sanctions strike only at those who acknowledge the right of the Church to administer them. Eternal sanctions? These are not for the Church to dispense. We only inform the faithful that such sanctions exist. No one will be saved without willing it, and no one will be condemned without being guilty. Even then there's a way out, thanks to God's compassion. The Church tells the individual: "You were mature enough and old enough to understand that here is a supernatural community joined by bonds of love, ready to render you every possible assistance. If you have received more, more will be demanded of you. Apart from that, think and act as you wish. The consequences of your actions, both good and bad, you will bear alone." . . . It is perhaps time to stop talking about the internal intolerance of the Church.[7]

7. Jerzy Turowicz, *Chrześcijanin*, pp. 89–90.

Turowicz here insightfully exposes several kinds of stupidities. Yet he speaks of the Church only in its role as depository of faith. The Church, however, is an organization that also has a more worldly dimension. And we must not stop talking about that. For only then can I ask why, as a result of pressure from the Church hierarchy, that wonderful book by Reverend Mieczysław Żywczyński, *The Church and the French Revolution,* was removed from the libraries some twenty-odd years ago and is still not allowed back on the shelves. The standard answer is that Father Żywczyński "voluntarily" agreed to the book's removal, as demonstrated by the fact that his superiors who "asked" him had neither prosecutors nor policemen to enforce their request. This answer, I am afraid, simply will not do. I am well aware that this is no simple matter. Reverend Żywczyński's book, a wonderfully written satirical account of the reactionary nature of the Roman Catholic Church in the era of the French Revolution, was published by PAX in 1951 during the period of high Stalinism, a time of brutal repression against the Church and the clergy. The aim of the book was quite clear. It criticized the close connections between the Church and the *ancien régime* and suggested that if only the Church had abandoned these ties, it could have come to an accord with the revolutionary government. Translating historical metaphor into contemporary reality, one could read the book as an appeal to Polish clergy to support the new government, or at least to abandon their anti-Communist beliefs. Żywczyński's close and long-lasting ties to PAX would only seem to confirm this interpretation. Indeed, such ties, together with his recent diatribe against Cywiński's *Genealogies of the Indomitable,* make Żywczyński a rather dubious political personality. No, let me be clearer: Żywczyński is a decidedly *unsympathetic* personality, at least to this writer. His review of Cywiński is a masterpiece of slander, a kind of personal denunciation addressed to the Party and the Church hierarchy alike. I fully agree that his criticism of the French clergy could have been used for contemporary anticlerical propaganda. The Polish bishops did indeed have a right to believe that his book might help "soften up" the Church in its struggle against the totalitarian government, might help strengthen capitulationist tendencies. In a word, they had a right to believe that Żywczyński's book could be harmful.

And yet it is my deep belief that in the long run the truth *cannot* be harmful to society. I take this position in regard to Father Żywczyński's volume, too. Actually, I think that a careful reading of the text could prove extremely useful. One can learn valuable lessons despite the perhaps ignoble intentions of the author. In particular, I think that a careful reading of the book would have helped the Polish bishops avoid many mistakes (such as their campaign against the nationalization of the forests) in their struggle with the totalitarian Communist authorities—a struggle, I repeat, that is to the Church's credit. And if not the bishops, then it certainly would have helped many priests and lay Catholics.

Here I seem to be touching once again upon intra-Catholic and intra-Church affairs just after I'd sworn this off. But the matter concerns me as well. For all of Polish culture, and not just its Catholic component, has been made poorer by the loss of Żywczyński's volume. And one cannot deny people outside of the Church the right to be concerned for the fate of our culture. I hope that in light of all that I've said, I will not be suspected of bad faith, demagoguery, or malicious nitpicking. I also trust that I will not be identified with those "freedom fighters" who criticize the lack of internal freedom inside the Church from the pages of the official Party press. Although the fate of Żywczyński's book is not (unfortunately) unique—I am aware of several other examples of its kind—I do not intend to compare this with the methodical devastation of Polish culture wrought by the Communist authorities. That would be absurd. Nevertheless, people of the Church must understand that all of their declarations about the need for cultural and scientific freedom will be fully credible when and only when there are no more examples whatsoever of this kind. One cannot demand the right to "build Catholic culture in this Catholic country" and at the same time confiscate books of Catholic intellectuals. It's either-or. You have to choose.

8

LIBERALISM AND THE CHURCH

To tell the truth, I'm not too fond of the argument that Catholics deserve rights (religious, cultural, political, etc.) because they constitute a majority of Polish society. And what if they were a minority? Would they then deserve less civil rights? Perhaps a little bit less? What exactly is the basis of the Catholic claim: the numbers of their followers or the principle of inalienable individual rights? My belief is that the rights and liberties of Catholics should be completely independent of the number of people who subscribe to the faith. Catholics are due the same rights as other citizens, whether Protestants, Muslims, or atheists. From the standpoint of state law, religious conviction should be a purely private matter.

Secularization to me means the following: complete separation of church from state, complete separation of state from church, and complete civil rights for all. Cardinal Wyszyński understands it quite differently. He has described secularization as "the purging of believers and of religious and Catholic elements." He developed this line of thought in the "Sermons of the Holy Cross." Secularization, he said,

is a tendency that arose near the end of the eighteenth century and grew powerful by the turn of the nineteenth century. Its aim was to create, with the help of the state, both secular schools and a secular morality, and to bring about the secularization of all state, social, and political establishments. Its very terms have been dredged up from the French. . . . The expressions *école laïque, morale laïque,* come from a time when liberals and Freemasons, scorning all moral principles, were intensifying their secularizing efforts, mainly in France. If we still read and hear so much about the secular state today, this is just so much reheating of the same old food, which a modern man simply cannot swallow. These are obsolete concepts. The state has no right to forcibly propagate, with the help of social and public institutions, secular rites or a secular morality, particularly in a society that is Catholic through and through.[1]

Perhaps there is a semantic misunderstanding here. If secularization is taken to mean censorship and the crippling of a nation's culture by the elimination of its religious traditions; if it is understood as the use of state force to eradicate Catholic customs and impose other ones; then it is hard to disagree with Cardinal Wyszyński. That kind of "secularization" is merely a mask for totalitarian terror. But the primate's remarks may also be understood as an attack upon the principle of the separation of church and state. There is a terrible confusion of concepts in our language today. Thanks to the work of our official propaganda, more and more words confuse matters rather than explain them.

Jean-Marie Domenach has called attention to the distinction made by French bishops between "secularization," or "the sovereignty of the state in the temporal world, . . . which is fully harmonious with Church doctrine," and "secularism," or "the philosophical doctrine entailing the dissemination of a materialist and atheistic philosophy to all of society." Domenach explains as follows:

Defending the rights of their Church, Catholics should understand that in the political struggle they are on the same plane as others and that the worldly values they recognize are not only for them but for all people living in the country. Increasingly widespread, this kind of secularization leads to reconciliation within the bounds of the nation. . . . Without the surrounding passions, secularization turns out to be something quite appropriate to the very nature of the state. As a necessary condition of every . . . political decision, secularization is for politics what methodological atheism is for science: not a dogmatic tenet but a prerequisite of investigation, a basis of knowledge, a requirement of action. . . . Catholics must make an effort here to untangle the notion of the state from their memories of the struggles surrounding the state in the last century. The secular state, like every state, has known the temptations of abuse of power and has even succumbed to those temptations, though to a lesser degree than the religious state or the state that is one-sided in its very foundation. . . . The state in and of itself is neutral. It becomes totalitarian when it surrenders to a certain idea. . . . And this concerns the

1. Stefan Cardinal Wyszyński, *Kazania Świętokrzyskie* [Sermons of the Holy Cross] (Rome: Rycerza Niepokolanej, 1975), pp. 51–52.

Church as well, insofar as it is tempted directly or indirectly to form a state apparatus.[2]

I fully accept Domenach's basic theses, although they are clearly not very appropriate to Polish realities. The Polish People's Republic is not a democratic and secular state; it has surrendered to the idea of a totalitarian state. The necessary condition for its secularization is the abolition of its totalitarian political structure. A secular state is a state in which the Christian is not compelled "to make the terrible choice between God and Caesar." It means that "he who chooses God . . . is not martyred by an idolatrous Caesar," and that no one else is "subjugated by an allegedly Christian Caesar."

Domenach here is in agreement with Reverend Jacques Leclerq, a professor at Catholic University in Louvain, for whom secularization means that "the state leaves the grip of the Church." Yet this kind of view is in conflict with a long tradition of thought on church and state. As Leclerq has written:

Throughout the nineteenth century, the majority of Catholics were captivated by the idea of a Christian state, nourishing hopes for a return to the ways of the past. Even today we can meet such people. When there's even a glimmer of movement in that direction, they pounce on it with enthusiasm.[3]

In April 1962, the Polish episcopate wrote the following: "We command no riches and have no material strength. And for this second deficiency we should be particularly grateful to God: lacking earthly power, we are free from the temptation of using it."[4]

In August 1963 (we quote this for the second time), the bishops declared:

We have heard enough of the charge that in old times the Catholic hierarchy and clergy used to support earthly kings and bask in their glory. Perhaps that sometimes did happen. As a result of such past experiences, therefore, let us now keep as far as possible from the kings and the mighty of this world.

In an episcopal document on secularization from 22 March 1968, we can read the following:

2. Jean-Marie Domenach, "Świadomość religijna i świadomość polityczna" [Religious and Political Consciousness], in *Więź*, no. 6, 1968. Quotation in the next paragraph is from the same source.

3. Jacques Leclerq, *Katolicy i wolność myśli* [Catholics and Freedom of Thought] (Warsaw, 1964), p. 186.

4. *Listy Pasterskie Episkopatu Polski* [Pastoral Letters of the Polish Episcopate] (Paris: Editions du Dialogue, 1975), p. 258.

We are well aware that in contemporary societies, people with different worldviews will be living side by side. . . . The Church is often accused of not wanting to recognize the existence of modern society with its diverse world outlooks. That is not true. It is true, however, that we cannot accept the use of state power to impose a materialist worldview upon citizens. The Church does not ask that secular authorities be concerned with the development of God's Kingdom, nor does it seek a privileged position for itself. The Church insists only on those rights that are its proper due. It insists on genuine freedom to carry out the works of Christ. . . .

More and more these days, it is said that the contemporary state should grant no privileges whatsoever to any philosophical system, ideology, or cultural or artistic current. When, however, as is the case with compulsory secularization, the state intervenes on the side of the materialist worldview, utilizing state institutions and the administrative apparatus in this effort, then we are forced to voice our objections. Social justice and the general welfare demand that people of different orientations live together, with the same rights in all areas, and without discrimination or administrative pressures on believers.[5]

If these statements mean that the Church has foresworn efforts to obtain earthly power, they meet the deepest wishes of secular leftists and calm many of our deepest concerns. I certainly hope that, in contrasting the words of Domenach with those of the primate, I am only fighting with windmills. But this does not alleviate other doubts raised by the primate's Sermons of the Holy Cross.

For example, I cannot make sense of the argument that certain ideas were "dredged up" from France. Surely the hostility to foreign ideas, simply because they are foreign, is one Polish tradition that is not worth saving. From there, it is only a small step to the charge of cosmopolitanism, a favorite of totalitarian dictatorships. Christians should be particularly sensitive here, since Christianity itself, of course, is neither Polish nor Slavic, but was also once "dredged up" into Poland from somewhere else.

The primate's assessment of liberalism also strikes me as unfairly one-sided. While it is true that liberal ideas in the nineteenth century were in sharp conflict with the teachings of the Church, it would be erroneous to reduce liberalism to anticlericalism, or to make this issue the sole vantage point for judging liberalism. The anticlericalism of the liberals most certainly played a key role in de-

5. *Pastoral Letters*, pp. 522–23.

termining the attitude of the Church. In the era of totalitarianism, however, that is not the most important point. Rather, we should remember that it was liberals who first formulated, in secular language, the principles of freedom of conscience and freedom of religion, the ideas of human rights, religious tolerance, and the parliamentary system. The Church teaches that man, as a free being, has the freedom to choose between good and evil but has a *duty* to strive toward God—that is, to choose good.

"The liberals are not concerned with God," says Reverend Leclerq. "They do not consider whether God imposes any obligations upon us. Rather, they are concerned with *politics,* and they want to know whether the *state* can impose or favor any specific beliefs. In the nineteenth century, people talked specifically about religion. And so the question was whether the state should support any specific religion. It was a purely political question."[6]

The course of the conflict was quite intense. The separation of church from state was brought about in France by brutal methods that cannot be approved. Does this mean that morality existed on only one side of the conflict? If so, how would we characterize the Church's support for various royalist conspiracies? Or its position in the Dreyfus Affair? Yet this is not the point. The most essential point, I believe, is that the overwhelming majority of French Catholics do not desire a return to the old state of affairs. They consider the present legal status of the Church to be perfectly natural.

From a doctrinal point of view, the Church cannot accept liberal ideas. But the doctrinal point of view is not the only point of view. The Church, after all, also rejects other religions from a doctrinal point of view, yet it still engages in dialogue with them. Let us remember that the principle of human freedom, according to the classic liberal thinker John Stuart Mill, is based on freedom of conscience and of religious conviction, freedom of thought and of feeling, and absolute freedom of opinion and judgment in all spheres, whether practical, philosophical, cultural, scientific, moral, or theological. Intrinsically connected with this is the freedom of expressing and publicizing one's opinions. According to Mill,

The principle requires liberty of tastes and pursuits of framing the plan of our life to suit our own character; . . . freedom to unite for any purpose not involving harm to others. . . . No society in which these liberties are not

6. Leclerq, *Katolicy,* p. 192.

. . . respected is free, whatever may be its form of government; and none is completely free in which they do not exist absolute and unqualified.[7]

Elsewhere, Mill added the following:

To be held to rigid rules of justice for the sake of others develops the feelings and capacities which have the good of others for their object. But to be restrained in things not affecting their good by their mere displeasure develops nothing valuable except such force of character as may unfold itself in resisting the restraint. If acquiesced in, it dulls and blunts the whole nature. To give any fair play to the nature of each, it is essential that different persons should be allowed to lead different lives. In proportion as this latitude has been exercised in any age, has that age been noteworthy to posterity. Even despotism does not produce its worst effects, so long as Individuality exists under it; and whatever crushes individuality is despotism, by whatever name it may be called and whether it professes to be enforcing the will of God or the injunctions of men.[8]

There is much here that is similar to the principles expressed in the Vatican councils and in the pastoral letters of the Polish bishops. The language is different, as is the initial point of departure. Yet the two traditions have a common way of evaluating human affairs, for both have their roots in a joint European and Christian cultural tradition. Not accidentally, Mill's splendid booklet, banned in the USSR, is basic reading for Russian dissidents fighting for human rights in their own country. Nor is it an accident that in the language of Communist propaganda, accusing someone of "liberalism" is one of the most damaging charges that can be made. The leaders of the Vanguard System understand perfectly well—better, in fact, than the Church—that the ideas of Mill's intellectual descendents strike right at the heart of the Party's totalitarian project and not at religion or the Church. Today the concept of a secular state is an antitotalitarian notion, not an anti-Catholic one. The conflict between the liberal intelligentsia and the Church is now a closed chapter of European history—and let us hope it stays that way. The ideas of the Church, of the Vatican Council, and of the papal encyclicals of John XXIII and Paul VI pose no threat whatsoever to those who espouse a liberal conception of human rights. On the contrary, with respect to the basic issues of the human order, and especially on the question of fun-

7. John Stuart Mill, "On Liberty," chapter 1; in *Essential Works of John Stuart Mill* (New York: Bantam Books, 1961), pp. 265–66.

8. Mill, "On Liberty," chapter 3 of the *Essential Works*, pp. 311–12.

damental human rights, the aspirations of Christians are identical to those of students of Mill.

Whoever in today's Poland fights against the Church in the name of human freedom is either an ignoramus, an idiot, or a knight of totalitarian reaction disguised in liberal phraseology. No liberal can wage such a struggle today. For a liberal is always on the side of those who defend human rights.

In this context, let me just say a few words about the Freemasons. The primate, it seems, influenced by a very old and unfair stereotype, did them an injustice in his sermon. From recent scholarly works, we know that freemasonry was an ideological and intellectual formation fully worthy of respect. Edward Abramowski and Jan Wolski, Szymon Askenazy and Marceli Handelsman, Stanisław Stempowski and Andrzej Strug—these are some of the prominent names of Polish freemasonry. And they were honest and honorable people, sincere patriots, consistent defenders of freedom and tolerance. The Freemasons were liberals. They sought to create a democratic, secular state, and this is what put them at odds with the Church hierarchy. But let us repeat: relations with the Church should not be the sole criterion for judging an intellectual tendency. Even the Church should accept this—perhaps especially the Church. For there have been many examples in history where the Church, to quote the Polish bishops, has "supported thrones." In the realm of earthly affairs, the Church has not always stood on the side of human rights. These very Freemasons, fought by the Church, have contributed glorious things to Polish history, through their cultural creations and their unswerving defense of human and civic rights. They have earned our respect, as well as an objective assessment. The actions of the Communist authorities, destroying our culture and customs under the banner of "secularization," have nothing in common with Masonic traditions. Masonic cults and rituals were never imposed on anyone by force. They guide the lives only of those who have freely and consciously chosen to be so guided.

It is not for obscure historical reasons that I take up this dispute here. Nor do I do so because Freemasons somehow need to be defended today—after all, there have been no Masonic lodges in Poland since the late 1930s. But in place of this we have something that is far more dangerous than all the lodges of the world—the myth of Masonic domination. This myth has been around for a long time, and its impact has always been pernicious. Suffice it to recall that the great anti-Masonic campaign of 1936 to 1938, which ended with the lodges disbanding themselves, was a key part of "Ozon's" campaign to destroy democratic rights.[9] Maria Dąbrowska wrote about this with anger and pain. Yet at least Masonic lodges really did exist, even if they were far from dominating anything. When there are no Masons, however, any person can be "exposed" as one by the press—just like any person could become a Jew in 1968. The myth of the "omnipotent freemasonry" can be very useful to the Communist government. It allows the government to blame each new economic disaster ("temporary difficulties") on some secret mafia. But the myth is a dangerous one. It promotes mindlessness and strengthens obscurantism. In crisis situations, it is even more dangerous. Like anti-Semitism, it can arouse anti-intellectual emotions, encourage the search for scapegoats, and pave the way for totalitarian demagogy.

Church attacks on "liberals and Masons" are part of a bad tradition. They are associated with attacks on values that secular leftists hold dearest: freedom, tolerance, and human rights. It is the sound of the past one hears here, full of anger and fury.

As has often been noted, the values of the secular Left grow out of the Christian tradition. Today these values are championed by the Church. This has been demonstrated by the constitutions of the Ecumenical Council, by the pastoral letters of the Polish bishops, and by the primate of Poland with his unswerving, if often lonely, defense of freedom, tolerance, and human rights. Nevertheless, for a great many years, the Church and the Left have understood and defended these values in markedly different ways. The Left has felt that these values needed to be protected *against* the Church, since human rights and the aims of the Church appeared to be on opposite ends of the field. This resulted in a bifurcation of the national culture: the "Polish radical" went one way, with his humanist ethics and his notions of the rights of man, while the "Polish Catholic," conscious of his responsibilities to God and Fatherland, went a different way. The result was a series of dramatic conflicts, so majestically described by Bohdan Cywiński in *Genealogies of the Indomitable*. The conflicts lasted long. It took Communist totalitarianism to push the Left closer to the Church, as the Left began to realize that many common values were in jeopardy. For it turned out that there *were* common values between the Church and the Left, something that both sides had denied. To-

9. "Ozon"—Obóz Zjednoczenia Narodowego, or Camp of National Unity, an influential right-wing political organization in the late 1930s.—TRANS.

day, probably no one from the Church would deny that the Left defends such values. For it was precisely in the name of these common values that the spiritual descendents of the "liberals and Masons," together with many priests, signed the protest letters against the constitutional changes proposed in 1975.[10] And the thrust of these letters was quite similar to the position taken by the episcopate. This similarity was a spectacular manifestation of what was to come. For the episcopate then made a most noble and farsighted gesture: it took under its wing and defended the persecuted signatories. Just as in Bonhoeffer's allegory, "mother and children once again recognized each other."

The road to this encounter has been roundabout and complex, filled with zigzags and misunderstandings. But such misunderstandings cannot be mechanically avoided. It takes a long time to resolve age-old tensions and animosities. If the encounter is to be authentic, however, the sole aim of the dispute over the past should be the joint search for truth. And let us hope that this is what it proves to be.

The historical sense of our encounter can be understood in different ways. For some, it is but a tactical accord or "temporary cease-fire." For others, including this writer, the encounter is a historic opportunity for Polish culture. It raises hopes that we might finally be able to smash the ghettolike culture of our intellectual life, that we can finally leave our endless controversies behind. It raises hopes that the rigid division into two camps, the Catholic and the secular, might finally be overcome, replaced by the pluralistic unity of our culture. Everyone would benefit from this. Catholics would remain Catholics, secular people secular, but the destructive ghettolike climate of our lives would at least partially disappear. In this unified—though not uniform—culture, there would be room for Catholics and "Freemason liberals" alike. Both are indispensable to our culture.

One may well reply that this is all some utopian fantasy. Yet as Antoni Słonimski has said, where would we be without fantasy?

10. The Party proposed changing the Constitution so as to formally guarantee the Party's "leading role in the state," as well as Poland's alliance with the Soviet Union. Intellectual oppositionists responded with a series of open letters in protest.—TRANS.

9

PATRIOTISM AND CULTURE

Yet is this proposal, with its special understanding of the idea of patriotism and more broadly of the idea of Polishness, really so very utopian? I have found similar ideas in one of the letters of the episcopate. This one, from 5 September 1972, concerns the notion of Christian patriotism. Defining patriotism as "love for one's country, properly understood," the bishops developed the Christian point of view as follows:

The foundation and source of Christian patriotism can be found in the teachings of Jesus on loving thy neighbor and on the equality of all people before God and amongst one another. We must love all people. And in order to reach this goal, we must first embrace with our love all those people with whom we share not only our land, but also our language, our loves, and our spiritual and cultual values with their diverse traditions from the past. Through love for our own country, we move toward love for the entire human family; and through the development of our national virtues, we enrich the entire human family. For the existing diversity of nations contributes to the richness and beauty of the entire human family. And this diversity derives from the Heavenly Father, the Creator of all nations, the Source of all good and beauty. . . . True love for one's country entails profound respect for the values of other nations. It requires recognition of all the good that is found beyond our borders, as well as readiness to improve ourselves on the basis of the experiences and accomplishments of other nations. . . . [But] it eschews hatred, for hatred is a destructive force that leads to a diseased and degenerated version of patriotism. Our epoch has supplied us in abundance with terrifying examples of distorted patriotism in the forms of racism, egotistical chauvinism, and diseased nationalism. In the name of an alleged love for one's nation, the biological existence as well as the economic, cultural, spiritual, and even religious values of other nations have been destroyed. It is often forgotten that the seed of hatred poisons also those who plant it. Hatred impoverishes one's own nation terribly, depriving it of the opportunity to gain from the achievements of the entire human family. . . . There is another danger here as well, occurring chiefly among those individuals or nations who have lost . . . a sense of God as the supreme value and the basis of human conduct. . . . For when "there is no God," nation and fatherland come to be seen as absolute values. They begin to take His place. Reality is thereby falsified, with terrible consequences. For although one may place one's nation very high on the list of dear values, one nevertheless must know that above all nations stands God, Who alone has the right to establish universal moral norms, independent of any particular nation. This is the true understanding of patriotism. Such an understanding purifies patriotism and allows one to fully comprehend the human family. It guards us against indifference to the fate of others and makes us sensitive to the needs of every person, regardless of what language he speaks or what nationality he professes. . . . True patriots do not speak much about their love for the fatherland. Those who claim to be true patriots yet only have their own interests in mind—such people never close their mouths.[1]

When patriotic ideals are formulated in such a way, we cannot disagree. Leftists raised on the writings of Żeromski and Dąbrowska will feel very close to this concept of patriotism, so free of chauvinism and empty boasting. Leftists will not, of course, say that "above all nations stands God," but we fully share the categorical rejection of idolizing one's own nation. Above solidarity with one's nation we place solidarity with the fundamental ethical values of European culture. Leftists feel closer to the German who joins with the allies to fight against the Third Reich than to the German who defends the Nazi state out of solidarity with his country. We believe that the "other Germans"—such as Dietrich Bonhoeffer, Willy Brandt, or Thomas Mann, who spoke out against their country—showed by their actions what true patriotism and true love of country is all about. Among them were Christians, but also nonbelievers whose secular ethics guided them to the proper decision. Thus leftists cannot agree that a Christian worldview is a necessary condition for honest patriotism. Too many Christians fought in the *Wehrmacht*, and too many non-Christians participated in the anti-Hitler Resistance. It was the same in Poland. All those people who have publicly proclaimed their Catholicism and noisily professed their patriotism—

---

1. *Listy Pasterskie Episkopatu Polski* [Pastoral Letters of the Polish Episcopate] (Paris: Editions du Dialogue, 1975), pp. 707–8.

people like Piasecki, Żukrowski, or Zabłocki—are they somehow "better patriots" than such secular leftists as Maria and Stanisław Ossowski, Edward Lipiński, or Antoni Słonimski?

In the Polish situation, the continuity of tradition and national culture is particularly important. As Cardinal Wyszyński has noted, "raising the young generation in the spirit of love for our country's history has enormous significance for the future of the Nation." It is hard to disagree with this. But the next part of the primate's commentary is far more controversial:

We must break with the widespread tendency to "dirty" our own history, to mock the sometimes tragic experiences of our Nation. If the young generation of Poland is to conscientiously fulfill its obligations and work for the future of our country, it must be raised in the spirit of deep veneration for our history. . . . Let us fear not that we might stray into chauvinism or misguided nationalism. That is something that has never threatened us. We have always shown our readiness to devote ourselves to the cause of freedom of other nations.[2]

I fully agree that respect for the historical traditions of one's nation should be an essential part of one's education. But it is only the *good* traditions that we ought to respect. We should know the entirety of our history, but we should value and preserve only those parts that deserve to be preserved. It is one thing to know the fascist ONR tradition and another thing to respect it; it is one thing to know the truth about Targowica[3] and another thing to pay homage to it. I do not quite understand what the primate had in mind when he spoke about "dirtying" our history. If he is referring to the Communists' attempts to defame the soldiers of the Home Army or to vilify former Foreign Minister Józef Beck as a Hitlerite stooge, then we can fully agree with him. But if the primate is suggesting that we ought not criticize the *policies* of the Home Army leadership or the *policies* of Beck, then we must disagree. A noncritical stance toward one's history is, I believe, incomparably more detrimental to honest patriotism than the most severe and uncompromising criticism. Speaking honestly about our not always glorious past is not the same as "dirtying" it. Tough criticism is a far more authentic expression of love for one's country than pseudopatriotic panegyrics. If anything can and

2. *Listy Pasterskie Prymasa Polski* [Pastoral Letters of the Polish Primate] (Paris: Editions du Dialogue, 1975), p. 545.
3. Refers to the eighteenth-century betrayal of Polish national interests, as gentry statesmen capitulated to annexationist demands of the Russian tsarist authorities.—TRANS.

does "dirty" our history for the younger generation, it is precisely the bombastic slogans and apologetic self-depictions. Such education produces either cynics or chauvinists. Therefore I do not share the optimism of the primate, who asserted in April 1967 that we have no reason to fear that we might "stray into chauvinism or misguided nationalism." The events that took place just one year later showed precisely our "reasons to fear" and demonstrated the broad range of chauvinism in our country. In one sense, these events were a continuation of previous political and ideological tendencies, a kind of degenerated mixture of Stalinist communism and ONR fascism. It seems that Poles have not always been able to resist the temptations of "misguided nationalism." Not even Polish Catholics have always been able to resist.

Unfortunately, contrary to what the primate says, Poles have also not always displayed a "readiness to devote ourselves to the cause of freedom of other nations." We have lacked this readiness in relation to our Eastern neighbors, the Lithuanians and the Ukrainians. We lacked it in 1938, during our actions against Zaolzie—and again thirty years later in our actions in Hradac Kralove.[4] It is not pleasant to write about this, but if we want to live in truth, we must not forget it. Father Jan Zieja, Władysław Bieńkowski, and Edward Lipiński have all spoken out on these matters with courage and dignity. Did they "dirty" our history by doing so? I think they did the opposite: they gave evidence of a noble and wise patriotism, just as the Polish bishops attested to their humanism and patriotic wisdom with their splendid letter to the German bishops.

Our conflicts over the past usually reflect disagreements over the nature of Polish national culture. The episcopate has frequently emphasized the Catholic nature of our culture. It has often declared that there is an intrinsic connection between Catholicism and Polishness. This connection can be understood in two ways. It can mean that Catholicism is an integral part of Polish culture, or it can mean that only that which is Catholic is truly Polish. If we say that the connection stems from Catholicism's long-lasting presence in our culture, this is obviously true and we can all agree on it. But if, by speaking of this connection, we mean to reduce Polish culture to only those parts that have been shaped by Catholic thought, this can be quite dangerous.

---

4. Zaolzie is a province in northern Czechoslovakia the Poles tried to seize by force in 1938. Hradec Kralove is the area of Czechoslovakia to which Polish troops were sent during the Warsaw Pact invasion of 1968.—Trans.

A Polish culture without its non-Catholic accomplishments means a Polish culture without, for example, the following people: Nina Assordobraj, Szymon Askenazy, Jerzy Andrzejewski, Tadeusz Borowski, Jacek Bocheński, Tadeusz Boy-Żeleński, Kazimierz Brandys, Marian Brandys, Władysław Broniewski, Włodzimierz Brus, Maria Dąbrowska, Henryk Elzenberg, Marian Falski, Gustaw Herling-Grudziński, Mieczysław Jastrun, Michał Kalecki, Leszek Kołakowski, Tadeusz Konwicki, Janina and Tadeusz Kotarbiński, Tadeusz Kroński, Ludwik Krzywicki, Witold Kuła, Oskar Lange, Edward Lipiński, Tadeusz Manteuffel, Czesław Miłosz, Zofia Nałkowska, Marek Nowakowski, Maria and Stanisław Ossowski, Julian Przyboś, Adolf Rudnicki, Bruno Schulz, Antoni Słonimski, Andrzej Stawar, Julian Stryjkowski, Andrzej Strug, Jan Józef Szczepański, Wisława Szymborska, Julian Tuwim, Adam Ważyk, Wiktor Woroszylski, Kazimierz Wyka, and Stefan Żółkiewski. Of course, we could make this list much longer than it already is. We might reach into the past and include such people as Stefan Żeromski, Aleksander Świętochowski, and even Mikolaj Rej and the Polish Brethren. For, oh, how crippled Polish culture would be without such people! How much less attractive! How much poorer!

I am deeply convinced that the strength of our culture is its pluralism, its variety. This is what lies at the heart of our culture's richness and beauty. It was not only Catholics who lived and created on this land of ours, but also Protestants, Greek Orthodox, Muslims, Jews, and nonbelievers, too. True, there has been more than one attempt to achieve religious homogeneity and mono-ethnicity. But such attempts were always carried out in ways that, to put it delicately, were not very conducive to the development of our culture. Its participation in these efforts constitutes a black page in the annals of Polish Catholicism, for I can in no other way describe the expulsion of the Arians or the limitations placed on the civil rights of Protestants. Although we did not burn anyone at the stake, the result of such policies was an increasing homogeneity of our spiritual life. Our culture was in danger of being smothered by sheer uniformity. This is what led Leszek Kołakowski to remark bitterly about the "curse of clerical, fanatical and dimwitted Catholicism, which has been strangling our culture for some four hundred years."[5] I do not fully agree with Kołakowski. During the partitions,[6] I feel, Catholi-

5. Leszek Kołakowski, "Jezuz Chrystus—prorok i reformator" [Jesus Christ—Prophet and Reformer], in *Argumenty* (Warsaw), 19–26 December 1965.

6. From 1795 to 1918, Poland was fully partitioned among the states of Russia, Germany, and Austria and did not exist as an independent political entity.—TRANS.

cism enriched our culture immensely. And Kołakowski's remarks are not at all relevant to the situation after 1945. Nevertheless, Kołakowski has touched upon an essential point, albeit with a touch of journalistic bravado. For the Roman Catholic Church did indeed win the battle for the "control of souls." Other faiths almost completely disappeared, leaving only small contingents behind. And yet this proved to be a Pyrrhic victory, for it came at a very high price—indeed, at too high a price. Standing alone on the battlefield, Catholicism triumphant became a shallow, anti-intellectual, and extremely conservative movement. In defending Polish national identity through the entire nineteenth century, it remained, to use Ksawery Pruszyński's expression, a "Saxon" Catholicism. And because of this, all the philistines and obscurantists clung to the side of the Church.

Of course, it was not the obscurantists who shaped the spiritual side of Polish Catholicism, despite what the anticlericalists assert. That side was shaped by the specific historical situation, in which the Church, whose very existence was threatened, was forced to be permanently on the lookout. In the nineteenth century, Catholic bishops had to defend themselves against Russian oppression and the German Kulturkampf, against the liberals and the socialists. They had to continually respond to slander and false accusations. The Church persevered through iron resistance, hardened from the inside, always aware that the slightest crack in its cohesion, ideologically or organizationally, could have incalculable consequences.

Twenty years of independent Poland were not enough to radically change this state of affairs. Then came the Nazi occupation, and it was necessary to resurrect the defensive model. Following the onset of the Vanguard System in 1945, things became even worse. The Church now found itself in lethal danger. Threats were constantly on the rise; attacks reached unprecedented frenzy. There was no crime of which Polish bishops were not accused. Such a situation was not conducive to a reconsideration of stereotypes. On the contrary, the dishonest and total attacks led to a kind of fundamentalist resistance. Self-defense turned into self-justification. The Roman Catholic Church withstood tremendous pressure. Not once did it betray the principles of the Gospels. It preserved its honor and strengthened its authority in society at large. Yet this admirable steadfastness helped perpetuate some negative features too, the effects of which can still be felt today. Let me illustrate with a quote from an episcopal statement of 22 March 1973, in commemoration of the 500th anniversary of the birth of Copernicus:

Over the centuries, the Church has always played the role of guardian of art and science. It has cultivated not only religious subjects but also secular ones, and has provided scholars with appropriate material conditions to develop their talents and devote themselves to research. So it was with Copernicus, who took full advantage of the care and assistance provided by the Church. . . . Not only did the Church not oppose his heliocentric theory, but, on the contrary, it helped him in his studies, in his research, and in the publication of his works which revolutionized science. . . . The image of Copernicus as a nonbelieving, secular man, completely unconcerned with church teachings and dogma, is groundless, tendentious, and damaging to the great name of a man revered by the entire world.[7]

The last of these sentences is undoubtedly true. Those of us on the Left cannot without embarrassment recall all the drivel written about Copernicus by people like Andrzej Nowicki, who spoke of the great astronomer as an atheist, an enemy and victim of the Church. And yet the episcopate's words are themselves tainted by a rather one-sided apology for the past. For surely the Church did not always play the role of "guardian of art and science"—unless by "guardianship" we understand the custom of burning books, sometimes together with their authors. The relationship of the Church to Copernican theory must also have been a bit more complex than presented here, since the works of the astronomer were listed in the Index of books banned by the Church.

In this minor but characteristic example, we see all the bad habits that arose in the period of "fundamentalist resistance." And the consequences have been disastrous, doing both Church and society far more harm than good. The problem, of course, is that no sensible person (and in such matters one cannot count on ignorance) will believe such a carefully crafted version of Copernicus in Church history. And so only one response will be forthcoming: "No one tells the truth," people will say. "The government and the episcopate both distort facts to their own advantage. One is as rotten as the other."

I understand the episcopate's difficult situation. Many lies are still being told about the Church and its history. Efforts to eliminate the Church from Polish history and culture continue. The prominent role played by Catholicism in the thousand-year history of our nation is passed over in silence. Naturally the Church's obligation is to re-emphasize this role. Yet the matter of which we are speaking has far-reaching implications.

7. *Pastoral Letters*, pp. 747–48.

The ruling Communists are carrying out a long-term cultural policy that is in essence a plan for the sovietization—devastation, "totalitarianization"—of Polish culture. If they succeed in realizing this program, Poles will be transformed into a people of broken backs, captive minds, and ravaged consciences. They will cease to be a nation and will become a collectivity of captives speaking a soviet dialect of Polish. The essence of this phenomenon—following Leszek Kołakowski, I call it "sovietization"—is its attempt to mold consciousness so that any idea about changing the existing state of affairs will seem to be an irrational absurdity. This is the most dangerous form of dictatorship, since it depends not only on depriving a person of physical freedom but on depriving the person of spiritual freedom as well. The soviet type of slave, after all, feels that he is free and is proud of his "freedom."

In a classic sovietized system, culture is not a creative source of tension producing new ideas. It does not inspire critical thought or activate human inclinations toward freedom and authenticity. Instead, it is a dangerous instrument in the hands of a dictatorial power—more dangerous than open terror. Through organized lies, and through the mass media which become agents for the mass destruction of human hearts and minds, sovietized "culture" blurs the boundaries between description and evaluation, between reality and its propagandistic image. It blunts social sensitivity and liquidates the capacity for autonomous thought. Sovietism entails the *"illiterization"* of society. For freedom of the press has meaning only where people truly know how to read; and one can meaningfully speak of freedom of expression only when a person is able to have his or her own opinion and to articulate it. *Homo sovieticus* is robbed of these faculties. He will not fight for freedom, for freedom is worthless to him. He will not even be able to explain the real meaning of this strange word "freedom," for he is the unknowing captive of sovietized language.

The sovietization of language is an essential stage in the sovietization of culture. Words lose their original meanings. Servitude is called "freedom," lies "truth," misery "prosperity." George Orwell labelled this "newspeak." Soviet newspeak shackles the citizen more effectively than terror. With newspeak, education is tantamount to taming, and all social criticism becomes impossible. The categories allowing one to analyze and evaluate social reality through an "external," "supra-systemic" point of reference disappear. Words themselves disappear. The word "pluralism" disappears, for the soviet world is marked by "unity of thought and deed." The word "dialogue" disappears, for in the soviet world truth is on one side only. The word "God" disappears, for here one worships only Caesar.

The progress of sovietization has been resisted by all people of goodwill, by all for whom words such as *truth, solidarity, freedom,* and *homeland* have not become empty phrases. The most consistent resistance has been posed by the Church. But today the Church stands at a crossroads. The program and direction of this resistance is now the question of utmost importance. People of the Church must decide, and here I repeat the ideas of Domenach: do they seek to replace the official, totalitarian, fundamentalist concept of "socialist" culture with an equally fundamentalist doctrine of "Catholic" culture? Or do they seek to create the conditions for the free development of the *entire* national culture? What exactly do they wish to defend: our ravaged culture with its inherent pluralism, or only a place for what they call "Catholic culture"?

Two observations come to mind here. First, in conditions where all other currents of intellectual and artistic life will have been eradicated, any social space that might possibly be wrested free for "Catholic culture" could only exist as if on a reserve. And just as the last bisons are dying out in the forest reserve of Puszcza Białowieska, so the last Mohicans of Catholic culture would soon die out in *its* own reserve. Second, the division into Catholic and non-Catholic culture is, I feel, arbitrary and socially detrimental. In our situation, it is simply a formal division. Catholic literature is that which is published in Catholic publications. All other criteria are too arbitrary.

As religion, Roman Catholicism may inspire, and has inspired, cultural diversity. But culture is one. There is no Catholic culture, Protestant culture, or nonbelievers' culture; there is only Polish culture. And it is precisely this culture—pluralistic, yet understood as a unity—that we must defend.

We on the secular Left must defend this culture regardless of what the Church does. Let us say it loud and clear: the confiscation of any book, even a religious book, we must treat as a confiscation of our own book. We must treat every act of police repression as repression aimed at us. We must defend every persecuted person as if he or she were our closest comrade. Only then will we be faithful to our ideals. All the rest is sham.

10

IN DEFENSE OF CULTURAL PLURALISM

The process of sovietization is waged on two fronts. The first is the attempt to destroy traditions. It is the effort to eradicate from the collective memory knowledge about the complex past of our country, about its culture and ethos. One result of these efforts is that the complete works of Zygmunt Krasiński or Stefan Żeromski, Karol Irzy-kowski or Stanisław Brzozowski have still not been published. Writers such as Marian Zdziechowski, Jan Kucharzewski, or Eugeniusz Malaczewski (so admired by Primate Wyszyński) are all unknown today. Because of this policy, we still lack new editions of such fundamental works as Feldman's history of Polish political thought, Askenazy's biography of Walerian Łukasiński, Mochnacki's history of the 1831 Uprising, the political writings of Klaczko, the memoirs of Witos, or Rosa Luxemburg's wonderful pamphlet on the Bolshevik Revolution. Entire dimensions of history remain unknown. It is impermissible to write the truth about Piłsudski and the Polish Legions, Dmowski and the National Democrats, Piasecki and his Falangists, Pużak and the Polish Socialist Party, Stefan Grot-Rowecki and the Home Army, Stanisław Mikołajczyk and the peasant movement, or about Adolf Warski and the tragic fate of the prewar Polish communists. The nineteenth-century history of the Catholic Church is covered by a complete ban, while the Uniate tragedy is clearly a sorer spot today than it was in the tsarist empire.

The result of such policy is that there are frightening gaps in the historical consciousness of Polish youth. We see a break in the continuity of tradition, a disappearance of the sense of responsibility for the nation and its fate. The average historical consciousness comes to resemble a formless lump of clay.

The second front of sovietization is the attempt to fashion a new, false shape of reality out of this lump of clay and to burn this falsified image into people's minds. This is the meaning of the regime's untiring practice of attaching new elements onto a castrated and devastated cultural tradition. Everything that happened in the past, yet might somehow serve to legitimate the present, is incorporated by the regime and written in a new ideological context. Grunwald and Jagiełło, Racławice and Kościuszko, Kołłątaj and the May 3 Constitution, Marie Curie-Składowska and Copernicus, Mickiewicz, Norwid, and Żeromski; as well as Edward Dembowski and Jarosław Dąbrowski, Ludwik Waryński and Stefan Okrzeja, Rosa Luxemburg and Feliks Dzierżyński, Wera Kostrzewa and Marceli Nowotko—all these names have been so transformed, brushed up, and officially prepared that they are scarcely recognizable anymore. It turns out that each one of them was a harbinger of the ideals of Communist power! At night they evidently dreamed of nothing else except how to create a totalitarian social order!

In this way, we now have a new canon of Polish history. It is a sham and bogus canon, yet an obligatory one, carefully guarded by the censors and popularized by official propaganda. The state insists on monopolizing the right to interpret the meaning of the May 3 (1791) Constitution, the novels of Stefan Żeromski, or the merits of a particular staging of Wyśpiański's *The Wedding*. The state insists on monopolizing the entire awful canon, the terrible canon of sovietized culture. On the one hand, therefore, we have a mess of random knowledge, the clay lump of the devastated tradition. On the other hand, from out of this mess, there is the basis of new myths and cults based on lies. The Christian would say that God has been replaced at the altar by Caesar. This is what sovietization leads to.

Authenticity is the defense. When the authorities seek to control the entire culture, then every authentic gesture, every authentic movement, and every artistic or scholarly work conceived in authenticity is antitotalitarian. Thus, in the Stalinist period, the stories of Adolf Rudnicki and of Jan Józef Szczepański, Julian Stryjkowski's *Voices in Darkness* and Antoni Gołubiew's *Bolesław the Brave,* the poems of Miron Białoszewski and the journalism of Stefan Kisielewski, the logic studies of Ajdukiewicz and the philosophical reflections of Elzenberg—all of these had an intrinsically antitotalitarian dimension.

Simplifying perhaps too much, we can say the following: Polish culture, seen from above, has long resisted the destructiveness of sovietization. The resistance has occurred on two levels: a persistent defense of the authentic canon of tradition; and a persistent, passionate polemic against the new, sovietized canon.

Above all, it is the Church that has stood out against the destruction of tradition. One need only study the episcopate's *Pastoral Letters* or the sermons of the primate to find the classical canon of thought on Polish affairs. Particularly instructive, from this point of view, are two volumes of the primate's sermons: *From the Eagle's Nest* and *In the Heart of the Capital.*[1] For those of us on the Left, more than a few of Wyszyński's formulations may seem simplistic, one-sided, or annoyingly self-congratulatory. Many phrases will grate upon us with their anachronistic, baroque style. I myself could quarrel with a few accents or choice of words. But for all my reservations, I laud the presence of the classical Polish canon in these sermons and in the pastoral letters. We need this canon. We need to be continually reminded that Poles once constituted a free and independent nation, able and willing, during 150 years of occupation, to fight for their rights. We need to continually think about what belief in a free and independent Poland might mean *today,* for this is a crucial part of the struggle to preserve our authentic national identity against the destructive process of sovietization.

This current of thought about Polish history and culture I call the *traditionalist current.* The superb and penetrating works of Antoni Słonimski belong to this tendency, as do the historical essays of Paweł Jasienica, the war stories of Marian Brandys, the editorial work of Juliusz Gomulicki, the artistry of Zbigniew Raszewski, the historical theater of Kazimierz Dejmek, or the historical literary studies of Stanisław Pigoń. It is an important current. It counterposes words to silence, order to nonsense, knowledge to ignorance, and genuine patriotism to cynicism.

The second current of our intellectual life—let us call it the *radical current*—also has enormous significance. If the essence of the traditionalist current is the reconstruction of the traditional canon of Polish culture, the goal of the radical current is the destruction of the official canon of sovietized culture. This second current aims to expose lies, lay bare hypocrisy, and mock the imprimatur of officialdom. In this current I would include the writings of Sławomir Mrożek, the journalism of Stefan Kisielewski, the stories of Marek Nowakowski, some of the books of Tadeusz Konwicki and Kazimierz Brandys, the productions of the Student Satirical Theater, the theatrical criticism of Konstanty Puzyna, and the poetry of the younger generation of writers such as Tomasz Burek, Stanisław Bar-

---

1. *Z gniazda orląt* [From the Eagle's Nest] and *W sercu stolicy* [In the Heart of the Capital] (Rome: Papieski Instytut Studiów Kościelnych, 1972).

ańczak, and Ryszard Krynicki. The radical current teaches us skepticism and critique. It gives us the ability to resist the ignorance of the official propaganda.

We need both of these currents. They each make the survival of authentic Polish culture possible. They are but two different ways for the nation to comprehend the truth about itself. They are essential to the nation and to each other. The traditionalist current, by reviving traditional Polish culture, keeps our national consciousness from sinking into the swamps of sovietization. If it is not subjected to constant criticism, however, it runs the risk of becoming provincial, parochial, complacent, and intellectually shallow. The radical current, on the other hand, by revealing the absurdity of official stereotypes and the language of propaganda, by mocking "reality according to the newspapers" and the little bits of tradition doled out for us *à la soviet*, prevents the false tradition from creeping unawares into our consciousness. Yet the reduction of antisovietism to antithesis alone may lead to absolute relativism and total negation, to a belief in the absurdity of all ethical norms, the absurdity of all activities and of all patriotism.

Thus one current is as necessary as the other. Marian Brandys is as necessary as Kazimierz Brandys. We need Dejmek's "canonical" National Theater as much as we need Jerzy Markuszewski's "absurdist" Student Satirical Theater. "Harmony," someone once wrote, "is possible only in diversity. One tone does not make a chord."

Conflicts between these two currents are as damaging as they are unavoidable. Ten years ago, many "radicals" considered Paweł Jasienica a nationalist supporter of the regime. Many of the "traditionalists," meanwhile, saw Mrożek as an antipatriotic blasphemer out to destroy the Polish spirit. Only the passage of time helped separate truth from stupidity, Jasienica from Zbigniew Załuski, the theater of Mrożek from the essays of Wiesław Gornicki or Jerzy Urban. Jasienica was no nationalist. He wrote many first-rate books that have much to teach us about political thought, books that probed popular wisdom about Polish history. Mrożek, meanwhile, in his *Death of an Officer,* was fighting not Mickiewicz (who could have been defended without the help of the national-chauvinist journal *Stolica*), but rather the aura created around the *myth* of Mickiewicz, an aura that is dangerous for rational thinking, an aura in which common sense was supplanted by pompous phraseology and concrete arguments were replaced by pseudopatriotic drivel.

So let us repeat: The traditionalist current reconstructs the past, with its spirit, its monuments, and its relics. It teaches respect for the familiar and tries to root itself in the national tradition.

The radical current seeks to disrupt the past. It mocks obscurantism, intellectual primitivism, and the familiarly banal and tries to uproot the increasingly familiar sovietized tradition.

The traditionalist current, seeking foundations in universal cultural values, finds them in the classical European canon, in the traditions of antiquity and Christianity. The works of Zbigniew Herbert, Jacek Bocheński, Zygmunt Kubiak, Mieczysław Jastrun, and Jacek Woźniakowski stand as examples of this.

The radical current finds support in the contemporary antiauthoritarian movements in the West. Western radicalism is its potential ally.

Western Radicalism and Poland

The Polish episcopate, in a letter of March 1970, came out strongly against Western radicalism: "The rising tide of faithlessness, social animosity, licentiousness, secularization, rejection of authority both human and divine, and the general rebellion against everything— this so-called 'radicalism' constitutes one vast frontal assault on the Church."[2]

At about the same time Cardinal Wyszyński issued his own "letter to the clergy and the faithful," commenting on the very same themes:

There has arisen in the world a numerically strong generation that might be called the "children of lies." Everywhere they foment doubt, negativism, and demented criticism. They seek to overthrow everything, yet know neither what they want to build nor how it is to be built. . . . We must guard against the tendencies of anarchy, disintegration, and deceit. We must defend ourselves against the various "rebels" who seek to undermine the truth and authority of Christ's Church. . . . We must keep the specter of social chaos far from the thresholds of home and country. We must ward off suspicion toward the Church and its authority, and deflect all this destructive prattle that is the conceit of the intellect but the bane of the soul. . . . Let us protect our youth and our Nation against this disorder. If other, more prosperous nations, knowing not what to do with their time and their money, allow themselves this anarchy, that is their business. We cannot afford it. We are a Nation rebuilding ourselves after long years of occupation and devastation. We

2. *Listy Pasterskie Episkopatu Polski* [Pastoral Letters of the Polish Episcopate] (Paris: Editions du Dialogue, 1975), p. 593.

live in a different historical situation. We must firmly hold onto the anchor that we find in the Church. It is our might, our strength, our perseverance. We must be serious and wise. We must not fall victim to the propaganda of people obsessed by the conceit of intellect, those who are a bit too sure of themselves, with their unstable convictions and their own ways of "saving the world." . . . Polish youth need not mimic the actions of their counterparts abroad. We have our own wonderful traditions and models worthy of following. With all our might, with all our care, we must protect our youth from this emotional and intellectual chaos.

Similarly, not everything that our brethren clergy does abroad needs to be imitated here at home. . . . Striving for renewal in the conciliar spirit, we must remember that genuine renewal is not newness so much as it is holiness in the spirit of Christ, beginning with the consecration of oneself. . . . Conciliar renewal is not a screen behind which one may propound ambiguous and irresponsible slogans of reform. It does not mean endless dialogue, ignorant and unconstructive chatter, or a spirit of negativism and disobedience. Such features simply cover up an unwillingness to work, to exert oneself, or to make sacrifices. . . . Our intelligentsia, expecting renewal from the Church, must not forget these truths. Renewal in the Church starts from inside. . . . When you demand progress from the Church, remember that "progress in the Church does not imply newness but holiness." Progress is not a fruitless discussion, the endless production of words, the pursuit of the new and different, the undermining of everything that was and is. Progress is a particular kind of holiness. And the holiness begins from within. . . . Renewal originates not so much from a change in church institutions as from a change in hearts and minds and in the style of personal life. You who would be teachers of the world: Become holy yourselves!

Anyone with a shred of decency should know that it is wrong to attack other people's faith, hopes, and loves. Rather than sunder ties with God and the Church through cheap talk and doubt, one should try to establish new ties—through prayer, confession, and the humble recognition of sins and errors committed. . . .

I appeal to you to take responsibility for your words. Put a finger to your lips. Consider every word before speaking. Do not utter words that undermine people's faith, moral principles, or religious way of thinking. Give up your fruitless chatter; it does not create, but only destroys. . . . I appeal to you finally to recognize God's truth. You must courageously accept the truth of Christ and His Church. You must have the courage to speak the truth, and to bear witness to the truth in both word and deed.[3]

3. *Listy Pasterskie Prymasa Polski* [Pastoral Letters of the Polish Primate] (Paris: Editions du Dialogue, 1975), pp. 614–17.

I have quoted at length both the statement of the episcopate and the letter of the Polish primate so as not to deform the main thrust of their arguments. It should be clear from my earlier position, however, that I look upon the phenomenon of radicalism in a quite different way from that of the Polish bishops.

I have pondered long and hard about whether it is worthwhile to even raise these issues. Is there room for such disagreement in a book conceived of as a sincere gesture of goodwill? Is it not better to avoid such matters in a text that is, after all, partly expiatory? Ought I pass over the issues in silence or dispense with them euphemistically? Ought a person without a clear conscience vis-à-vis the Church, someone aware of the complexity of the issues and of the well-substantiated mistrust on the part of the clergy—ought such a person engage in a debate over such fundamental matters, with the risk that he will be misunderstood, his motives doubted, and his actions deemed suspect?

I have considered all of these objections. But I have decided that an intellectual encounter based on bad faith would have little value for anyone. I need to explain why I consider the Church's position on these matters to be wrong. I trust that my polemical comments will be read with the same goodwill with which they are written.

There are three aspects to this problem of radicalism, which I will discuss in order. The first is the question of radicalism within the Church itself; the second deals with radicalism as a phenomenon embracing the entire Western world; the third concerns the matter of transferring the ideals of Western radicals onto Polish turf.

As I have mentioned earlier, a full discussion of the question of internal Church reform is completely beyond my competence. It is difficult for those outside of the Church to speak on this issue, particularly since the primate has warned—correctly, no doubt—against applying secular language to Church matters. I will restrict myself, therefore, to simply noting, in secular categories, what it is about these documents that is so striking to the nonbeliever. To a nonbeliever who once accepted Marxist-Leninist doctrine, who has had many dealings with Party authorities, and who has come into sharp conflict with those authorities, the primate's letter raises unfortunate associations. It reminds him of those times when the Party hierarchy would call for discussion, and then promptly accuse all critics of being "irresponsible" and "muddle-headed grumblers," people engaged in "useless chatter" and "destructive activity," bent on "total negation," etc., etc.

I am no expert on theological language. In secular language, however, one cannot appeal simultaneously for silence and for speaking the truth. The vagueness and generality of these invectives (one cannot say there are any substantive arguments here) indicate a desire to render impossible a discussion in which opinions contrary to those of the party hierarchy may be expressed. Attributing evil intentions and intellectual incompetence to one's opponents ("unwillingness to work," "ignorant and unconstructive chatter") only hinders a dialogue in advance. Telling opponents to stop dreaming up ways of correcting the system and to work on correcting themselves instead is a well-known method of prohibiting discussion in Communist parties. Let me repeat: I am outside the Church. Perhaps inside the Church such words have some other meaning. But I, outside the Church, have been told not by a bishop but by a high Party functionary that my "cheap talk and doubt" shake "other people's faith, hopes, and loves." I replied at the time that faith, hope, and love are not attained by "cheap talk" and so cannot be lost because of someone else's cheap talk. Moreover, nobody has ever been able to defend faith by prohibition, hope by command, or love by abuse. The only result of all these bans, commands, and invectives, I argued, would be the atrophy of intellectual life and the departure from the Party of all those who wish to conscientiously search for truth. In secular language all of this is obvious; whether it is equally obvious in church language, I do not know. I do know, however, that the bishops are wrong to define today's radicalism as a "general rebellion against everything," constituting a "vast frontal assault on the Church." The radical phenomenon is so diverse and complex that it cannot be reduced to any simple formula, much less to an anti-Catholic conspiracy.

Here again we have a disturbing similarity to how the Communist government views the democratic opposition. Everywhere the authorities speak of secret plots and conspiracies. All human history shows that the portrayal of great social movements as the product of secret plans of secret forces is a complete misunderstanding. Western radicalism is a powerful social movement of youth against the general system of values of advanced capitalist societies. The radicals have, it is true, written a good deal of nonsense. Sometimes they have committed acts that warrant unequivocal condemnation. This means that to the fundamental questions they have often answered falsely; it does not mean that the questions themselves are false. It is difficult to engage in a substantive debate here, since the formulations of the episcopate and the primate offer much general indignation but few concrete accusations. Let me say briefly then: we cannot accept a struggle against consumerist civilization that entails the senseless destruction of libraries, laboratories, or works of art. We must, however, seriously consider the Western radicals' analysis of the mechanisms and stupefying effects of mass culture and the educational system. We cannot accept totalitarian ideologies such as Maoism, but we must carefully study the radicals' concrete criticisms of the system of parliamentary democracy. The worries of "the West," after all, may soon be our worries as well.

Thus I cannot agree that Western radicalism is merely a "tendency bringing anarchy, disintegration, and deceit," or that an entire generation of people often quite desperately seeking truth and authenticity in a world of violence, hypocrisy, and self-interest deserves to be dismissed as the "children of lies." I am not convinced by the argument that "they have it too good," for it simply does not follow that when people have an automobile and a nice apartment they have all they are interested in, or that only these things provide meaning to one's life. Nor am I convinced by the claim that radicalism is a "destructive" tendency, for I believe that there are political structures in the world for which "destruction" would be a good thing (Soviet totalitarianism and the Soviet empire, for example). More dangerous today than "doubt, negativism, and demented criticism" is fanaticism, total affirmation, and a demented absence of criticism. More than the "licentiousness" of the radicals I fear the puritanism of state officials. A greater sin than long hair is the state's order to cut it.

Father Bruckberger, a French Dominican far removed from the liberal wing of the Church, once put it this way:

Satan is a puritan, a very refined being, and in this respect the Antichrist will surely be the same. His followers will be "virtuous" in the popular sense of the term. The women will knit and do charitable works, while the men will drink milk instead of alcohol and keep no mistresses. Collaboration with Satan in crime does not occur on the level of commonplace sins.

I do not completely defend the radicals. I think that they do go astray. But they stray in the search for truth. Such people deserve careful attention, a friendly dialogue, comradely conversation. It is particularly important for Poles to talk with the radicals. It is worth talking to them not only because they are searching for truth, or because they are fighting against problems similar or identical to our own, but also because the *Western radical Left may soon prove to be a valuable ally* in the struggle to free the nations of Eastern Europe from Soviet rule.

On the surface this appears absurd. How, one might ask, can the youthful adherents of Mao Zedong's thought ever be our allies? The sympathy of some left-wing Western youth to Maoism is based on ignorance. They mistake their own illusions for reality. Consequently, their support for Maoism, although it irritates us, is merely a mirage. The real issue for them is their condemnation of the morality (or rather amorality) of the policies of the capitalist states. Among those policies today is détente and extensive trade with the Soviet Union. In the course of this trade, as Aleksandr Solzhenitsyn recently reminded us, the USSR obtains modern technical equipment facilitating eavesdropping and surveillance and thus the persecution of Russian dissidents. Such a policy, the product of amoral business, must surely be challenged, but neither the establishment parties nor the pro-Soviet communist parties are going to do so. The so-called Eurocommunist parties, however, might do so. These parties call for the full respect of democratic rights, not only in Western Europe but also in Eastern Europe and the USSR. The radicals might also do so. By challenging such policies, they challenge the international Holy Alliance governing the world.

It seems to me—here I move to the third aspect of the matter—that Poles should not fear radical ideals understood in this way. Skepticism, criticism, and the ability to doubt are characteristics that can be extremely useful for Polish youth. Against what kind of radicalism must we protect the "thresholds of home and country"? Against the "specter of social chaos"? For that we have the secret police and the vigilante journalism of magazines like *Law and Life!* No one fears "social chaos" like the rulers of our country. And no one condemns "destructive prattle" like they do, for no one knows as well as they that if something can be toppled by "prattle," then that "something" is in pretty bad shape. And so I think that the Church, in defending freedom and truth, need not fear "destructive prattle" and the "spirit of doubt." Nor need it fear skepticism.

"What should contemporary poetry be?" Stanisław Barańczak, a writer from the "generation of '68," responded to this question as follows:

1) It should be skeptical.

2) It should be skeptical because only skepticism can justify poetry's existence today. The wider the reach of a form of speech, the more it disaccustoms us from thinking. It tries to convince us of one set of absolute truths

or another, to bring us in line with a particular system of values, to force us to behave in a certain manner. Poetry, as everyone well knows, has a rather narrow reach these days. And herein lies the possibility of its revival, the "initial capital" from which it can grow. There is a chance that we can make poetry the frontline of the struggle for an unfalsified image of the world in which we live. This is possible precisely because poetry is addressed not to the passive recipient stupefied by television or casually turning the pages of the newspaper, but to the person who, by taking the book of poems to hand, has already demonstrated that he or she wants to think.

3) But there is another reason. Poetry is not the anonymous voice of Grand Manipulators, but the voice of an individual. Individual thought is skeptical thought. It is critical vis-à-vis collective faiths, sentiments, and hysterias. The innate individualism of this literary form, which has been both rekindled and re-stifled by poets over the centuries, today gives poetry one more chance for an active relationship to the world.

4) Nor is that all. For poetry also has a certain innate partiality to the concrete (a partiality that may be developed or ignored). Poetry always seeks to verify, to check wishful thinking against actual facts. "What do you *really* mean?" This is the question the poet needs to ask today, as he or she listens skeptically to empty slogans, hollow myths, and false descriptions, all trying to gloss over difficulties and camouflage conflicts. The poet should check everything at the level of the individual, and discover, on the basis of this singular example, just what remains from the grand generalities.

5) And so poetry should be skeptical. Skeptical, critical, aiming to expose. Poetry should be all of these things until the moment when the last lie, the last demagoguery, and the last act of violence disappear from the Earth. I do not think that poetry itself is going to bring this about (if anything at all can bring it about). But I believe that poetry can play a part, by teaching people to think in terms of rational skepticism about lies, demagoguery, violence, and everything that threatens the world. Poetry will play this role when it is completely and consistently skeptical, when it tears down the masks of false appearances not only from the external world but also from itself, when it tries to reveal—not only in what surrounds it but also in itself—the conflicts, disunity, and ambiguity lurking behind the appearances of harmony, agreement, and perfect clarity.

6) From this it must begin. From skepticism, which clears the path for that which we need most. And what I am talking about here—it's nothing new, I admit, yet we've all seemed to forget just what it is we should care for most—is, of course, truth.[4]

4. Stanisław Barańczak, *Jednym tchem* [In One Breath] (Warsaw: Orientacja, 1970), pp. 3–4.

Skepticism is dangerous only for the adherents of arrogance, might, and deception. It is a valuable weapon in the fight against the totalitarian tendencies of the world in which we live. In 1972, in a sermon to Polish youth from London, Cardinal Wyszyński said the following:

Polish youth must be courageous and able to make sacrifices. It cannot be a mere sponge, shapeless and formless. . . . We saw how in 1968, on the sidewalks of Warsaw, in front of the Church of the Holy Cross, young people demanded freedom of speech, freedom of thought, a free judiciary, freedom of studies, freedom to worship God and to love one's Fatherland. The young were able to fight for these things. We were witnesses to their struggle.[5]

From this it would follow that the necessary conditions for courage and self-sacrifice were intellectual independence, criticism, and creative mistrust. Courage and self-sacrifice were offshoots of a universal questioning of the officially proclaimed system of human values and the officially propagated, false, and apologetic vision of social reality. Without criticism, without creative mistrust, this would have been impossible. Such characteristics, so typical of young radicals, are completely unnecessary for those who do not seek truth. Yet for Polish youth who in the name of truth reject conformism and choose the path of rebellion and civic disobedience, these features have been, are, and will continue to be essential. In fact, I think that the most radical ideas in our political reality are Christian ideas, and that the greatest "rabble-rousers" have been the bishops themselves. If, after all, people reared in mendacity are urged to "live in truth," how can they do so if not through criticism, doubt, and skepticism? How can they embrace new values if not by challenging and undermining existing obligatory truths and authorities? Not everyone can accept the truths preached by the Church, since not everyone is a believing Christian. But secularization is a social fact, not the product of an anti-Christian conspiracy. The primate urges us to "firmly hold onto the anchor that we find in the Church." It is not for me to advise the Church what position it should take regarding secularization and secular social circles. Yet I feel justified in saying that the Church can become a moral authority for these circles only when it addresses the problems that genuinely bother them and when it replaces its attitude of defensive hostility by one of friendly dialogue.

5. Stefan Cardinal Wyszyński, *Z gniazda orląt*, pp. 137–38.

PART THREE

TOWARD A NEW DIALOGUE

11

WHAT IS DIALOGUE?

I have spoken much here about "dialogue." This is a word with many meanings, often misused, and diversely interpreted. It is an idea easy to explain, but difficult to achieve.

Historically speaking, the first ones to call for interaction and dialogue between Catholics and nonbelievers were the adherents of PAX. In 1945, just after the war, Bolesław Piasecki and his comrades from the proto-fascist ONR-Falanga began a new stage of their political careers on the pages of the weekly *Dziś i jutro* [Today and Tomorrow]. The facts surrounding the origins of Piasecki's new career in People's Poland are today well known. We know that General Serov, one of the chief officers of the Soviet NKVD (forerunner to the KGB), sponsored Piasecki's activities in the first postwar years and that PAX was conceived by its Soviet protectors as a kind of front organization.

If we consider the ideological development of PAX as well as the psychology of its leaders, it would seem that three factors were crucial. First, there was a recognition of political realities. The Falangists understood very quickly that in the changed geopolitical situation they could survive only as faithful executors of Communist and Soviet policies. There was no room for any other political line in the conditions of that time. Thus, *Dziś i jutro* repeatedly spoke out on behalf of a "progressive Catholicism," which it contrasted to the "reactionary Catholicism" of other groups of Catholics, including, of course, the episcopate.

Second, as I mentioned earlier, the Falangists found it rather easy to accept a program of state control of the economy and a strong state power. They had put forth similar positions in their prewar programmatic documents—the difference being that they had previously felt someone else should be guiding the totalitarian state ship: namely themselves.

Third, Piasecki and his group undertook a clever attempt to "build a bridge between Catholicism and the camp calling for radical social reconstruction." Stefan Kisielewski, the author of these words in June 1946, defended the former Falangists against charges that they were pro-totalitarian with only an instrumental attitude to Catholicism. And if a savvy political fox like Kisielewski could believe in the honesty and sincerity of the *Dziś i jutro* group, how can we be surprised that others believed in them too? I have already discussed the reasons pushing secular intellectual circles toward the Vanguard Ideology in the 1945 to 1947 time period. Similar reasons pushed young Catholic intellectuals too. Just as in secular circles, many Catholics considered the PPR's program as the basis for the modernization and democratization of the country. *Dziś i jutro* appealed to these attitudes. Championing progressive slogans, it managed to bring together a rather large group of young and idealistic intellectuals, who took seriously both the official governmental reform program and PAX's attempt to "reconcile" Catholicism with socialist transformation.

These people played their own part in the tragedy of the young Polish intelligentsia. Just as many of their peers were taken by the ideals of secular humanism and universal brotherhood, so these young Catholic intellectuals were fascinated by French personalism. From their pens came the first articles on personalism and Jacques Mounier. The problem was that their work within PAX did not contribute to the building of a personalistic reality. In the name of honest personalist ideals, they served totalitarianism. Thinking they were serving the Church, they actually worked against it. For people of the secular Left, and so also for the author of these words, it is hard to pass judgment on their activities. The situation was very complex, as were the motives of the people involved. Some years later, Tadeusz Mazowiecki, one of the leaders of this group of young intellectuals, wrote the following:

Judging from historical distance, it is impossible to deny that the Church was opposed, if not downright hostile, to the basic social reforms of the first postwar years, such as the nationalization of industry and the agricultural reform. This position was a reflection both of the Church's opposition to the government, which it considered atheistic and arbitrarily imposed, and the powerful influence of socially conservative elements in the Church's ranks.

On the other hand, looking again from a distance, it is hard not to see that in the period of Stalinist errors, it was the Church that gave particular support to the idea of freedom and human dignity.[1]

Considering the censorship of the time, it would have been hard to come up with a more honest self-appraisal. In the "October" period of 1956–57, Mazowiecki, though of course not only he, was making a public reckoning of his own activities in PAX. He had broken with PAX in 1955, after a sharp internal battle. The parting of ways was the result of complete political incompatibility. Mazowiecki and his co-thinkers wanted to serve personalistic ideals and the Church; PAX, an organization with a totalitarian internal structure, was a tool of the government designed to break up the Church. This was, and remains, the price paid for the existence of PAX. And so it is no surprise that for PAX, "dialogue" was simply an ideological label, a justification for collaboration with the government as well as a way to win concessions from it. For society and the Communist authorities alike, PAX represented the extreme pro-Soviet tendency. It was also the most consistent mouthpiece for the "totalitarianization" of public life. Catholicism and the teachings of the Gospel were no obstacle to the leaders of PAX, but then they were no obstacle during the "high and mighty" years of the Falangists either.

The "Official" Understanding of Dialogue

In place of the democratic principles of religious freedom and religious pluralism, PAX substituted the concept of the co-superiority of two worldviews: Catholicism and Marxism, each defined as "Promethean." The "Prometheanism" of Marxism and Catholicism (that is to say, of "true" Marxism and Catholicism, the ones associated with the government and PAX, respectively) were said to be based on their "cognitive optimism." This sorry and absurd nonsense was supposed to mean, in "PAX-speak," that the ideal political leadership was the union of progressive PAX Catholics with the "cognitive-optimist" wing of the Party. Which wing of the Party was this? At times of political crisis, PAX's answer was clear. In 1956 PAX allied with the hard-line Natolin faction, sponsored by the Soviet embassy and openly hostile to all liberal tendencies; in 1968 PAX sided with

1. Tadeusz Mazowiecki, *Rozdroża i wartości* [Crossroads and Values] (Warsaw: Biblioteka Więzi, 1970), p. 57.

the so-called Partisans, the xenophobic adherents of the police method of governing.

During one of the PAX-sponsored "dialogues" with Marxists, a PAX representative spoke as follows:

It is no accident that we are discussing the matter of cooperation between believers and nonbelievers . . . precisely with the editorial board of the journal *Wychowanie* [Upbringing]. Your journal represents the tendency in contemporary Polish Marxist thought which recognizes the importance of moral inspiration in social activity, and which was the first to propose, in a courageous and constructive manner, that the dialogue between the Catholic and Marxist worldviews not be isolated from the concrete patriotic reality of People's Poland.[2]

Considering that the biweekly *Wychowanie* has always specialized in attacks on educated and persecuted people, that it embodies the most reactionary and obscurantist tendency of Polish intellectual life, and that it is a magazine lacking even the slightest influence in society, it is hard to imagine PAX's choice of partner as a mere coincidence. In the PAX way of thinking, "dialogue" is an encounter between totalitarians, drawing inspiration from a peculiarly understood Catholicism and a specific, very Soviet understanding of Marxism. The masthead of *Wychowanie* and of PAX journals alike could very well bear the common slogan: "Totalitarians of both world-outlooks, unite!"

Another PAX publicist noted that, thanks to the existence of PAX, "socialism has not become entangled in a total struggle with the Church."[3] This is obviously untrue. "Socialism" (and by this PAX means the policies of the ruling communist party) has "entangled itself" more than once in a total struggle with the Church, and in every one of these conflicts PAX played the role of assistant to the atheist authorities. This is no surprise, since amelioration of the Church-state conflict would only undermine PAX's *raison d'être*. That the Church survived intact was due not to PAX but to the firm and decisive stance of the episcopate.

Relations between the episcopate and the state have sometimes been referred to as a "dialogue." This is a misunderstanding. It would be more accurate to treat Church-state relations as a permanent con-

---

2. Mikołaj Rostworowski, in *Dialog i współdziałanie* [Dialogue and Interaction] (Warsaw: Instytut Wydawniczy PAX, 1970), p. 55.
3. Maciej Wrzeszcz, in *Dialog i współdziałanie*, p. 98.

flict interrupted by short periods of compromise. Each side, the Party and the Church, has always treated the other as a necessary evil. The leaders of the Party have never seriously considered abandoning their antireligious policies, and the Catholic bishops have never considered passively accepting the consequences of these policies. The rest is tactics and diplomacy.

And yet there does exist a political tendency within the Catholic movement which strives for a lasting accord between Church and state. I am speaking here of the group known as ODISS (Center for Documentation and Social Studies) and of its leader, the Znak parliamentary deputy Janusz Zabłocki.

Zabłocki was for a long time the only Catholic politician in Poland to maintain equally good relations with both the Party and Church authorities. A PAX activist until 1955 and then for many years the associate editor of *Więź*, Zabłocki demonstrated his differences with other Znak activists during the events of March 1968. Although he signed the important parliamentary interpellation along with other Znak deputies, he soon began publicly to distance himself from them. "We seek neither allies nor applause in Bonn or Tel Aviv," stated Zabłocki at one meeting of the Catholic Intellectuals Club.[4] Those alleged to have sought that applause were his Sejm colleagues Zawieyski, Stomma, and Mazowiecki. This precipitated a split in *Więź*. Supported in its efforts by certain elements in the Party hierarchy, Zabłocki's group left the *Więź* editorial board to form ODISS and publish the new bimonthly journal *Chrześcijanin w świecie* [Christian in the World]. Zabłocki's program was simple: to drive a wedge between the oppositionist intelligentsia and the Church hierarchy, and thus help bring about an accord between the nationalist "Partisan" wing of the Party (which used patriotic phraseology while closely following instructions of Soviet officials) and the episcopate.

In June 1969, Zabłocki offered a clear presentation of his programmatic point of view:

Our goal is to help broaden and consolidate a sphere . . . for Church-state cooperation in place of hitherto existing conflicts. In this way we will try to create the conditions for a long-term accord between the government and the episcopate and, in the future, between the Polish People's Republic and the Holy See. . . . The Church should avoid allying itself with any oppositionist political forces. And yet anti-Communist circles have always been proposing

4. Founded in 1957 in cities throughout Poland, the Catholic Intellectuals Clubs were public discussion groups affiliated with the Znak and *Więź* milieu.—TRANS.

such alliances. I am speaking here not only of classic anti-communism, which seeks to turn back the historical clock to old systemic forms, but also of the new and more subtle variety. The Church cannot be indifferent to the question of freedom. But it must serve the cause in the proper way, by training the person for freedom. It is not for the Church to enter the political arena or to make political alliances.[5]

Let me make only the following comment: Nobody is claiming that politics is the Church's calling. Obviously the Church has a different mission. Yet it is not "politics" to defend persecuted and brutalized people. "Training people for freedom" is well and good, but it is only a fraudulent and empty declaration if accompanied by silence in the face of the brutal repression of freedom. In Polish conditions, the conflict between Church and state is a religious conflict. It necessarily arouses a great many emotions. There is no one for whom the eradication of such conflicts is more important than those of us on the secular Left. No one can be more alarmed by the seeds of future intolerance that lay within each one of these conflicts. For the lack of religious freedom that provokes these conflicts is both part of, and caused by, a much deeper phenomenon: a complete lack of civic freedom. Thus, in our view, the way to eradicate religious conflict and tension is to struggle for basic human rights. The problem cannot be solved by an alliance of the Church with a totalitarian regime hostile to the people. The Church might, on the basis of such an alliance, be able to obtain a few more institutional rights, but it would be forced to betray the teachings of the Gospels every step of the way.

Nevertheless, Zabłocki has raised one of the most controversial issues facing the Church. Cardinal Wyszyński discussed the problem, in the context of the 1968 events, in a sermon devoted in part to the fate of Archbishop Szczęsny Feliński, who was exiled to Siberia for his part in the 1863 uprising against the Tsar. In Primate Wyszyński's view, Archbishop Feliński

established a model for the pastor to follow. He showed how one must work in a new situation in order to respect the rights of the Nation. . . . He demonstrated, by his own example, that the bishop must always be true to the difficult obligations of his calling, a calling that demands courage and unswerving conviction. Such obligations have nothing in common with subtle political maneuvers that aim to please God and devil alike. That is impermissible! The people watch the bishop, and the bishop's behavior must be pure.

5. Janusz Zabłocki, "Nasza rola w odnowie soborowej w Polsce" [Our Role in the Conciliar Renewal in Poland], *Chrześcijanin w świecie*, no. 2 (1969): 12–13.

Archbishop Feliński accepted exile, but he did not bend to the pressures of the authorities. And so, Wyszyński continued,

Even today, one hundred years later, the program of the banished priest is still relevant in Warsaw. It is relevant in the archdiocese, in the bishopric, indeed in all of Poland! . . . But if the banished priest left us a program, he also taught us that in difficult times one must be willing to take risks in order to remind the authorities of the rights of the people. . . . Is this politics? . . . No, it is not. It is the bishop's duty to address the worldly authorities in times of great public misfortune, and to remind those in power that they do not have complete power, and that people have God-given rights that every ruler must respect.[6]

These are the words of a Polish bishop. In 1972, a German bishop, Cardinal Joseph Hoffner, wrote:

It is legitimate to counterpose Church to state or Church to the world, but one should not take this to mean that the Church exists apart from the world. The Church is obliged to cry out and protest when basic human rights, such as the right to life, to freedom, and to personal inviolability, are violated in society and in the state.[7]

Zabłocki is well aware of the truths contained in the pronouncements of both of these bishops. Cardinal Hoffner's words, after all, were published in the journal of ODISS. Zabłocki therefore knows perfectly well that political protest by the Church is an essential part of "training for freedom." And so it was surely not freedom that Zabłocki was so concerned about in his 1969 speech. The real aim of the speech seems to have been something else: to lay out the conditions of a *concordat* between the Church hierarchy and the party-state leadership. The result of this alliance would be a new pro-state loyalty on the part of the Church hierarchy and an expansion of the state's political base by allowing into government the representatives of a new Catholic party revolving around ODISS. Catholics were to be "admitted to power" the way Jacek Kuroń once suggested they might:[8] the hospital director (or factory manager, ambassador, local militia leader, etc.) who used to have his child christened in secret,

---

6. Stefan Cardinal Wyszyński, *W sercu stolicy* (Rome: Papieski Instytut Studiów Kościelnych, 1972), pp. 110–14.

7. Joseph Cardinal Hoffner, "Nędza i nadzieja czwartego świata" [Misery and Hope of the Fourth World], *Chrześcijanin w świecie* (Warsaw), no. 2 (1974): 29.

8. Jacek Kuroń, "Opozycja polityczna w Polsce" [Political Opposition in Poland], in *Kultura* (Paris), November 1974.

would now be able to do so in public. Zabłocki's program was no more than a modernized version of PAX's vision for Poland.

Zabłocki presented himself to the national-chauvinist "Partisan" wing of the Party as an "honest patriot of the people's state" (in contrast to an "antipatriotic oppositionist"), as a realist (and not a "political adventurist"), and as the man able to placate a recalcitrant episcopate. He presented himself to the episcopate as a faithful follower of Catholic social teaching (and not a "Godless intellectual" like Słonimski or Kołakowski; or a "Catholic corroded by liberal secularism" like his colleagues from Znak), as a proponent of moderation in the postconciliar Catholic renewal (and not an "adventurist reformer" like his colleagues from *Więź*), and as an authentic Catholic (and not a "suspect innovator" like Turowicz or Mazowiecki). To both sides, Zabłocki claimed to embody the "true patriotism" of the Polish Catholic, in contrast to the "rootless cosmopolitanism" and "Zionism" supposedly embodied by others. On the basis of such an ideological program, Zabłocki hoped to receive a mandate from both sides for the formation of a Christian political party. ODISS's idea of "dialogue" has always been subordinated to this goal. Theirs would be a dialogue with the ruling powers and the ruling ideology, a dialogue of fundamentalist Catholicism with officially codified "Marxism-Leninism," a dialogue between two inflexible doctrines, two dogmatic worldviews, conducted by two well-organized political camps.

I tend to consider these far-reaching plans of Zabłocki and ODISS as completely unrealistic. There is no indication that the ruling Communist party would like to share power with even its most loyal and obedient ally. Nevertheless, this latest version of alliance between altar and throne can be quite dangerous for society—not because it might offer Zabłocki something more than the dubious satisfaction of shaking hands with the head of the Bureau for Religious Affairs, but because it might provide the authorities with a way to completely destroy religion in Poland and to subordinate church to state as has been done in the Soviet Union or Czechoslovakia.

In the language of the ruling Communists, the concept of compromise does not exist. Every concession is treated as an opportunity to raise the ante and make even more far-reaching demands, as can be seen in government policy to the literary and academic communities and in the history of Church-state relations. The only effective way to deal with the communist authorities is through firm resistance and the uncompromising defense of one's principles. It is precisely this attitude on the part of the episcopate that is responsible for the survival of the Polish Catholic Church and for the moral authority it presently enjoys. The approach suggested by Zabłocki would, if accepted by the Church hierarchy, lead to a crisis for the Church and to the collapse of its moral authority.

One might ask why people of the secular Left should care about the defense of religion and the honor of the Roman Catholic Church. My answer is that the defense of values is important to us, or at least should be important to us. We have traditionally believed that religion and the Church were but synonyms for reaction and dim-witted obscurantism. From that perspective, we considered indifference to religion to be a natural by-product of moral and intellectual progress. This view, which I once shared, I now consider false. Although the Church has, through its conduct, frequently lent credence to Kołakowski's old characterization of Catholicism as "traditional, obscurantist, fanatical and dim-witted, with a decidedly provincial character,"[9] the experience of Christianity's confrontations with Hitlerism and Stalinism demands the revision of such stereotypes. From a humanist standpoint, the secular Left should be neutral on the question of religious indifference. Nonbelief can promote tolerant humanist attitudes, but it can also promote totalitarian attitudes. It is one's practical attitudes that are essential, not their moral or ideological basis. Religious indifference entails no particular practical attitude. For anyone other than the fanatical atheist, therefore, nonbelief is not in itself desirable. It is merely an existential fact, the social consequences of which may be quite diverse.

It is the same with religious belief. The simple act of believing in God is as inconsequential as the act of not believing in God. Only those forms of religious belief that are "anti-values," that lead to fanaticism and intolerance, are objectionable—as objectionable as the intolerance of official governmental atheists. Religiosity can promote various kinds of practical behavior. In the name of religious belief, some people perished at the stakes and other people burned them. There was no single rule. Nevertheless, there is one obvious fact of which the Left must be fully aware: although religious belief does not always lead to good, the persecution of religious belief always leads to evil. Where religion is suppressed by force, force will necessarily be used to crush everyone who thinks differently. Freedom of worship is the most visible sign of civil rights. An attack on this

9. Leszek Kołakowski, *Notatki o współczesnej kontrreformacji* [Notes on the Current Counterreformation] (Warsaw: Książka i wiedza, 1962), p. 53.

freedom by the state is always a sign of the totalitarianization of intellectual life. There is no exception to this rule, for only a totalitarian power will refuse to accept Peter and the Apostles' declaration that "We ought to obey God rather than men" (Acts 5:29). In secular language this means that a human being possesses, by virtue of his or her humanity, certain inalienable rights that no authority may annul. This is why the secular Left should care about the defense of religious rights.

The secular Left must also be ready to defend the Church. "The anticlericalism sparked by the old alliances of the Church with the privileged classes," wrote Leszek Kołakowski in 1962, "has largely lost meaning today. . . . The Church is no longer a great feudal landlord, and Catholic theorists no longer concern themselves with justifying the need for class hierarchy." [10] It has been many years since the Catholic Church in Poland has tried to protect the wealthy of this world. The Church now stands stubbornly on the side of the persecuted and the oppressed. The enemy of the Left is not the Church but totalitarianism. The central conflict in Poland is the conflict between the totalitarian authorities and a society systematically deprived of its rights. In the struggle against totalitarianism, the role of the Church cannot be overemphasized. No conscious person can fail to recognize the aptness of the episcopate's characterization: "when conditions for the nation have been good, the Church has enjoyed its freedom; but when the Church has been persecuted, the people have been deprived of the freedom and justice they deserve." [11] Unfortunately, by not always being aware of this connection, the secular Left has for too long been lamentably blind.

One might also ask whether there isn't a tendency in the Polish Church that seeks to recover its former privileges and to gain total control over public life. My answer is that if such tendencies exist, and it is highly probable that they do, they do not constitute any real danger to the aims of the secular Left. Under present conditions in Poland, there is no danger of theocracy. The secular Left should support an open and tolerant Catholicism (though neither open to nor tolerant of totalitarianism). In Poland today, even Catholic conservatives are condemned to do battle with the Communist authorities, just as they are condemned to fight for an expansion of democratic rights.

10. Kołakowski, *Notatki*, p. 73.

11. *Listy Pasterskie Episkopatu Polski* [Pastoral Letters of the Polish Episcopate] (Paris: Editions du Dialogue, 1975), p. 709.

For the Left, the only kind of Church that poses a danger is one that, as Zabłocki would have it, renounces both resistance and the Gospels, conducts a friendly dialogue with the government, and preaches from the pulpit that people must serve and obey even totalitarian authorities since all earthly power derives from God. Only in the face of such a Church will an anticlerical (though not antireligious) attitude be justified.

Tadeusz Mazowiecki and *Więź*'s Concept of Dialogue

Zabłocki's ideas inexorably led to a split with *Więź*. For the latter, dialogue was an encounter not of doctrines but of people. Tadeusz Mazowiecki, chief editor of *Więź*, formulated it this way:

A dialogue is made up of three components: people, a common platform, and values. A conversation may be nothing more than a transfer of information; a discussion may be merely a debate between differing positions; practical cooperation may entail no more than pragmatic activity pure and simple. A dialogue, on the other hand, depends on the communication and transfer of values. Each of these forms of contact becomes a dialogue to the extent that it is marked by the transfer and mutual confirmation of values. A dialogue thus occurs whenever there is a readiness to understand the validity of someone else's position and to enter into a different way of thinking; that is, whenever there is an openness to the values embodied in other points of view. . . . A dialogue is not a compromise; the tension of contradiction still exists. It is, instead, an attempt to discover a new dimension of the matter at hand, to find a new plane of discourse in which it is possible to meet. . . . Dialogue is a method by which an ideologically diverse society can learn to live together. Based on continual interaction, it is a way to overcome mutual human isolation.[12]

The editors of *Więź* have remained loyal to this difficult conception of dialogue ever since the journal first began publication. Mazowiecki and several other of the editors (such as Juliusz Eska, Wojciech Wieczorek, and Stefan Bakinowski) began their political careers in PAX. In other words, they had accepted socialist slogans for ideological reasons, and not, like *Tygodnik Powszechny,* for geopolitical ones. "Our approach to socialism," wrote Mazowiecki,

had as its starting point a moral motivation. We were attracted by the socialist tradition of social rebellion, or, to put it another way, by the social ques-

12. Tadeusz Mazowiecki, *Rozdroża i wartości*, pp. 82–86, 96.

tion, understood as the need for the transformation of society. We felt that the road to socialism would develop in such a way as to open up to personal values. This was the basis of our involvement and the standard by which we judged the unfolding events.[13]

Such motives that led them into PAX were the same motives to lead them out of PAX some years later. During the thaw of 1956, Mazowiecki and other discontented "Frondists" from PAX publicly attacked their organization's pro-Stalinist policies. They declared solidarity with the "democratizing forces" in the ruling PUWP. *Po prostu*, the weekly paper of the secular Left intelligentsia, opened its columns to the anti-PAX statements of the Catholic journalists. This was an important precedent. Regardless of the later activities of the paper's editors—and the majority, unfortunately, would behave like scabs—*Po prostu* remains even today a legend among the oppositionist secular intelligentsia. Allowing Mazowiecki and his co-thinkers onto the pages of *Po prostu* was a sign of a new kind of community, a community of people with similar political values motivated from different theoretical traditions.

Other publications of the secular intelligentsia also opened their pages to Catholic journalists in the autumn of 1956. *Nowa Kultura* [New Culture], for example, published the articles of Jacek Woźniakowski and Stefan Kisielewski, while *Przegląd Kulturalny* [Cultural Review] ran a piece by Stanisław Stomma.

From the very beginning, *Więź*'s situation was difficult and complex. Its attack on the traditional identification of "Pole" with "Catholic" (Juliusz Eska wrote a magnificent article on this) immediately rendered the journal suspect in the eyes of many Catholics. Its bold program of internal Church reform, often anticipating the ideas of Vatican II, caused problems with the Church hierarchy. This did not make *Więź*'s situation any easier. Nor was it made easier by the changing political situation in the country. Together with all of Polish society, *Więź* had supported Gomułka and the new Party leadership installed in October 1956. Leftist Catholic intellectuals saw Gomułka as the leader of socialist renewal, as a spokesman for the consistent democratization of the system. *Więź* became part of the Znak movement. In 1961, Mazowiecki himself became a deputy to the Sejm and a member of the Znak Parliamentary Caucus. In the Sejm and on the pages of *Więź*, this group of Catholics tried consistently to bring about a dialogue with enlightened elements of the Party. Soon, however, it became necessary to define anew exactly which

13. Mazowiecki, *Rozdroża i wartości*, p. 195.

elements and which people this referred to. As the conflict between Gomułka and the revisionist circles intensified, the dilemma grew more and more pronounced. As relations between the Party leadership and both the Church and the creative intelligentsia grew more and more strained, *Więź* became increasingly critical of the Party. Although the Znak circle was not, with the exception of Stefan Kisielewski, as openly critical of government policies as were people on the secular Left (such as Dąbrowska, Słonimski, Kołakowski, and Brus), it never opposed the oppositionist activities of the secular intelligentsia. Moreover, at the crucial turning point of March 1968, the entire Znak group demonstrated an admirable solidarity with the persecuted intelligentsia. Now it was *Więź* that published the essays of writers placed under public anathema, such as Krzysztof Pomian and Wiktor Woroszylski. The dialogue and community with Gomułka and his followers had become a dialogue and community with their vanquished opponents.

Więź's basic understanding of dialogue remained the same. It still referred to a substantive encounter of real people with real people, and not some perfunctory meeting where the representatives of one philosophical-political doctrine shake hands with the representatives of another. The formula, however, now took on a new political meaning. In the course of a discussion of Mazowiecki's book, *Crossroads and Values*, Zdzisław Szpakowski, one of the editors of *Więź*, argued that

> the division of Polish society into Catholics and Marxists is, from a sociopolitical point of view, . . . a superficial distinction, long obsolete. . . . I see a different kind of division in this society, one that runs at crosscurrents to the division between Marxist and Catholic. . . . If we understand dialogue to mean the search for, and realization of, basic social values, or as the community of such values, then the salient distinction is not Catholic versus Marxist but Right versus Left.[14]

While sharing Szpakowski's intentions, I feel a few reservations are in order. First, in present Polish conditions, the idea of a "Marxist camp" has lost all meaning. The only sensible definition would be the tautological one: whoever considers himself a Marxist is a Marxist. But people are increasingly unwilling to use this label, since few words have been as effectively compromised by official propaganda. Moreover, Catholicism as a religion concerns a separate sphere of human sensibility. It need not conflict with the application of the

14. *Więź*, no. 1 (1972): 38.

Marxist method to the scientific analysis of historical phenomena. For me, it remains an open question whether one can identify a Marxist method in contemporary historical science. But "Marxism" simply becomes too large a sack if it bags together people as diverse as Kazimierz Kąkol and Leszek Kołakowski, Seweryn Żurawicki and Włodzimierz Brus, Wojciech Pomykało and Karol Modzelewski, Andrzej Werblan and Jan Strzelecki.

Clearly, it makes more sense to use the distinction of Right and Left. Yet here too one must be very careful. It is quite easy, after all, to reduce even this division to absurdity. Szpakowski, for example, mentions egalitarianism as one issue that cuts "at crosscurrents" to the Catholic-Marxist distinction. Yet the dispute over egalitarianism has occurred on two separate planes that are continually being confused. On the one hand, egalitarianism means support for the notion of equality. On the other hand, it means support for the totalitarian state, whose policies are officially *labelled* egalitarian. This is not the place to develop my own views on such complex and snarling matters. I will only note that in a totalitarian state, egalitarian slogans can play a destructive and demagogic role. It is no accident that those who opposed the relative liberalism of the pre-1968 authorities, and who opposed the idea of economic reform, did so under the slogans of egalitarianism. If such people are "left-wing," it is only in the way that Röhm and others made up a "left-wing" faction of the Nazi Party. Such people, to use Lenin's well-aimed aphorism, "are to the left of common sense." They are in no way allies in the struggle for progressive causes; for the central component of leftist thought in a totalitarian state is, and can only be, antitotalitarianism. It is in this sense that the old distinctions, formed in conditions of bourgeois democracy, are now obsolete. In the changed political situation after 1945, the struggle for leftist principles is first and foremost the struggle for freedom and human rights. Without freedom, all grand projects of social reform are either lofty-sounding utopias or masks for totalitarianism.

With all of these reservations, I understand and sympathize with Szpakowski's remarks. Just as PAX does not want to carry on a dialogue with all Marxists, neither does *Więź* want to carry on a dialogue with all Marxists. The latter is certainly uninterested in "dialogue" with the orthodox Marxists from *Wychowanie*. PAX, however, is uninterested in dialogue with anyone *other* than *Wychowanie*. But perhaps this is because nobody else will talk with PAX.

12

THE SECULAR LEFT'S ROAD TO DIALOGUE

But let us give the secular Left its due: it never had any illusions about the nature of PAX. In the fall of 1956, Jan Kott wrote that whereas he and the other editors of the revisionist journal *Kuźnica* had always had respect for Jerzy Turowicz and *Tygodnik Powszechny,* they had felt nothing but contempt for PAX and Bolesław Piasecki. I think Kott was telling the truth. To anyone on the secular Left, whether pro-Communist or anti-Communist, PAX must have seemed like a specter from the darkest of Polish traditions. Nevertheless, such respect for *Tygodnik Powszechny* did not yet mean the secular Left was ready to enter into dialogue with Christianity.

Official Communist propaganda popularized an opposite thesis, arguing that revolutionary parties have always been ready to subordinate antireligious principles in the cause of united struggle against exploitation. This, of course, is true, although it is impossible to find anything in the works of Marx and Engels, not to mention Lenin, that would in any way suggest the need for a dialogue with religion. Nevertheless, the radical atheism of the Left has always been tempered by tactical political considerations. Pronounced hostility and brutal attacks on the Church have often been replaced by pleasant euphemisms and short-term political compromises, because the former were seen as bad tactics. What has *not* changed, however, is that secular leftists have continued to see the Church as a stronghold of backwardness and reaction. They have continued to view religion as superstition and believers as persons who have not fully learned to use their innate faculties of reason. Religion has been treated as a distressing remnant of feudalism and capitalism, as a decidedly decadent phenomenon. In the Left's vision of the future society, there has been no place for such relics of the past. Needless to say, this position precluded the possibility of dialogue. Contact with believers was valid only if it helped the cause of indoctrination. The Communists in power have been capable of making tactical alliances (such as in 1956), but they have never been willing to enter into a genuine and honest dialogue of equals. Unfortunately, others on the Left were also uninterested in pursuing a dialogue. And so the only ones to talk with *Więź* were the professional atheists from the journal *Argumenty*.

Perusing the Christian-Marxist discussions from 1958 to 1968 makes for some pretty depressing reading. The sincere and candid comments of the *Więź* group were answered by people who proclaimed a deep humanist ethos and claimed a profound solidarity with the principles of freedom, brotherhood, and tolerance, but who seemed completely unaware that they were living in a totalitarian country where the Church was persecuted and where the Party based its power solely on force—and not necessarily on Polish force, either.

Of course, I am not speaking here of people like Jan Strzelecki or Leszek Kołakowski. Strzelecki was a rare breed, a man of extraordinary moral and intellectual depth who pushed for genuine dialogue with Christianity long before it was popular. Kołakowski took a much different road to dialogue. He began his political career during the Stalinist years as an extreme atheist, a "personal enemy of God." His critique of religion and the Church was total. Even in 1956, during the October "thaw," he expressed views that we have previously called antireligious obscurantism. Equating belief in God with belief in Stalinist rituals, Kołakowski argued that a critique of one faith was simultaneously a critique of the other. In "The Priest and the Jester,"[1] a splendid and important essay written in 1958, Kołakowski came out as an adherent of the jester: in favor of relentless criticism and skeptical relativism of all priestly ideologies and all grand visions of the world, including Christianity. For the same reason, he was also an enemy of primitive, dim-witted atheism, as he showed in his 1959 article, "Theses on the Sacred and the Profane":

From the point of view of secular socialist humanism in Poland, the rise of religious indifference is certainly desirable. . . . From the same standpoint, however, the progress made by open Catholicism at the expense of fanatical and conservative Catholicism is also desirable, even though this leads not to popular indifference but to a deepened and modernized religiosity.[2]

1. Leszek Kołakowski, *Toward a Marxist Humanism,* translated by Jane Zielonka Peel (New York: Grove Press, 1968), pp. 9–37.
2. Leszek Kołakowski, *Notatki o współczesnej kontrreformacji* [Notes on the Current Counterreformation] (Warsaw: Książka i wiedza, 1962), p. 53.

In the same essay Kołakowski derided the infantile "exposé" kind of atheist propaganda, capable of convincing only those who don't need to be convinced.

The next phase in Kołakowski's evolution can be seen in his beautiful 1965 essay, "Jesus Christ: Prophet and Reformer." There he renewed his attacks on fanatical Catholicism and primitive atheism, repeated his hopes connected with the rise of open Catholicism, and, most important, paid great homage to the moral teachings of Jesus Christ and the fundamental values of Christianity. One can find a similar tone in his 1966 collection of essays, *The Presence of Myth.*[3] In his writings after 1968, after leaving Poland to live in England and the United States, Kołakowski evolved even further: he now spoke of religion as one of the few guarantors of the continuity of culture and the survival of interpersonal norms.

I hope that none of Kołakowski's disciples will be too angry with me for this journalistically superficial synopsis of his ideas on religion. After all, in my generation each of us is to some extent Kołakowski's pupil—a rebellious, disloyal, and critical pupil, but a pupil nonetheless. For my generation of secular thinkers, Leszek Kołakowski has been our model of civic courage, moral purity, and intellectual honesty. Our thoughts on Christianity and the Church were frequently a product of his views and his writings. This, of course, is no excuse for our own mistakes. It is only an explanation of the roots of the ideological road we have traveled: a crooked road with snarling traffic, but in the end a rather honest road to a dialogue with Christianity.

The dialogue we are interested in is not at all like the conversations between *Argumenty* and *Więź*. What we are talking about here is more like the type of dialogue with Christianity that Kołakowski initiated in his article on Jesus Christ. Our dialogue is also quite different from the encounters that Western European Christians have had with representatives of the Italian or French communist parties, for it has not been initiated by people who decry the cruelties of capitalism and bourgeois parliamentarism while arguing that support for the Soviet bloc is the acid test of a "progressive worldview." Therefore, reading this book as the Polish version of the *Paulus Gesellschaft* would be a gross misunderstanding. Unfortunately, the progressive, pro-socialist Western European Catholic participants do not explain what their discussions mean to a Pole, a Russian, or (God

---

3. Leszek Kołakowski, *The Presence of Myth*, translated by Adam Czerniawski (Chicago: University of Chicago Press, 1989).

forbid) a Lithuanian. That is, how can *we* be "progressive Catholics," too? And until we get a clear answer to this question, I do not think the discussions of "progressive Catholics" abroad (excluding groups like "Esprit" in France) will be very relevant to Eastern Europe.

I do have great respect for some of the Catholic participants of those Western encounters, people such as Johannes Baptist Metz and Jürgen Moltmann. Unfortunately, I cannot say the same for their Communist counterparts. I cannot trust people who are able to find exploitation, oppression, and injustice only within carefully defined geographical borders, who can discourse long on the evils of Christianity and the Church yet pass over in silence (or at best with a few euphemisms) the realities of Communist rule in the Soviet Union. Until they begin to clearly and unequivocally denounce Soviet totalitarianism, I will continue to suspect them of subscribing to Montalembert's maxim: "When weak I will demand freedom from you, for that is your principle; when strong I will take freedom from you, for that is my principle."[4] It should be said, however, that certain European communist parties, particularly in Italy and Spain, seem to be evolving in a genuinely antitotalitarian direction.

As a socialist, I am an opponent of capitalism. But as a socialist I consider not capitalism but totalitarianism to be the greatest nightmare of our times, the greatest enemy of progress, democracy, and socialism. All totalitarian regimes are the enemy: whether capitalist or communist, Chile, the USSR, China or anyplace else where basic human rights are trampled upon and people are beaten down and oppressed in the name of higher ideals, religious or secular.

When I speak of "dialogue" with Christianity I am not speaking of intellectual swordsmanship or a tactical play for power. I am speaking of basic human values. The Polish dialogue between the secular Left and Christianity must be based on union in antitotalitarian resistance.

The Left's encounter with Christianity takes place on three different levels: an encounter with God, an encounter with the Church as an institution, and an encounter with Christianity as a system of values. The first two we will look at in this chapter. The encounter with Christian values is the subject of the next chapter.

4. Cited by Jacek Woźniakowski, *Laik w Rzymie i w Bombaju* [A Layman in Rome and Bombay] (Warsaw 1965), p. 90.

The Encounter with God

From a Catholic perspective, the most important level of contact is the encounter of many former atheists with God, which frequently leads to conversion. The question of conversion is a difficult, personal, and intimate matter. I feel unqualified to write about it and incapable of explaining it. Ignoring it, however, would distort and impoverish the problem at hand.

Lately in Poland there has been a noticeable rise in religious interest and religious conversion among people who were, until recently, devout nonbelievers. The phenomenon about which I am speaking has nothing to do with tactics. It is not an attempt to subordinate religion or the Church to specific political ends (a tendency that I will comment on below.) I am writing here about people who seek, in transcendence, an internal moral order, about people who have found in God a new meaning for their lives.

I must ask my secular friends to bear with me in goodwill. I know that I am touching matters that are, for a nonbeliever, practically impossible to imagine or comprehend. Simone Weil has written on the topic as follows:

If an island completely cut off had never had any other than blind inhabitants, light would be for them what the supernatural is for us. One is tempted to think at first that for them it would be nothing, that by creating for their use a system of physics with all theory of light left out, one would be giving them a complete explanation of their world. For light offers no obstacle, exerts no pressure, is weightless, cannot be eaten. For them, it is absent. But it cannot be left out of account. By it alone the trees and plants reach towards the sky in spite of gravity. By it alone seeds, fruits, all the things we eat, are ripened. . . . That which escapes the human faculties cannot, by definition, be either verified or refuted.[5]

The well-known poet Anna Kamieńska experienced a similar feeling several years back, as she noted in her diary in August 1970:

A sort of intellectual fever—the kind you're supposed to get only in youth, when you suddenly discover some great book or philosophy. It's like a new awakening. I would have been terribly surprised if someone had told me, not long ago, that I was going to experience this all over again. I always

---

5. Simone Weil, "Is There a Marxist Doctrine?" in *Oppression and Liberty*, translated by Arthur Wills and John Petrie (London: Routledge and Kegan Paul, 1958), pp. 175–76.

thought that intellectual breakthroughs were the exclusive privilege of literary heroes.

The world glistened as if after a flood.

To me, the call sounded like this: Humans cannot be the measure of things. We are restricted by reason. We cannot cut ourselves off from reason, but we must try to transcend it at the place where it ceases to serve knowledge, where it becomes an obstacle to knowledge.

Of course the same thought could have come to me differently. It was not the form that was important, but the character of the thought, as if it demanded something from me. Is it possible that a single idea striking in the middle of a sleepless night can transform everything, in me and all around me? No, it had to be present within me for a long time, latent in the form of a possibility, or perhaps an impossibility.

Maybe the long years of cutting myself off from metaphysical questions were necessary so that I could experience this revelation, this great awakening, this openness to feelings and ideas. I reached within to draw something from my cast-off childhood faith. And so it must have existed somewhere deep inside me, for how else could I so suddenly find the source within? . . .

The moment of breakthrough is what I find particularly interesting. How are radical spiritual transformations possible? Why are they so sudden and so violent? We have heard many explanations of so-called conversions, and yet in essence they are ineffable. For someone on the outside they always seem inadequately grounded, insufficiently motivated. There is something about them both too much and too little. The effect never seems to live up to the power of the cause. *Gustavus obiit. Conradus natus est.* A psychological analysis could no doubt isolate many of the rational and emotional factors leading to this process of internal death and rebirth, yet I am afraid that the crucial element will somehow always remain hidden, suspended in space, ineffable.[6]

Anna Kamieńska writes here about matters that we cannot understand, about feelings incomprehensible to nonbelievers. "To be sure," she notes, "nonbelief is easier to justify than belief." We should accept the truth of her testimony. We should, in the name of a proper dialogue, display maximum goodwill and try to comprehend what we can. As to what we are unable to comprehend, we should respect those who genuinely seek the truth about such matters. By this I understand something more than the simple tolerance of differences. I imagine this rather as the recognition that there exists a di-

6. Anna Kamieńska, *Notatnik, 1965–1972* (Poznań: W drodze, 1982), pp. 120–21.

mension of feeling and motivation that is personally incomprehensible to me, but that enriches and gives meaning to the lives of others.

Clearly, this requires a good deal of rethinking. We have grown accustomed to thinking that belief in God necessarily impoverishes a human being, limits and undermines one's essential humanity. At the same time, however, we know from everyday experience that faith often inspires people, promotes heroism, moves mountains.

We have also come to think—following the classics of rationalist and revolutionary thought, following Voltaire, Feuerbach, and Marx—that religious belief is a sure sign of psychological disability, an expression of spiritual weakness and lack of faith in humanity, an abdication of responsibility for the world. To be sure, more than a few Christians have helped us think this way. Yet even a cursory reading of Christian theological writings (Bonhoeffer, for example) demonstrates how shallow and inaccurate such a view really is.

In the pages of *Więź,* Father Roman Rogowski wrote as follows:

> The Second Vatican Council strongly emphasized that "believers may play a considerable role in the development of atheism," if only by their presentation of a false image of God. A Catholic is therefore obliged to continually reassess his understanding of God, to cleanse the image of God of all exaggerated anthropomorphisms and geomorphisms. This is a task incumbent on every believer as long as he lives, since, as Eckhart has said, "only the hand that wipes the slate clean is the hand that can write the truth."
>
> We must continually remind both ourselves and others that . . . God does not "do" things so much as He causes things to be done; that faith is not a safeguard but a challenge. God is no simple panacea for the problems of earthly human existence. Rather, He is someone who, as Love and as Truth, summons man to this Grand Adventure, places before him tasks, demands from him responsibility. "A religion that is neither disquieting nor strenuous, seeks neither perfection nor the absolute, and is not to some extent tragic, is no religion at all," writes Mahomed Talbi. Of believers, meanwhile, Charles Péguy comments: "Because they lack the courage to take up earthly affairs, they believe they are taking up God's. Because they are afraid to be part of humanity, they think they are part of God. Because they love no one, they delude themselves into thinking they love God." In general we may say that atheism today . . . is a challenge to believers, and particularly to Christians—a challenge for us to examine ourselves.[7]

7. Roman Rogowski, "Wiara i niewiara" [Belief and Nonbelief], *Więź,* no. 11 (1975).

To this we may answer that Christianity today is also a challenge to nonbelievers, and particularly to the secular Left—a challenge for *us* to examine ourselves. The comments in this book are an attempt at such an examination. For leftists, the Christian principle of triumph through love is a challenge and an appeal, the most basic way of checking our plans and intentions. How barren our existence would be without a spiritual dimension! How much less good and virtue there would be in such a life! Rejecting the spiritual dimension together with its implications would mean accepting the rule of brute force.

Looking from the outside, I have the impression that it is not easy to maintain an authentic Christian disposition. Christianity, wrote Bruckberger,

is not some complete, harmonious kit of ready-made answers. It is continuous anxiety caused by questions that lie deep within the nature of man. The crisis of every human being takes the form of a question. We may not be required to find an answer, but we are obliged to guard our question with honor until our very last breath. For the answer can be found only outside of this world.[8]

The human condition as described by Bruckberger is identical to the one faced by the heroes of Camus and Malraux. Bruckberger's description shows us that the traditional secular alternative, "God or man," is a false dichotomy. It is obvious to Christians that God's love must be realized in the human world, in relations between human beings. We read in the First Epistle of John, "If a man say, I love God, and hateth his brother, he is a liar: for he that loveth not his brother whom he hath seen, how can he love God whom he hath not seen? And this commandment have we from him, That he who loveth God love his brother also" (1 John 4:20–21). And elsewhere in the same letter: "If ye know that he is righteous, ye know that every one that doeth righteousness is born of him" (1 John 2:29). We can read these texts to mean that true belief in God requires loyalty to the biblical teaching that there is no road to God except through other people and that every person living a just life lives in harmony with God. Clearly there is no room here for a "God or man" dichotomy.

Nor is there room for such a dichotomy in secular thought (assuming, of course, that faith results from a completely free act). To a nonbeliever, this dichotomy is the product of a perfidious imagina-

8. Father Bruckberger, *Dzieje Jezusa Chrystusa* [The Life of Jesus Christ] (Warsaw, 1972), p. 353.

tion. That is, only nonbelievers with a perfidious imagination can consider the Christian God a threat to their freedom and human dignity. And it is the refusal to comprehend the mystery of faith that begets such an imagination. Unable to put concrete content or personal experience into the concept of faith, the nonbeliever is tempted to reduce the whole matter to a self-evident proposition. But this, of course, is impossible. However reluctant we may be to do so, we must recognize our limitations in these matters and not assume a stance of superiority. From Christians, in turn, we expect a similar recognition that nonbelief can also add an enriching dimension to human life.

It is this aspect of the new dialogue, the secular Left's encounter with God, that is most important for Christians and most difficult for secularists. It is easier to accept the existence of a visible and tangible Church than of an invisible and incomprehensible sphere of intangible phenomena. Yet true pluralism is impossible without accepting the latter as well as the former. Otherwise the Christian will view the nonbeliever as an invalid or a cynic, while the nonbeliever will treat the Christian as a charlatan or an ignoramus. In that case, our confessional and ideological ghettoes will continue to exist, and our lives will be impoverished by the loss of all the benefits that come from the intellectual confrontation of people who think differently, people traveling separate roads toward common goals of humanism and truth.

The Encounter with the Church

The second aspect of the new dialogue is the encounter between the secular Left and the Church as an institution. The origins of this encounter have been discussed extensively above. Before asking what each side expects, or ought to expect, from this encounter, let us first make clear what ought not be expected.

Our new approach to the Church and our rejection of political atheism should not be confused with apostasy. The secular leftist is not a renegade ready to reject the entire set of values he professed only yesterday. We already have too many renegades in our intellectual circles, people who go from one extreme to another, denouncing everything identified with the Left and adopting a classic conservatism as their own. Yesterday's Party member becomes today's champion of the Middle Ages: out of hatred for communism he now espouses the virtues of serfdom. As someone has aptly put it, such a person merely replaces "yesterday's stupidities with those from the day before yesterday." He is more Catholic than the pope, more pro-Church than the primate, yet markedly reluctant to speak out publicly in the defense of civil rights.

I do not question the personal integrity of some of the representatives of this tendency. Still, I am inclined to see a number of dangers in their ostentatious anti-communism and their exaggerated pro-Catholicism. Their anti-communism, it seems to me, is more antidemocratic than antitotalitarian. These people use anti-communism to mask a hostility to democratic public life, opposition to civic equality, and support for conservative paternalism as the ruling principle of society. Such an intellectual position allows one to combine everyday conformism with patriotic phraseology. According to this view, the Roman Catholic Church is the nation's only safeguard against sovietization; therefore the people should resist through religion alone. What we have here, I believe, is a dangerous reduction of religion to nonreligious functions and a dangerous abrogation of responsibility for the fate of one's country. The Church cannot replace political and civic activism, and the effort to make it do so entails an instrumental approach to both religion and the Church.

It is worth mentioning here the case of Charles Maurras, the conservative French nationalist from the early twentieth century and founder of *L'Action Français*. Maurras was a nonbeliever. Christianity, he said, was the work of "four suspicious Jews" (namely, the evangelists). With its concept of inalienable individual rights and its principle of compassion, Christianity was, for Maurras, a "destructive" doctrine "leading society towards anarchy." Yet Maurras was a consistent conservative, and he highly valued the Roman Catholic Church for supporting discipline and order, the restoration of the monarchy, and the return of the *ancien régime*. "A Catholic atheist" is how Maurras described himself. This distinction between Catholicism and Christianity led Maurras to espouse national chauvinism in public life while rejecting the teachings of the Gospels as dangerous drivel. He deified the nation-state with its traditionally conservative internal structure, and he considered Catholicism a fundamental part of this structure, an instrument in the hands of national-chauvinist state authorities. For Maurras, in other words, the Roman Catholic Church was to be supported to the extent that it was a purely political institution that did not try to carry out the teachings of the Gospels. The analogy may not be exact, but I fear that a shadow of "Maurrasism" exists over Polish intellectual life today.

The new approach by the secular Left could lead to a Maurrasism *à rebours*. For many years, the Roman Catholic Church was our political opponent, something of a hostile political camp. Today's change in attitude should not mean that we now begin to treat the Church as a political ally. The Church is not a political party, and any attempt to make it act like one is as unrealistic as it is harmful. This holds true regardless of whether such a party would be pro-government or anti-government, rightist or leftist, conservative or revolutionary. The role of the Church is to propagate the teachings of the Bible, and these teachings cannot honestly be made the property of any one political tendency. Asserting otherwise will only lead to the abuse of religious institutions and of religion itself. The teachings of the Gospels are something other than political ideology, both wider and narrower, neither Right nor Left. While there is a specific current of right-wing thought that appeals to these teachings and seeks to be loyal to its principles, similar tendencies exist within the leftist camp as well. The tenets of the Gospels have been inscribed on the banners of both Right and Left, but they have also been trampled by both rightist and leftist governments. The Bible belongs to no one. For Christians it is the Word Revealed; for nonbelievers it can be the basis of a moral code of fundamental rights. If the secular Left will be loyal to the teachings of the Gospels, the Gospels will be on the side of the Left. In this sense, we may speak of a community of values between the Church and the Left. But this community is in no sense a political alliance, and it would be wrong if anyone understood it as such. That would be an attempt to identify religion with politics, to subordinate the timeless functions of the Church to the current political interests of the Left. We know from experience that such efforts lead to no good for either religion or politics. Left-wing Maurrasism would be a repudiation of the entire tradition of the European Left.

This tradition, however—let us be frank—is not in every way laudable and does not in every aspect deserve to be maintained. In fighting against the alliance of altar with throne and the confusion of "God's" with "Caesar's," the Left promulgated the thesis that "religion is a private affair." It was a thesis that communist totalitarianism appropriated with zest. According to Communist propaganda, the "privacy" of religion hinges on the complete separation of religious values from political realities and on the Church's total abdication from involvement in the political sphere. Surely such an understanding of the "privacy" of religion, such a "separation" of church and state, the secular Left should not accept. For this would be nothing more than the separation of the church from the real world, the consigning of the church to the sacraments alone. The assertion that "religion is a private affair" is acceptable only insofar as it means that the state neither forces nor prevents anyone from choosing, or not choosing, the religion of their choice. It most certainly does not mean that religion must succor only the "private" realm of human life or that the Church must be silent when biblical principles are violated in public life. Understood in such a way, the "privatization" of religion would lead to a generalized double standard, to the elimination of moral norms in political affairs. In Poland that could only mean the sovietization of the Church, and that is something only a totalitarian government desires.

So what should the secular Left expect from the Church? We must first of all recognize the unique, suprapolitical, and otherworldly apostolic mission of the Church. I am appealing not for conversion but for the acceptance of reality. As long as the Left considers the pastoral mission of the Church to be bogus, it will find neither support nor understanding from people of the Church. And as long as the Church judges people solely on the basis of their participation in religious activities, it will continue to have the Left as its principal opponent. This can only be avoided if both sides accept pluralism as a lasting component of Polish reality. Secular leftists must understand once and for all that religion and the Church are not ephemeral and dying relics from the past, but permanent and inextinguishable parts of the social, moral, and intellectual reality of the nation.

Even so, as the German Catholic theologian Heinrich Fries has written:

To the challenge presented by pluralism, Christianity and the Church cannot respond with the defensive tactics of trench warfare or a war of position. It cannot stop up all of the holes and turn the Church into a fortress. A Church that lives by faith must move onto the open field and swim in the open sea, risking storms and high waves with the knowledge that *fluctuat, nec mergitur*. It must not resort to apologetics in the face of every critical remark, or defend at all costs the various events of past and present, for doing so will only erode the Church's credibility. . . . The Church cannot live in the anachronistic hopes of rebuilding the past. It should not strive to recreate the supposed splendor of the old *Imperium Christianum*. Even where external conditions may be favorable, the Church should not attempt to realize such goals locally in the form of a state religion. This, of course, does not mean that the Church should not have its own associations, unions, and institutions, but such organizations should not . . . impose their will without regard for others. That which is clear and apparent to Christians may not be so to others, and such values may not be imposed on these others. . . . In today's pluralism the Church may not cut itself off and try to flee from the world, conducting an independent religious and cultural life. The Church must instead turn *to* the world, armed with faith, hope, and love. . . . The Church should involve itself on behalf of the people in the service of universal solidarity, ready to cooperate to make the human world a humane world, so that peace and justice may prevail on earth.[9]

Fries's comments provide a wonderful answer to the question of what the secular Left should expect from the Church. It should expect an active presence. Another German theologian, Johannes Baptist Metz, has elaborated on this answer as follows:

The sociocritical attitude of the Church in our pluralist society cannot consist in the proclamation of one particular social order as the norm. It must consist in the Church acting effectively in society, and on society, through an emancipatory critique. The task of the Church is not to create a systematic social doctrine, but to engage in *social criticism*. The Church, as a particular social institution, can only formulate its universal claim with regard to society if it presents this claim as effective *criticism*. Two important points follow from this position. *First,* that the Church, as a sociocritical institution, cannot be transformed into a political ideology. No political party can have criticism as its sole plank. Moreover, no political party could possibly encompass, within its sphere of activity, all that is the object of Church criticism, for Church criticism concerns the entirety of human history under God's eschatological proviso. A party that did try to encompass all this would drift into either romanticism or totalitarianism. *Second,* it is precisely this critical function of the Church that creates the possibility of *cooperation* with non-Christian institutions and groups. Cooperation *cannot* be based on agreement about how society should develop, or on shared views about the future free society. On such matters there will always be differences of opinion, and this pluralism cannot be eliminated without totalitarian manipulation. Therefore, cooperation must be based primarily on negative criticism and shared experience: the experience of threats to humanity, freedom, justice, and peace. And we should not underestimate the power of this negative experience, for therein lies a crucial mediating moment. For although we may not immediately and directly agree on the positive meaning of freedom, peace, and justice, we all share a long-standing and common experience of what these things are *not*. And so this negative experience offers us an opportunity to unite—not so much in the positive planning of freedom and justice but in our critical opposition to the horror and terror of unfreedom and injustice.

9. Heinrich Fries, *Wiara zakwestionowana* [Faith Contested] (Warsaw, 1975), pp. 163–64.

The solidarity bred by this experience, the possibility it suggests of a common front of protest, must be understood and put into action. . . . The irrational factors in our social and political conduct are only too clearly visible. We have not erased the possibility of "collective blindness." The dangers of . . . unfreedom and injustice are too great to allow us to remain indifferent on such matters for indifference will inevitably lead only to more criminal behavior.[10]

Discussing the critical and emancipatory functions of the Church, Metz distinguishes three kinds of tasks, which he defines as "the defense of the individual," "criticism of totalitarianism," and "love as a principle of revolution." With regard to the first, Metz writes:

Because of its eschatological proviso over against any abstract concept of progress and humanity, the Church defends the individual of the present moment against being used as the material or means for the building up of a technological and totally rationalized future.[11]

This also refers to revolutionary utopias and great social movements:

Here the eschatological proviso of the Church with its institutional power of social criticism must protect an individuality which cannot be defined by its value for the progress of mankind.

. . . The Church must constantly use this liberating power of criticism with regard to all political systems; it must stress that history as a whole is subject to God's eschatological proviso. It must demand recognition of the truth that history as a whole can never be contained in a political idea in the narrow sense of the word, and therefore can never be limited to any particular political conduct. There is nothing within this world that can be designated as the subject of all history, and whenever a party, group, nation or class sees itself as such a subject and consequently tries to dominate the whole process of history with its particular political interpretation, it must necessarily become totalitarian.[12]

Concerning the third task, or "love as a principle of revolution," Metz writes:

Today more than ever, the Church must mobilize the potentiality of that Christian love that lies at the heart of its tradition. This love must not be

10. Johannes Baptist Metz, "The Church's Social Function in the Light of a 'Political Theology,'" in Johannes B. Metz, ed., *Faith and the World of Politics* (New York: Paulist Press, 1968), pp. 17–18. [I have substantially retranslated this and later passages in the interests of clarity and in line with the Polish version.—TRANS.]

11. Metz, "The Church's Social Function," pp. 12–13.

12. Metz, "The Church's Social Function," p. 13.

confined to the interpersonal contact of I-and-thou. Nor should it be understood as a kind of philanthropy. It must be interpreted in its social dimension and made operative. This means that it must be understood as the unconditional commitment to justice, freedom and peace *for others. . . .* Love *. . .* demands a firm criticism of pure force. It does not allow us to think in terms of "friend" and "enemy" because it commands us to love the enemy, and even to bring one's opponent within the sphere of one's own universal hope. Of course, the credibility and effectiveness of this criticism of pure violence will to a large extent depend on whether a church that presents itself as a church of love can avoid the appearance of being itself a religion based on force. The Church's mission is not to assert itself, but to affirm in actual history that salvation is there for all. . . . [This mission] forces the Church into impassioned criticism of all force, and thus also into criticism of the Church itself, when, as so often in its history, the Church criticized the powerful of this world too meekly or too late, or when it hesitated to stand up for *all* persecuted persons, or when it did not forcefully reject the denigration of the human individual. . . .

[When] Christian love . . . operates socially as the unconditional commitment to justice and freedom for others, it may in certain circumstances demand the use of *revolutionary force*. Where the social *status quo* is filled with no less injustice than might possibly result from its revolutionary overthrow, then revolution, in the name of love, for the justice and freedom of "the least of the brethren," cannot be forbidden.[13]

There is not much that a man of the secular Left can add to the perceptive and penetrating reflections of these two Catholic theologians. Perhaps only a wish that the Roman Catholic Church was precisely the kind of Church proposed by Heinrich Fries and Johannes Baptist Metz. With such a Church, the secular Left would feel a deep bond of solidarity. It would join with such a Church in the name of defending all persecuted peoples, in the name of defending truth, freedom, and tolerance. The result would be not a political alliance but a community in humanist values, whose consistent advocate would be a Church loyal to the spirit of the Gospels.

Let us repeat: The necessary conditions for such a community are the rejection of political atheism and an understanding of the nature of the religious tasks of the Church. These very same conditions are the basis for a harmonious coexistence between the secular Left and the Catholic Left.

13. Metz, "The Church's Social Function," pp. 13–14.

RESPONSIBILITY AND VALUES

Just prior to the March events of 1968, Tomasz Burek, a young left-wing secular literary critic, wrote these lines in an essay characteristically titled, "On the Razor's Edge":

Perhaps we have already lied to ourselves so thoroughly, lived pretences with such nauseating abandon, that whatever we might say now—however wisely, pathetically, coyly or clearly—we end up, ironically but inevitably, back at the basic questions, questions so obvious that they offend the educated mind. And I'm speaking here of us, the young generation, who haven't lived out a single thought on our own account, haven't pursued a single notion through to the end—to the end, I say, to the point where problems squeeze together in your brain like knots, not letting you go on living until you finally find some satisfactory solution. Do we even have the right to speak, we who have not yet found a foundation for our own lives? . . . We speak, we write, we grow up, we grow old, but does a single one of us really know what to do with his life? I have a sense that we will end badly—moral capitulation, intellectual defeat, something all the more merciless since it is precisely in intellectual growth that the best of us seem to have placed our hopes—if we cannot manage to think through to its basic truths even a single day of an honest life.

The final judgment comes every day: this is the first and chief consequence of secular thinking. Since there is no hope for a divinely just reckoning after the end of time, it follows that we must make a unique and meaningful life from the one we have whether we want it or not. It also follows that there are no meaningless moments or deeds in history, that history happens at every moment, is determined in every gesture of every individual life. This sense that we live by finalities, definitively, on the razor's edge, totally and ruthlessly, believing that everything about us is always the result of human choice and the drive to humanity within each person—this is not theology or historical determinism but a realistic approach. For it is impossible to wait oneself out, put one's self at a distance, mediate the self, or hide from fate behind anyone's back, not even behind the backs of history, since history, as our great teacher has said, is "nothing other than purposeful human activity." Here, every bit of life is considered invaluable, every loss is mourned as irreplaceable, even as we know that there is no way to create one's self, one's values, or a history that can facilitate the survival of those values other than through what is known as work, which is a way to carve out one's fate at the cost of one's life.[1]

This essay by Burek, first published in a selective literary journal, played a significant role in the spiritual education of my generation. It was a brutal accusation, a radical call for us to live our own kinds of lives, to take responsibility for our lives, to live in truth. In the years since the publication of this essay, people of my generation have produced a great many artistic, intellectual, and political works that run counter to Burek's predictions and prophecies, works that can in no way be described as "moral capitulation" or "intellectual defeat." And yet more than one of these works were inspired and shaped precisely by the writings of Burek.

The main point of Burek's essay, its statement of faith, is particularly striking in juxtaposition with another text, this one by Dietrich Bonhoeffer:

We have been the silent witnesses of evil deeds. We have eaten breads from many ovens, and learned the art of deception and of evasive speech. Experience has made us suspicious of others; we have often had to deceive people who needed to hear the truth. Bitter conflicts have made us corrupt, perhaps turned us into cynics. Can we still be of any use? It is not the genius that we shall need tomorrow, nor the cynic, the misanthropist, or the adroit tactician, but honest straightforward people. Will our spiritual reserves prove sufficient, our self-candor remorseless enough, to enable us to recover the path to simplicity and straightforwardness?[2]

Elsewhere, Bonhoeffer writes:

The only way to be honest is to recognize that we must live in the world *etsi deus non daretur.* So our coming of age forces us to a true recognition of our

1. Tomasz Burek, "Na ostrzu noża," in *Zamiast powieści* [Instead of a Novel] (Warsaw: Czytelnik, 1971), pp. 313–14.
2. Dietrich Bonhoeffer, "After Ten Years," in *Letters and Papers from Prison*, edited by Eberhard Bethge, translated by Reginald H. Fuller (New York: Macmillan, 1953), p. 34. Much of this translation has been revised by me.—TRANS.

situation vis-à-vis God. God is teaching us that we must live as people who can get along very well without him. The God who is with us is the God who forsakes us *(Eloi, Eloi, lama sabachthani)*. The God who makes us live in this world without using him as a working hypothesis is the God before whom we are ever standing. Before God and with God we live without God. God allows himself to be edged out of the world and on to the cross. God is weak and powerless in the world, and that is exactly the way, the only way, in which he can be with us and help us.[3]

The Christian theologian seems to be saying here that the Christian duty is to live in the world "as if there were no God," as if humans themselves bore total responsibility for the shape of the human world. At the same time, the leftist critic associated with Marxism asserts that one's moral obligation is to live in the godless world as if God did exist and was judging us daily. What an apparently paradoxical contrast this is! "Apparently," I say, since both voices are fervent protests against two kinds of escapism, two kinds of flights from freedom and responsibility. Bonhoeffer rejects a Christian morality that reduces resistance against evil to prayer. He rejects the common Christian practice of transferring responsibility for "the shape of this world" onto God, the habit of looking to God as the only salvation and thereby refusing to take one's fate into one's own hands. Burek, meanwhile, protests against the kind of morality that Anna Morawska has aptly called "streetcar atheism," which is but a secular version of the renunciation of responsibility for creating a humanist world. He rejects that version of Marxist historiography that allows one to pass off personal moral decisions as mere consequences of historical laws. There are no laws of history, Burek seems to be saying, that can invalidate an ethic of personal duty and responsibility.

I am juxtaposing here two very different texts: the reflections of a German theologian written in the nightmare of the Nazi hell with an essay of a young Polish critic published safely in a literary monthly. The relevance of the contrast, I believe, can be seen in the Polish intellectual context of recent years. The journals of Bonhoeffer, published here a few years ago, provided a crucial new dimension to "open Catholicism" in Poland. The literary essays of Burek played a very important role in shaping the moral consciousness of the literature of the young generation. In juxtaposing these texts, the

3. "Letters to a Friend," in *Letters and Papers from Prison*, pp. 219–20. Translation revised.—Trans.

point of contact becomes clear: we see two concepts of responsibility
that differ in their origins yet are still somehow alike.

It is this concept of responsibility that is the basis of the dialogue
between Christianity and the secular Left. It is here, around this issue, that we find the most precious achievements in Polish literature
of the postwar period. Here there is room for the poems of Herbert,
Miłosz, and Słonimski, for Stanisław Ossowski's *Moral Norms* and
Maria Dąbrowska's *Reflections on Conrad*, for Jan Józef Szczepański's *Before the Unknown Tribunal* and Kazimierz Brandys' *Unreal-
ity*, for Gustaw Herling-Grudziński's *Another World* and the concen-
tration camp stories of Tadeusz Borowski, for Hanna Malewska's *Sir
Thomas More Refuses* and Wiktor Woroszylski's *Dreams in the
Snow*, for Tadeusz Konwicki's *The Calendar and the Hour-Glass* and
Jerzy Zawieyski's *Between the Wheat and the Chaff*. Here we can
find Kołakowski's philosophical essays, Strzelecki's *Continuations*,
Kuła's *Considerations on History*, Woźniakowski's *A Layman in
Rome and Bombay*, the essays of Tadeusz Mazowiecki and Anna
Morawska, and the literary work of the young generation of writers
such as Barańczak, Krynicki, and Zagajewski. And here we can also
find Bohdan Cywiński's *Genealogies of the Indomitable*.

I have cited here various names and books that teach the difficult
art of honest thinking and dignified living. To the last of these titles
my book is particularly indebted, for *Genealogies of the Indomitable*
was my initial inspiration. In a multicolored and beautifully constructed historical fresco, Bohdan Cywiński outlined the historical
background of the encounter between "unhumbled" Christians and
the "unhumbled" on the secular Left. Sharply criticizing Church history, Cywiński tried, perceptively and honestly, to explain leftist values to Christians and Christian values to the secular Left. In his con-
clusion, we read the following:

In reflecting on the perpetually new social ethos, it is worthwhile returning to those traditional values that guided the Polish intelligentsia in the
extraordinarily difficult epoch when the nation regained its freedom. . . .
The ideals that the unhumbled radicals of the time invariably proclaimed on
their banners seem to retain their relevance today. These radicals brought
together the ideals of genuine social progress with values such as commitment to social action, respect for other human beings and their views, democracy understood not as a fact but as a process of struggle between social
consciousness and ideological inertia, an ability to critically assess one's
own views along with a willingness to revise them, and finally a noble non-

conformism, inevitably producing a sense of moral responsibility for the future of society.

The greatest wish of a Catholic is that each proponent of these values might find a deep Christian inspiration and an ally in the Polish Church. . . . We wish to be a Church loyal to our mission, and thus free from the temptation of Neo-Constantinianism. We seek to stand firm in defense of the freedom and dignity of the human individual. We want to be a Church of people able to bear witness, yet aware that bearing witness can sometimes be difficult and that defending one's Truth can sometimes exact an extremely high price. At the same time we wish to be a Church open to all genuine human values, including those we find outside of the Church.

This is why in the transition from our wishes to specific ethical attitudes we do not hesitate to make use of those traditions that have arisen apart from direct Christian inspiration, but that are, in their lasting and truly essential values, quite close to the spirit of Christianity. . . . We can, to some extent, find such values in any authentic humanism. It seems, however, that the humanist ethic of social involvement professed and lived out by the Polish indomitable should, despite its secular character, be particularly close to us, since it arose from a common historical experience. An awareness of the existence of this moral-intellectual tradition, a recognition of its authentic ethical values, a respect for the memory of the people who bore witness to these values—all of this must find a place in our contemporary Christian attitudes about service and in our ethic of social activity. This is an essential and necessary step toward an honest dialogue between believers and nonbelievers in Poland—a step aimed at burying the century-old divisions, today so irrelevant, that keep a sizable and valuable sector of the indomitable Polish intelligentsia apart from the Church.[4]

When I read Cywiński's book, I realized it was unique. I could not counterpose it with a single work, a single article, in which a leftist intellectual had written about Christianity and the Church with the honesty, sincerity, and goodwill of Cywiński's *Genealogies*. This does not speak well for the people of the secular Left, and it presents us with a special responsibility: to bear witness ourselves. The fragmentary sketches of the present work do not, of course, fulfill this function, but they were begun out of an awareness of this responsibility. The dispersed, quarrelsome people of the secular Left, searching simultaneously for truth and for each other, must understand once and for all that Christianity is not their enemy. It will become their

4. Bohdan Cywiński, *Rodowody niepokornych* [Genealogies of the Indomitable] (Warsaw: Biblioteka Więzi, 1971), pp. 518–19.

enemy only when they themselves put ends over means, defile truth and freedom, and pay homage to Caesar—in other words, when they themselves stop being the Left.

The secular Left is in a particularly difficult situation in Poland. It must defend its socialist ideals in the face of an antipatriotic totalitarian power shouting socialistic slogans. Yet it is precisely for that reason that the defense must be firm, consistent, and uncompromising, free from sectarianism, fanaticism, and obsolete scenarios. Leftist thought must be open to all antitotalitarian and pro-independence ideas, and thus open to Christianity and the riches of the Christian tradition. People of the secular Left should want to unite in brotherhood with all people of goodwill. We should want to join with Christians not in spite of their religious beliefs but because of those beliefs. We should want all persecuted Christians to see us, the proponents of secular humanism, as their closest and most sincere friends. Only then will the secular Left be worthy of its noble antecedents. Only then will we be faithful to our own principles. Only then will an authentic socialist thought be revived in Poland. Socialism, which I understand as a moral and intellectual movement, will be revived in Poland not as a result of dubious alliances and questionable compromises with inner-party circles but through an uncompromising struggle for freedom and human dignity and through a full and honest reevaluation of the road socialists have traveled so far.

The study of undaunted Christians in totalitarian states awaits its secular leftist author. Such a study will certainly arouse much conflict and debate, but then a great deal of debate was provoked by *Genealogies of the Indomitable,* too. Characteristically, ideological divisions completely overtook religious divisions in the controversy surrounding Cywiński's book. The book was denounced, often quite violently, by Party officials and PAX Catholics alike. On the Party side, these included people such as Stefan Pełczyński, editor of the Party monthly *New Roads,* and Janusz Wilhelmi; while Cywiński's critics from PAX included Professor Mieczysław Żywczyński, author of the book on the Church in the French Revolution, and Maciej Wrzeszcz, chief editor of the PAX weekly, *Directions.* The heart of the conflict was revealed precisely by Wrzeszcz, who wrote that Cywiński's book

is interesting in that it shows the search for a point of departure and a basis for alliances on the part of the group of Catholic intellectuals revolving around *Więź* and the Catholic Intellectuals' Clubs. For years this group has been searching for a "third road" between [PAX's] ideological acceptance of socialism from a Catholic standpoint and the neopositivism of the older generation of activists found in Znak and *Tygodnik Powszechny* (though of course *Tygodnik Powszechny* has also for some time been publishing the words of the "unhumbled believers" from former secular liberal circles). . . .

Cywiński's concept of "ethos," as something distinct from ideology and political programs, which he considers of secondary importance, is not the author's own invention. It is simply the latest version of the thesis presented by the *Więź* group already in 1957. At that time, the idea of substituting a moral and philosophical worldview for a clear political and ideological position was presented under the slogan of a "personalist dialogue." *Więź* rejected the natural scheme of things, according to which philosophical values can be realized only by coming to grips with the actual state of reality and by committing oneself to the optimal political and ideological solution. Instead, it replaced program with personalism, which it saw as a bridge to selected Marxist intellectuals. . . . Today, many years later, that same idea has returned as an "alliance of the indomitable," bringing together people from the Left and the Right against the "artificial divisions" of ideology. The goal remains the same: to create an alliance on the basis of values other than patriotism or socialism, on values supposedly more universal and more modern than these. . . . [On the contrary,] it is the dialogue and cooperation of communists with progressive Catholics that gives a true picture of the balance of social forces. The proposal to replace this with the nonideological encounter of the "indomitable" in both camps . . . reminds us of various old Western conceptions of dialogue directed solely to selected "good Marxists." In reality, this was nothing other than revisionism.[5]

The PAX publicist undoubtedly thought that this denunciation of Cywiński and other "indomitable" intellectuals, Catholic and secular alike, would provide the authorities with important inside information on the revisionists' latest play for power. But Mr. Wrzeszcz, so quick to denounce, made a mistake this time—and a big one. *Genealogies of the Indomitable* and the controversy surrounding it played an immensely important role in the overcoming of closed religious circles and in the reorientation of the Polish intelligentsia. This was not a new political game but a clear and emphatic demonstration that there were now new conceptual conflicts far more fun-

5. Maciej Wrzeszcz, "Niepokorni katechumeni i pokorni recenzenci" [Indomitable Believers and Humbled Critics], in *Życie i Myśl* [Life and Thought], no. 6 (1972): 36–37.

damental than formal religious distinctions, new conflicts that had nothing in common with the division into believer and nonbeliever.

The controversy surrounding *Genealogies* revealed a new dimension of the dialogue between Christians and the Left. For the Left, it should be clear that the religion of Cywiński and others like him is no "opiate of the people" but a source of progressive and humanist ideas. For us in the secular Left, there is nothing opportunistic about meeting with Christianity in service of such values as freedom, tolerance, justice, human dignity, and the search for truth. This is a chance to build an ideological community of a new type, so important in the struggle for democratic socialism. The Polish experience in this matter, and in particular the ability for a secular Left free from crude atheism to coexist, in respect and solidarity, with a Christianity free from religious intolerance, can be useful for other left-wing antitotalitarian movements in other countries and in other parts of the world.

"We nonbelievers hate only hatred," wrote Albert Camus. "As long as a breath of freedom remains alive in France, we will not ally with those who hurl insults and innuendoes. We will stay with those, whoever they may be, who give testimony to the truth."[6]

I cite these words of the great French writer in a spirit of deep solidarity. Camus's credo should become the credo of all those in Poland's secular Left; of all those "for whom the words truth, love, faith, hope, patriotism, and progress have neither died nor turned into stone" (Jerzy Andrzejewski); of all those who continue to ask themselves that most fundamental and most trivial question of our times: How ought one live? This is a question directed to each one of us. And each one of us, individually and independently, must sincerely and painfully set out on that difficult road back to the simple questions and the elementary answers, the difficult road of moral and intellectual reevaluation.

In Polish intellectual circles it is common to complain about the restrictions on our rights, about the lack of freedom, about censorship. Far be it from me to minimize the importance of these issues. And yet it is not only the political authorities who are responsible for our moral and intellectual life. We all share responsibility. The authorities can expand or restrict the boundaries of freedom, but they cannot make people free. Our freedom begins with each one of us, not with the authorities. If we do not circulate our carbon-copy book

6. Albert Camus, *Eseje* (Warsaw, 1971), p. 251.

manuscripts, if we do not publish in uncensored émigré publications, if we are silent in the face of persecution, injustice, and the lies of official propaganda, then it is not the authorities who are responsible for this but we ourselves. It is we who are faint-hearted, we who acquiesce in totalitarian evil. We do so even though today we do not risk very much: no gulag, torture, or secret executions await us today. I fear that tomorrow may be too late. It will be impossible to douse the flames of the burning home with ink; only the ashes of our ideas will remain.

We live as prisoners of our myths and patterns. We accept the official system of relations and values. We live each day in lies, among others immersed in their lies, and it is increasingly difficult to look one another in the eye. In despair and helplessness we accuse only each other, and if any one of us tries to throw off the burden of conformity and to shatter the web of lies, we immediately say, "this one has a dirty past." (Who is without guilt?) Or we question that one's intentions, saying that he only seeks dissident fame, easy popularity, celebrity on the cheap. How often we forget that the price of such fame is the barred window of a prison cell. We do not even have the courage to quarrel honestly among ourselves, for every polemic is censored, every criticism takes on a new and unintended meaning, and every critical voice can become like clean water poured into a dirty glass.

We are condemned to impotence.

"Surely," said Bonhoeffer,

there has never been a generation in the course of human history with so little ground under its feet as our own. Every conceivable alternative seems equally intolerable. We try to escape from the present by looking entirely to the past or the future for our inspiration. . . . It may be, however, that the responsible, thinking people of earlier generations who stood at a turning-point of history felt just as we do, for the very reason that something new was being born which was not discernible in the alternatives of the present. . . . Who stands his ground? Only the man whose ultimate criterion is not in his reason, his principles, his conscience, his freedom or his virtue, but who is ready to sacrifice all these things when he is called to obedient and responsible action in faith and exclusive allegiance to God. The responsible man seeks to make his whole life a response to the question and call of God.[7]

7. Dietrich Bonhoeffer, "After Ten Years," in *Letters and Papers from Prison*, pp. 16, 19.

We expect "the success of our cause with confidence and calm," Bonhoeffer adds. I envy all Christians this confidence and calm. My confidence and calm are not so deeply rooted and have no supernatural legitimacy. They do, however, have a legitimacy that I am inclined to recognize as absolute: the basic canon of values of European culture in its specific Polish form. This is a human authority, since it was created by people, and yet also suprahuman, since the eradication of this canon would mean the annihilation of all the principles of human existence for which it is worth living and suffering.

"Since the realm of the absolute order remains inaccessible to our understanding," writes Jan Józef Szczepański, "we should at least be faithful to the order that shaped us, whose legacy we recognize with pride as our own, and to whose laws we should be loyal. Maintaining that loyalty should be our goal and our reward."[8]

It is in this sense that my path has also been an answer to a "question and call." It is an answer that I give inconsistently—often cowardly, often unwillingly and with trepidation—and yet an answer that I cannot refrain from giving if I am to look at myself in the mirror without shame. I feel, as Antoni Słonimski once wrote so beautifully, that moral right is not only in me but above me. This is why it is my duty to answer the question, to respond to the call. No one can answer for me. No one can absolve me from my responsibility. The road that I choose and seek to follow, while fearing the police, malicious gossip, and my own conscience, is a road on which, my teacher Słonimski taught me, "there are no final victories, yet also no final defeats." I have found this road thanks to the determination, and the writings, of many different people who shared a stubborn insistence on living in truth. On this road we of the secular Left can meet with Christians, and together we can recite Zbigniew Herbert's prayer of free people:[9]

Go where those others went to the dark boundary
for the golden fleece of nothingness your last prize

go upright among those who are on their knees
among those with their backs turned and those toppled in the dust

you were saved not in order to live
you have little time you must give testimony

8. Jan Józef Szczepański, *Przed nieznanym trybunałem* [Before an Unknown Tribunal] (Warsaw: Czytelnik, 1975), pp. 27–28.
9. "The Envoy of Mr Cogito." © John and Bogdana Carpenter 1977. Reprinted from Zbigniew Herbert, *Selected Poems*, translated by John and Bogdana Carpenter (1977 by permission of Oxford University Press), pp. 79–80.

be courageous when the mind deceives you be courageous
in the final account only this is important

and let your helpless Anger be like the sea
whenever you hear the voice of the insulted and beaten

let your sister Scorn not leave you
for the informers executioners cowards—they will win
they will go to your funeral and with relief will throw a lump of earth
the woodborer will write your smoothed-over biography

and do not forgive truly it is not in your power
to forgive in the name of those betrayed at dawn

beware however of unnecessary pride
keep looking at your clown's face in the mirror
repeat: I was called—weren't there better ones than I

beware of dryness of heart love the morning spring
the bird with an unknown name the winter oak

light on a wall the splendour of the sky
they don't need your warm breath
they are there to say: no one will console you

be vigilant—when the light on the mountains gives the sign—arise and go
as long as blood turns in the breast your dark star

repeat old incantations of humanity fables and legends
because this is how you will attain the good you will not attain
repeat great words repeat them stubbornly
like those crossing the desert who perished in the sand

and they will reward you with what they have at hand
with the whip of laughter with murder on a garbage heap

go because only in this way will you be admitted to the company of cold
    skulls
to the company of your ancestors: Gilgamesh Hector Roland
the defenders of the kingdom without limit and the city of ashes

Be faithful Go

AFTERWORDS

1977–1987

1977

TRANSLATOR'S NOTE:
In June 1976, the government unexpectedly announced major price increases on basic food items. When the authorities had earlier tried to raise prices, in December 1970, the move precipitated major strikes and protests that resulted in dozens killed and the ouster of Władysław Gomułka as Party Secretary. This time the move again sparked strikes, and although the authorities quickly rescinded the price hikes, they also dismissed and arrested hundreds of workers who had participated in the strikes. Oppositionist intellectuals, who had done little to support workers in 1970, this time organized in defense of the persecuted strikers. In late 1976 they formed the Workers' Defense Committee, or KOR, an organization of engaged intellectuals that would go on to play the leading role in the resurgent political opposition of the late 1970s. With Jacek Kuroń and Adam Michnik as its chief theorists, KOR ultimately played an important role in the Solidarity movement as well. The following brief afterword was written soon after the events of June 1976 and the founding of KOR.

INITIAL REAPPRAISAL

Several months have passed since completing this book, months filled with events very important for our nation, months perhaps constituting a turning point.

The events have not led me to revise my ideas. The articles on "socialism, politics, and Christianity," sent from Poland and published by my friends in the journal *Aneks* (issue no. 12) fully match my own way of thinking. Each one of us has his own point of view, but the most important thing is that an authentic dialogue now exists. I am especially pleased that I find myself in complete agreement with the ideas expressed in this issue of *Aneks* by my teacher and friend, Leszek Kołakowski.

Public life in Poland over these last months has revolved around the so-called "workers' question." It has been made clear once again that political divisions have nothing in common with religious differences. On one side can be found the overwhelming majority of the Polish intelligentsia, secular and Catholic, while on the other side stand regime apologists both Catholic (PAX and ODISS) and secular (the entire Party press).

The activity of the newly founded Workers' Defense Committee (KOR) deserves particular note in this context. In the ranks of this committee, whose members have by their actions written some of the most splendid pages of Polish history, can be found men and women of diverse traditions and orientations, those openly proclaiming their Catholicism as well as nonbelievers.

Underneath the text of numerous appeals in the defense of persecuted workers stand the signatures of prominent Catholic and secular intellectuals alike. In statements of the episcopate as well as in the sermons of the primate and other bishops, we find demands for justice for the prisoners together with condemnation of the brutality used during investigations. Staying within the framework of their pastoral duties and without engaging in political actions, the Polish bishops have clearly and unambiguously—and in loyalty to the teachings of the Gospels—condemned the violation of moral norms in our country. This is but the logical consequence of the long-term, often misunderstood policy of the Roman Catholic Church in Poland.

By their behavior in the recent events, PAX and ODISS proved themselves well worthy of my criticism. In fact, I am now inclined to consider my assessment of their activities as rather too mild. Thus I have all the more respect for those people connected with these circles (I am thinking chiefly of Anka Kowalska) who were able to maintain their own opinion of events and to take an independent position.

On the other hand, the honest and courageous comportment of the Znak milieu, and in particular of Tadeusz Mazowiecki and Stanisław Stomma, is in keeping with the profound respect enjoyed by such people in Polish society.

I showed the first draft of this book to several friends, both Catholics and nonbelievers. Each of them had serious reservations. I do not consider this a bad thing, for I see my book as but the beginning of a conversation that is important for all of us.

Let me take the opportunity here to thank all of those friends of mine who took the time to familiarize themselves with the manuscript and to send me their comments, all of which affected the final form. For the book as a whole, of course, the responsibility is mine alone.

Paris, February 1977

1979

TRANSLATOR'S NOTE:
In October 1978, Cardinal Karol Wojtyła of
Kraków became Pope John Paul II, the first
non-Italian pope in over four hundred years. In
June 1979, the pope made his first pilgrimage
to Poland. Michnik wrote this essay soon after
the pope's visit and had it included as an afterword to the 1981 Polish edition of *The Church
and the Left*.

A LESSON IN DIGNITY[1]

The pope has departed. The government has breathed a sigh of relief.

It will be a long time before we are able to grasp the full impact of this nine-day visit. The old phrase of Julian Stryjkowski keeps coming to mind: "the second baptism of Poland." Something very strange happened here. The same people who are so frustrated in everyday life, so angry and aggressive when queuing for goods, suddenly transformed themselves into a buoyant collective of dignified citizens. Discovering dignity within themselves, they became aware of their own power and strength. The police vanished from the main streets of Warsaw; as a result, exemplary order prevailed all around. A society deprived for so long of its rights suddenly recovered its ability to take care of itself. Such was the impact of Pope John Paul II's pilgrimage to Poland.

In this way, the thirty-year strategy of the Polish episcopate, developed chiefly by Primate Cardinal Stefan Wyszyński, was vindicated. All observers of the welcoming ceremony at the airport could see for themselves the enormity of the road traveled by the primate: from imprisonment [between 1953 and 1956] to this great symbolic scene. It was he who shaped the attitude of the Polish Church, one marked by determined resistance against sovietization yet tempered by the realist's feel for the situation, in which there was room for firmness and heroism yet also for reasonable compromise. It was this stance that led to the present situation, in which the Roman Catholic Church in Poland could reveal to the world its true nature. The traditional view of the Church as fanatical and obscurantist has been

---

1. A previous, slightly abridged translation of this essay appeared in Adam Mich nik's *Letters from Prison and Other Essays,* translated by Maya Latynski (Berkeley: University of California Press, 1985).—TRANS.

radically undermined. It is now quite clear to everyone that the Church in Poland is a force against which it is impossible to exercise power.

For some this is cause for alarm: Will this not lead to a new version of the old alliance between altar and throne? I do not share such worries. There is no rational basis to believe that the Church has abandoned its usual oscillation between diplomacy and speaking the truth in favor of diplomacy and capitulation—especially today, when the significance of speaking the truth has been brought so dramatically to the fore.

The Polish pilgrimage of Pope John Paul II has given a new meaning to the Vatican's Ostpolitik. In 1950, when news of the accord between the government and the episcopate reached the Holy See,[2] a leading Vatican official is said to have cried out in despair. The accord, felt the official, constituted an improper concession by the Church, given the conditions of total conflict at the time. Years later, however, when the Vatican began its own "opening to the East," the line of the Polish Church was considered to be too harsh. In fact, despite nuances and subtleties, that line had remained essentially unchanged: to consistently defend the principles of the Gospels while not losing contact with reality, to secure basic rights for the Church while insisting on the principle of dialogue and compromise in Church-state relations, and to transform reality through *fait accomplis*.

In this context, the behavior of the pope and certain of his gestures toward the government become perfectly clear.

The authorities this time displayed a modicum of reason. Although the television coverage of one mass was simply scandalous (a French acquaintance said it reminded him of a broadcast of a soccer match that shows everything but the ball), and although radio reports from Częstochowa or Gniezno could be heard in Warsaw only by tuning in Vatican radio via Munich, still the media did provide information. National television transmitted two of the masses and local television carried others; papal texts were published in the press with minimal interference from the censors. Although here and there they imposed absurd restrictions, still, let us acknowledge that the police and security forces did not behave provocatively. Although Jacek

---

2. In April 1950, the Polish episcopate signed an agreement with the Communist government—the only Eastern European Church to do so—aimed at defining the terms of coexistence. This is discussed more in Part One.—TRANS.

Kuroń found himself practically under house arrest—there were more people guarding him than the pope—still, the authorities did not impose a massive preventive detention against the democratic opposition.

The best the government could do—and this is what it did do—was to put a good face on a bad situation. That is, it pretended that the millions of happy faces pressing together to see the pope did not prove the complete failure of its thirty-five years of governing and did not demonstrate that it had lost all moral right to exercise power.

The fact remains that there were no violent outbursts. This is what we all, for various reasons, feared most. Some people were perhaps overly worried about this: Radio Free Europe, for example, simply stopped broadcasting information about arrests of oppositionists, leaving the latter, understandably, somewhat bitter.[3]

Democratic opposition circles fully respected the religious character of the pope's visit and did not try to take advantage of it for political activities. This does not, of course, mean that the visit lacked a political dimension. Prior to the event, the Western European press had occasionally compared the pope's visit to Khomeini's return to Iran and the struggle against the Shah, an analogy meant to symbolize a conflict between a dictatorship with modernist tendencies and a vast protest movement expressing itself in a language of anachronistic ideas and reactionary utopias. I cannot imagine a more fundamental misunderstanding. The values and views expressed in the pope's homilies had nothing in common with Catholic fundamentalism. He did not urge a return to a time when the Church not only had access to the wealthy but chiefly served them, too. "There is no imperialism in the Church," the pope specifically stated. "Its only mission is to serve." The Church, he said, seeks to attain its goals through nonpolitical means.

Most Poles experienced the pilgrimage as their chance to demonstrate their true longings and aspirations. In this sense, it was a national plebiscite. The choice, however, was not a simple alternative of Catholic versus atheist. I saw Catholics who gritted their teeth while listening to the pope, and I saw atheists swept away by his profundity. "What do you stand for?" he asked of us all. "For accept-

---

3. This is not an attempt to disavow RFE or an appeal for a fundamental change in its line. We understand all the reasons for its moderation. Nevertheless, we feel that this need not entail the censoring of information about repression.

ance of totalitarian coercion or for inviolable rights to freedom and dignity?" The overwhelming majority of Poles chose the latter.

The words of the pope were impressive. Any attempt to reconstruct their meaning runs the risk of simplifying and eroding it, particularly when such an attempt is made by one who is not and never has been a Catholic. Yet if, full of brashness, I make such an attempt here, I do so out of the feeling that Pope John Paul II spoke to all of us in general and to every one of us in particular, and thus also to me. Let me try then to say what it is I heard, what I understood, what I learned.

•   •

Just as the Polish historical experience is unique, so is the experience of Polish Catholicism. "When national and state structures were lacking," said Pope John Paul, its mostly Catholic society

found support in the hierarchical order of the Church. And this helped society through the times of partition and occupation; it helped society maintain, and even deepen, its understanding and awareness of its own identity. . . . The Episcopate of modern Poland is in a special way the heir and representative of this truth.[4]

After 1945, the Catholic hierarchy became "the center of the Church's pastoral mission [and] also a strong support for society and for the nation, increasingly conscious of its rights. This nation, overwhelmingly Catholic, seeks support in the hierarchical structures of the Church."

Church-society relations, according to the pope, take precedence over Church-state relations. The normalization of the latter must be based on "basic human rights, among which the right to religious freedom has an indisputable, and in a certain way a fundamental and central meaning. The normalization of relations between State and Church is evidence of the practical respect of this right and all that it entails in the life of the political community."

In this context the pope mentioned the cult of St. Stanisław, who is for Polish bishops "a model of firm and fearless courage in the propagation and defense" of the faith, demonstrating again the depth to which Christianity is inscribed in the Polish consciousness. "That

4. From Pope John Paul's address to bishops in Częstochowa, 5 June 1979; as translated in *Origins* 9, no. 5 (21 June 1979): 68. I have slightly amended this and other translations.—TRANS.

which the nation has brought to the development of man and humanity, as well as that which it brings today, cannot be understood without Christ. It is impossible to understand this nation, with a past so glorious and yet so terribly difficult, without Christ."

What do these words mean for me, someone outside of the Church? They mean that although we can explain history in various ways, such as through social or economic conditions, we should remember that none of these factors can tell us why Janusz Korczak or Father Maksymilian Kolbe chose to die as they did, or why we celebrate their deeds today with such deep veneration.[5]

Jarosław Dąbrowski and Romuald Traugutt, two nineteenth-century insurrectionists, differed greatly in their political and ideological views. But in one way they were alike: their readiness to work for the highest human and patriotic values even at the cost of their lives. This readiness gave the Polish tradition a specific ethos of sacrifice. In the name of this ethos, our fathers and forefathers fought uninterruptedly, over many generations, for national and human dignity. And this ethos cannot be understood apart from the persisting presence of Christianity in Polish spiritual life.

Polish culture is founded on another ethos as well—that of a diversified republic in which nationalities coexist in conditions of equality and tolerance. And even though this equality and tolerance have not always prevailed, they have always remained the dream of the best citizens of this land. With his warm words to the non-Catholic Christians of Poland, the pope seemed to hark back to this very ethos of tolerance.

It is in this way that I understand Pope John Paul's comments about the unique experience of Eastern Europe, an experience as dramatic as it is instructive for the entirety of this continent. Eastern Europe, he said, has made a vital contribution to a joint cultural legacy, to the "spiritual unity of Christian Europe made up of the two great traditions of East and West."

One can say much about the meaning and essence of this historical experience. Here let us mention only one aspect: these societies were subjected to "modernizing" experiments in conditions of totalitarian repression. Rapid industrialization, for many years the crowning argument in support of the system, was carried out simulta-

5. Both were victims of the Nazis. Janusz Korczak, head of the orphanage in the Warsaw ghetto, went with the children to be gassed at Treblinka rather than save himself. Father Kolbe sacrificed himself in Auschwitz in order to save the life of another.—TRANS.

neously with the elimination of the most fundamental rights of the working people, the eradication of their dignity and the dignity of their labor. The pope called attention to these sacrifices in his sermon in Częstochowa, and even more so in his homily at Mogila. Recalling the history of Nowa Huta, and the struggle to build a church there,[6] the pope noted that "the history of Nowa Huta has also been written by the cross"—a symbol of Good Tidings, as well as of suffering.

The workers' struggle for the Cross, for a church in Nowa Huta, was a struggle for dignity and identity, testimony that men and women "do not live by bread alone," even when there is hardly any bread. The contemporary problems of human labor can ultimately be reduced not to "technology or even to economics but to a fundamental category: the category of the dignity of work, that is to say, of the dignity of man."[7] "Christ," said the pope,

will never allow man to be considered, or to consider himself, merely as a means of production, or to be appreciated, esteemed, and valued in accordance with that concept. . . . He had himself put on the cross . . . in order to oppose any form of degradation of man, including degradation by work. . . . This must be remembered both by the worker and the employer, by the system of work as well as by the system of remuneration; it must be remembered by the state, the nation, the church.[8]

The problem of the liberation of labor currently lies at the center of many debates in Western Europe. It is precisely here that the pope from the East can make a unique contribution, by bringing to bear his knowledge of the experiences that shaped the features of that "other face of Europe," to quote Tadeusz Mazowiecki. The pope says he "comes before the Church, Europe, and the world to speak about these often forgotten nations and peoples. He comes to issue a great appeal." What does this mean? It means, I dare to believe, that the picture of a crippled and divided Europe—a Europe without Warsaw and Kraków, Budapest and Prague, Vilnius and Lvov—has now been challenged. This was the picture painted by the world powers at the Yalta Conference, due to the military balance of power. Today it is challenged, with all possible force, by a person who rejects the use of force, in the name of One who for some people is God and for

6. Nowa Huta was built as a model socialist city during the Stalinist period. The government was particularly stung by the residents' ultimately successful effort to build a church there.—TRANS.

7. Homily in Mogila, 9 June 1979, in *Origins* 9, no. 5 (21 June 1979): 77.

8. Ibid.

others is a symbol of the fundamental values of European culture, and thus for both is a source of moral standards and hope.

The Polish experience in Europe is one in which we have been called "subhuman" and the "scum" of history. We have been betrayed by our allies, deprived of our rights and our might, and have persevered in a struggle for national and human dignity carried out in such harrowing solitude that the only bastion of strength is simple human conscience. It is impossible to understand this experience without Christ.

So anyone who today repeats Stalin's question, "How many divisions does the pope have?" should remember that this question signifies approval of a system based on "the rejection of faith in God and in man; and on the eradication not only of love but of all signs of humanity," a system based on "hatred and contempt for man, in the name of an insane ideology."

By recalling the tragedy of insurrectionary Warsaw deserted by her allies, and by declaring that "there can be no just Europe without the independence of Poland marked on its map,"[9] Pope John Paul II rejects the principle of "national egotism" and the reduction of politics to a calculation of forces. In this way he introduces a moral factor into politics, without which many states can become superpowers but no nation can progress. Unfortunately, this century has not spared us examples of this basic truth.

The words spoken by the pope in Auschwitz before the commemorative plaques in Hebrew and Russian are a logical consequence of his universalist system of values. They are also a message to his countrymen: "No nation may develop at the expense of another, at the cost of another's enslavement, exploitation, or death." This message of Pope John XXIII and Pope Paul VI was uttered anew by Pope John Paul II, their successor and "at the same time the son of a nation that has suffered in its history, distant and near, at the hands of neighbors, distant and near. . . . Permit me, however, that I do not mention the latter by name. . . . We are standing at a place where we want to think of every nation and of every human being as a brother."

It is at this "Golgotha of the modern world," a place that reminds us of the victims of all systems of hate, where we think of loved ones gassed in the Auschwitz crematories and frozen in the Siberian labor camps, that we are challenged to be brotherly and conciliatory, re-

9. Mass in Warsaw, 2 June 1979, in ibid., p. 57.

jecting a however justified spirit of hatred and revenge. "I speak," said the pope, "in the name of all those people, anywhere in the world, whose rights are violated and forgotten. I speak because truth obliges me, as it obliges every one of us."

• •

This incomplete and perhaps inept reconstruction of a few lines of thought from the pope's speeches and homilies has been told in the only language I know, a secular language. It is in this language that I ask my own questions as well: Has the Polish cult of St. Stanisław never been abused for purposes having little to do with the defense of faith but a great deal to do with the Church's worldly aspirations? Is the hierarchical structure of the Church not threatened by its special role in the life of the nation? Has the Holy See always spoken with such clarity about the political systems which created death camps and slave labor camps?

I ask these questions because I know that others are asking them too, others who were also so moved by the words of the pope.

The most moving parts of the pope's homilies, and the most difficult to define, were the words addressed in a personal tone to his listeners. For if we accept that "in our time Poland has become a land of particularly responsible testimony," then one cannot avoid the pope's question as to whether we have really lived up to our "enormous tasks and responsibilities." More precisely, have I lived up to them?

The following words spoke to me:

A human being is a free and reasonable being, a conscious, autonomous, and responsible subject, who can and must seek the truth, who can and must make choices. . . . The whole historical process of a person's knowledge and choices is closely bound up with the living tradition of his or her nation, where down through the ages the words of Christ echo and resound along with the testimony of the Gospel, Christian culture, and the customs founded on faith, hope and love. . . . Can one cast all this off? Can one say no? Can one reject Christ and all His contributions to human history? Of course one can, for man is free. But the basic question remains: Is it permissible to do this? In whose name is it permissible? By virtue of what rational argument, what value close to the will and the heart, is it possible to stand before yourself, your neighbor, your fellow citizens and your country, in order to reject all that we have been living by for a thousand years?

In other words, is it permissible for me to reject a culture based on Christian values, on "faith, hope, and love"?

Any answer to this most important of human questions may sound false. Each must answer for himself. But it seems to me that this system of values is rejected not only by those who, through positions of power, violate inalienable human rights—or those, like Pontius Pilate, who silently allow them to do so—but also by those who, while proclaiming their solidarity with such values, defend them in dishonorable ways.

I will not enumerate those ways here. I will say only that while listening to the pope in Kraków, I had a strange feeling. When he asked the Catholic faithful "never to forsake Him," I felt that the pope was also speaking to me, a pagan. He was asking me to shun those dishonorable ways.

June 1979

1981

TRANSLATOR'S NOTE:
By the time this afterword was written in the summer of 1981, Poland had changed in several dramatic ways. The role of the Church expanded considerably as a result of the selection of a Polish pope, whose pilgrimage to his homeland in June 1979 became the most spectacular public celebration of Catholicism in Poland since the end of World War II. Then, in the summer of 1980, workers in Gdańsk, Szczecin, and throughout the country went on strike for the right to form independent trade unions. With the creation of Solidarity, the fight for a democratic Poland became the urgent issue of the day. Although Michnik did not play a direct role in the events of the summer of 1980, he soon became a leading theorist of the Solidarity opposition. He wrote the following afterword for inclusion in the 1981 edition of his book, which was being published in Poland—still only semilegally—for the first time.

A RESPONSE TO CRITICS

I finished writing *The Church and the Left* exactly five years ago. I greeted the suggestion for its re-edition with as much pleasure as uncertainty. With pleasure, since young readers, enriched by quite different experiences, will be able to read it. But also with worry, for can the book still be relevant today? Is it not already a complete anachronism? In a sense, it became anachronistic almost immediately. The growing democratic movement of recent years has overcome the old divisions between those who learned their political radicalism in theology schools and the Catholic Intellectuals' Clubs, and those who found inspiration in clandestine study groups reading Marx, Abramowski, and Ossowski, ragged old collections of *Po prostu,* worn-out editions of Kołakowski and Brus, and the latest issues of Paris *Kultura* with the articles of Gombrowicz and Miłosz, Herling-Grudziński and Mieroszewski. A new ideological formation arose before my eyes, one I am unable to describe in detail here but the broad outlines of which can be easily found in the literature of the "generation of '68," in the cinema of "moral anguish," in modern theater, journalism, and art, and finally in the political activity of the democratic opposition from 1976 to 1980. We will witness many kinds of divisions in Polish public life in the years to come, but these will almost certainly no longer revolve around one's attitude to Christianity. We need only look at the present ideological complexion of the democratic opposition, at the remarkable visit of the Polish pope to Poland, or at the evolution of events since the rise of Solidarity last August. In its diagnosis and predictions, my book, I tend to think, has proven to be on the mark.

I would certainly write many pages differently today. I would be more careful in some of my judgments of people and institutions; I would be more precise in some of my statements. It is not a good habit, however, to rewrite one's own biography. Let the book stay in its original form.

I beg the reader for indulgence in one matter only: to please accept my explanations of the book's terminology. In particular, the term "secular Left" has often been understood in a manner contrary to my intentions. I coined the term in order to describe an intellectual current, not a concrete political formation. There has never been a precise political movement with that name, and I was not trying to call one to life. A common misunderstanding has been to identify the "secular Left" with the Polish Socialist Party, with groups of ex-Stalinists, or with KOR. For me, the term referred not to any particular political formation but to an intellectual tendency marked by radical anticlericalism and a hostile attitude toward religion. I was including here people persecuted by Stalinism (such as Adam Ciołkosz, Ludwik Cohn, Maria and Stanisław Ossowski, Antoni Pajdak, Adam Pragier, Kazimierz Pużak, Zygmunt Zaremba, Paweł Hostowiec, Gustaw Herling-Grudziński, Konstanty Jeleński, and others), as well as those who for a certain time succumbed to the "Hegelian temptation" only to subsequently become firm defenders of democratic liberties and human rights. I was trying to argue against the stereotypes shared by all of these people concerning religion and the Church.

I also used the term "democratic socialism" in my book. Today I use these words carefully and with great reluctance. Not because I have changed my ideological orientation, but because in Polish public life today these words are virtually meaningless.

Many friends ask whether I don't regret my book today. No, I do not regret it. For those outside the Church, the book's importance consisted in its new view of the nature of religion and its attempt at a new reading of modern Church history. Even if I exaggerated and painted perhaps too bright a picture of the Church, I was justified in doing so by the complete absence of objective work on this topic. Today, after the publication of richly documented works by Andrzej Micewski and Peter Raina,[1] I of course have a more nuanced view of things. But the question has a more immediate sense as well: Have I not changed my views of the Catholic Church in light of the events of the past year? The answer once again is no. I do feel, however, that a deeper and more subtle analysis is necessary for understanding

1. Andrzej Micewski, *Współrządzić czy nie kłamać?: PAX i Znak w Polsce 1945–1976* [To Co-govern or Refuse to Lie?: PAX and Znak in Poland] (Paris: Libella, 1978). Peter Raina, *Stefan Kardynal Wyszyński, Prymas Polski,* 2 vols. (London: Poets' and Painters' Press, 1979).

the Church's strategy in recent years. That strategy, based on a dialectic of resistance and participation in official public life, necessarily entails partial gestures and actions. Consequently, it is often misunderstood and must therefore be assessed from a longer perspective. In my view, the record from 1976 to 1980 is a decidedly positive one. I might only mention the episcopate's strong defense of the imprisoned workers from Radom and Ursus after 1976, its defense of persecuted activists of the democratic opposition, or the beautiful letter written by the Polish primate about the "Flying University."[2]

The symbolic triumph of the Church's strategy came with the [1979] visit of the pope to Poland and the large cross erected on Victory Square in Warsaw.

For church members this is obvious and banal, yet they may be interested to see how their own affairs look through others' eyes.

I write these words soon after the death of Primate Cardinal Stefan Wyszyński. With his death ended an epoch in the history of the Church and our nation. Cardinal Wyszyński was a man of uncommon form, of great courage and sensibility. He was always so alive, with such true human characteristics, as shown by his often controversial decisions. It is too early to put together a complete picture of his role and accomplishments. It would be unfortunate, however, if admiration for the primate's accomplishments prevented an objective assessment of modern Church history, an honest account of its low as well as its high points. That this is a real danger is evident from the recent tone of the Catholic press, in which apologetics and hagiography have taken the upper hand. In this way, a great deal of truth manages to get lost. Where can we read, for example, about the complicated problem of the 1950 concordat with the state, or the episcopate's odd behavior after the 1953 arrest of Primate Wyszyński, or the tragic history of the martyr priests, or the sorry legacy of the "patriots-priests" during the Stalinist years? After 1956 it was no longer a "Church of silence," yet many priests were still repressed, and the episcopate itself remained an object of severe attack. There were internal differences within the Church as well, concerning issues such as the Conciliar reforms, the cult of the Virgin Mary, the influence of Western Catholicism (from Holland, for example), or the role of the laity. These matters await their historian.

The last ten years have seen an end to the pattern of frontal as-

2. This refers to the independent lecture courses organized by opposition circles in various Polish cities in the late 1970s. The lectures were held at private apartments and the location frequently changed; hence the name. The first "flying universities" in Poland began during the tsarist Russian occupation in the nineteenth century.—TRANS.

sault on the Church. Gradually abandoning its policy of harassment, the regime began to specially solicit the views of the primate and the episcopate. The objective situation of the Church began to be different. Although nothing changed on the outside, the episcopate, the clergy, and the entire Catholic community began to ask new questions of the new situation. The emergence of the democratic opposition and of independent social institutions prompted these questions. But the activities aimed at promoting social self-organization and the formation of social ties independent of the state were also quite indebted to the Church. What was important was not only the Church's de facto "security umbrella," which helped curtail the repression, but also its model of civil disobedience, carried out most effectively by Father Ignacy Tokarczuk, Bishop of Przemyśl, who in this way facilitated church construction in his own diocese.

The general stance of the Church can be seen in the communiques of the episcopate. Individually, the responses are quite diverse: from Father Tokarczuk's civil disobedience to a certain bishop demonstratively taking part in elections to the Sejm; from Cardinal Wojtyła defending Kraków youth who participated in commemorations for the slain student Stanisław Pyjas to a certain bishop accusing hunger-strikers of "cynically trespassing" on church grounds; from Father Kantorski acting as chaplain for hunger-strikers in Podkowa Leśna to a certain priest whose critical comments on KOR and KPN were cited approvingly by the Soviet press. The diversity is very great indeed.

I do not want to lightheartedly dole out grades here, but we must look at the picture in its full complexity if we want to understand the present dilemmas of the Church. Since the formation of Solidarity the situation is even more complex. The very problem of the relationship between the Church and Solidarity is still far from settled. Should the trade unions be Christian in spirit, or Catholic in letter? How will the clergy relate to this new social force? How will it seek to influence the unions? How will it react to clerical tendencies within the union, or to the occasionally appearing signs of fanaticism and intolerance? Which will prevail in practice, the spirit of the papal homilies or the completely different spirit served up in the leaflets of Grunwald?[3] A certain prominent unionist is said to have commented on nonbelievers in Solidarity as follows: "Behind me stands my Catholic faith, but what stands behind them? Probably only foreign

3. "Grunwald" was a national-chauvinist, anti-Semitic, pro-regime organization established in March 1981.—TRANS.

money." How many priests will applaud such attitudes? How many will recognize this as dangerous drivel? I do not feel able to answer these questions. I do feel obliged to ask them. I also feel obliged to warn that we have certainly not seen the last attempt at the manipulation of religion, the Church, and Christian values. We should be prepared, so as not to be shocked when we find people defending the Church against "antisocialist elements." In the pages of *Trybuna Ludu,* Ignacy Krasicki already defends the episcopate against criticism from the émigré journal *Kultura.* We can expect more of this in the times to come.

I cannot complain of a lack of reader response. I have been flattered by the comments, reviews, and criticisms of many leading experts on the subject, Catholic and secular alike. I would like to thank all of them. I am in their debt. I am grateful not only to their far more sophisticated view of the Church's past and present, but also to the deeper picture they present of their own metaphysical outlook.

Published in 1981, Father Józef Tischner's book, *The Polish Nature of Dialogue,* provides a rare example of the fully uncensored opinions of a prominent priest and intellectual.[4] The virtue of the book lies not only in its historical description of the sometimes stormy encounters between Catholics and Marxists, but in its authentic presentation of the consciousness, phobias, and complexes peculiar to a certain type of Catholic intellectual. This is particularly evident in Tischner's account of Leszek Kołakowski, where a perceptive and insightful analysis of Marx and Marxism goes hand in hand with a rather malign settling of accounts with one of the greatest Polish philosophers of our time. I see Tischner as an intellectual of the highest order; his essays, particularly his study of Dostoyevski's Grand Inquisitor, I consider among my most important readings of recent years. But Tischner fails in his account of Kołakowski and his contemporaries. He is unable to describe their intellectual and spiritual experiences the way, say, Miłosz was able to do in his sketches of Borowski and others in *The Captive Mind.* I do not want to argue here about the Stalinist experience, although I might say that, for one who is an expert in the Inquisition and a specialist in Heidegger, the superficiality of Tischner's analysis is rather surprising. While I share all of his moral judgments on the question, his account of the mechanisms by which Stalinism took over intellectual life reminds me of

4. Translated in English as *Marxism and Christianity: The Quarrel and the Dialogue in Poland* by Marek Zaleski and Benjamin Fiore, S. J. (Washington, D.C.: Georgetown University Press, 1987).

the shout of the surprised little girl who, having seen her first giraffe, cries out, "It's not possible that somebody can have such a long neck!" The totalitarian temptation of the mind is a specific illness of our time, and we should be aware that new totalitarian utopias wait all around us, in new phraseologies and alluring forms, whether egalitarian or elitist, nationalist or universalist, atheist or religious.

Fear of the totalitarian temptation was one of the main inspirations for my book. The encounter with Christianity and the Church is a crucial part of the creation of an antitotalitarian community. For me, the attitude toward totalitarian movements and systems is the acid test for institutions, political parties, and human behavior throughout the world. This distinction is more important than the division between Right and Left, more important than any other distinction. It is a shame that Tischner did not recognize this.

I must admit that I myself was treated generously and sympathetically in Tischner's book. I agree with the majority of his criticisms. Not without reservations, however, which I will enumerate here:

1. The picture of Catholicism that emerges from Tischner's book is so idyllic that any appeal to the Catholic conscience—especially today, in the era of the Polish pope—might seem a bit tactless. Yet I do not retract my remarks: As long as the Church refuses to recognize the dubiousness of its interwar alliance with nationalist chauvinism, it will continue to be susceptible to a triumphalist attitude that leads to intolerance and will continue to run the risk of interpreting the Gospel in the language of political fanaticism. As long as the Church maintains a siege mentality, truth will give way to tactical considerations, and all Poles will be the worse off for it. Let us speak openly: How many private discussions among Catholics concerning the situation of the Church and within the Church are kept secret, and not in the least because of state censorship? How many Catholic intellectuals still speak with an internal censor lurking within?

2. Tischner criticizes the concept of "democratic socialism." Democracy, he writes, means that "the ultimate source of power is the entire nation—people regardless of social class." Socialism, however, means that the "source of authority is above all the 'vanguard class of the nation,' the industrial proletariat. Thus, the concept of democratic socialism, from a purely logical point of view, is identical to the concept of a square circle."[5]

---

5. Tischner, *Marxism and Christianity,* translated by Zaleski and Fiore, p. 153. (Translation slightly revised.—TRANS.)

In my understanding, the adjective "democratic" is the complete opposite of all forms of political despotism, including all forms of dictatorship that go under the name of socialist. "Socialism," meanwhile, is for me the continual movement toward the self-determination of labor, a movement for the liberation of labor, a movement based on the ideas of freedom and tolerance, human rights and national rights, a just distribution of the national income and an equal start in life for all. My definition is completely arbitrary and does not have much in common with the Leninist notion of the "dictatorship of the proletariat." The dominant position of the industrial proletariat was supposed to hinge on its actual place in the process of production and the social structure. It did not entail the limitation of the political rights of any other group of people. I do not see a square circle here.

3. Tischner notes that the concept of socialism

[is also used] in the official language of those with whom Michnik is in conflict, in the language of the Party, the propaganda apparatus, the language of ideologues. A question arises: To what extent does this concept convey the same meaning to both sides? Could the word perhaps be the same but its contents diametrically opposite? Or is there perhaps a common denominator? These are not only theoretical questions; the issue is whether Michnik's thought, in spite of everything, bestows approval upon what came to exist in Poland after World War II, or whether he considers everything to have been in error. Does he perhaps believe that only the beginnings were good? Does he thus, in spite of his whole criticism and opposition, grant a moral sanction to the groundwork of the current system? I think he does. There is no indication to the contrary.[6]

"I do not know," continues Tischner, "whether there is another social theory apart from Marxism that can so utterly blunt man's natural sense of reality."

Theory functions through people who believe. And there is surely more than one Catholic, in more than one matter, who, like the Marxist, also has a blunted "natural sense of reality." Tischner, whom I really do not suspect of ill will, demonstrates this in the passage above.

But, good God, I have spoken out on this subject hundreds of times, orally and in print. I have taken a drubbing for my words from Communists, Catholics, and nonaligned people alike. The state pros-

6. Tischner, *Marxism and Christianity,* translated by Zaleski and Fiore, pp. 153–54. (One missing sentence restored to translation.—TRANS.)

ecutor has formally accused me of slandering the state, and one fine priest has announced that the Church, neither now nor in the past, has had anything in common with such rabble-rousers as myself. And all because I've called attention to the illegitimacy of Communist power in Poland, because I've spoken about Yalta, which sold out Poland's right to self-determination and de facto approved Stalin's imposition of a foreign system on the Polish people, who have been defending themselves against it ever since. And today I am asked if I give moral sanction to the "beginnings" and to the "groundwork" of this system! Which beginnings? September 17? Katyń? The trial of the sixteen? The falsified referendum? The falsified elections? The persecution of Home Army soldiers? The persecution of PSL activists?[7] And which framework? The principle of a political monopoly for the Communist party, which, supported by foreign force, took power against the wishes of Polish society?

No, I give no moral sanction to any of this. My view is that this system, from the very beginning, has been founded on lies and coercion. Have I expressed myself clearly enough?

4. Tischner writes: "Michnik focuses chiefly on a dialogue of the elite, on the level of Episcopate—government—bishop—premier, on the Church and Party apparatus. Yet this level has always been secondary, of lesser importance. The real dialogue and the real decisions have taken place on the level of the people, the so-called 'simple people,' who have packed the churches and flocked to pilgrimages. It is they, the nation, who have defended themselves against the building of socialism."

I accept the charge that I made use chiefly of official documents of the episcopate and the government, that my book lacks analysis of the sociology of Catholicism in Poland. This is due not to a fascination with power but to the absence of any meaningful empirical data.

7. On 17 September 1939, less than three weeks after Nazi Germany invaded Poland from the West, Soviet troops invaded from the East and divided up the country with the Nazis. Katyń is the site of a Soviet massacre of thousands of Polish army officers in 1941. The "trial of the sixteen" refers to the Red Army's arrest of sixteen non-Communist Polish political leaders in Warsaw in 1945, soon after the expulsion of the Nazis. The men were deported to Moscow, tried by Soviet authorities, and sentenced to long prison terms or death. In 1946 and 1947, respectively, the Polish Communist authorities staged, and falsified, a referendum and an election in an attempt to legitimize their rule. Veterans of the Home Army, the non-Communist resistance group, and members of the Polish Peasant Party (or PSL), the main opposition group in the early postwar period, were mercilessly persecuted by the government at this time.—TRANS.

Anything I might have said on this subject would have been too speculative, tainted by its lack of rigor. As it was, I felt I was stepping onto virgin soil. Still, I should have made the appropriate qualifications, which I carelessly omitted.

Tischner substantiates his main theses through reference to philosophical discourse. His comments on the "simple people," however, must be taken on his word. I have no objection when Tischner tries to reconstruct his own ideas and those of his circle. But when he tells me that he knows the consciousness of the so-called "simple people"—excuse me, but here I maintain my skepticism. Popular consciousness in societies under totalitarian pressure is always difficult to gauge. Intellectuals who believe that they have figured it out are usually just doing some wishful thinking, confusing their own desires for reality. This applies to Marxists and Catholics alike. In my thirty-five years of living under this system, I have learned that things are never as bad as we fear and never as good as we would like to believe. Two characteristic features of the Stalinist dictatorship were its destruction of social bonds and its falsification of language. There is no question that the Church was a foundation for the nation—I wrote about this at length—but the actual scope of its influence should be a topic for serious research. From all accounts we have of life under Stalinist dictatorship, the experience of loneliness and fear comes through most sharply. Religious pilgrimages did not negate this experience. We still await the monograph about daily life in the Stalinist period, but even such a book will not entitle us to conclude who truly "lived Poland" and who merely lived in it. Many people have told me their "flawless methods" for discovering who represents the true Poland—so many, in fact, that I vowed never to use this kind of argument against anyone. Naturally, I do not find the argument very persuasive against me.

5. Tischner considers the terms "secular" and "Left" to be rather compromising ones. "I cannot imagine," he writes, "that in free elections a candidate appearing under the banner of 'secular Left' would . . . win many votes in this country."

I have already written on questions of terminology. I agree with Tischner that linguistic confusion is hard to avoid. There is a broader dimension involved, however. The distinction between Left and Right is relevant for societies in a parliamentary system. In such parliaments, the Communists are often said to be coming not from the Left but from the East. For societies in totalitarian systems, the distinction has lost its social significance. But what about societies recovering from the ruins of a totalitarian system? The experiences of Germany, Italy, Portugal, or Spain seem to indicate that these divisions somehow resurface. So far, that is all the empirical evidence we have. We do, however, have the Polish experience of the past year. Without going into specifics, it is hard not to see that along with democratic and open-minded attitudes, authoritarian and dogmatic attitudes have also appeared. Over time, there will develop a great diversity of views concerning the desired social order. Without quarreling over terminology, it is hard to deny that a social movement based on the traditional values of the Right is presently emerging in Poland, or that political supporters of Grunwald or the Katowice Forum[8] will continue to organize themselves in the future. Other groups based on other social visions are also coming forth, such as those focusing on self-government and human rights. My book is part of the intellectual current that has existed at least since 1968 and has, by its actions, achieved a certain moral authority in society. This diverse and multifaceted movement played no small part in the evolution of the Polish August. The movement continues to exist today. I leave it to others to name this tendency as they please.

One more thing: I wrote this book with the idea of striving for the truth, not with the hope of winning a parliamentary seat. The latter is something that is really not important to me. I hope, however, that I do not live to see the day when to win such a seat it will be necessary to declare oneself a Catholic. That would be a great setback for Polish democracy as well as for Polish Catholicism. It would also, I am convinced, be a great setback for my friend Father Józef Tischner.

6. I do not accept the charge that my chief concern was the coexistence of the Church with the apparatus of the Communist government. I wrote my book so that people of goodwill could come together with one another. This can be seen on every page, heard in every sentence. I was interested in two types of Poles: the Polish Catholic and the Polish radical. In the biography of the Polish radical, Marxism-Leninism was but an episode, playing a role far less fundamental than anticlericalism. In the encounter between these two types of Poles, one's attitude toward communism was certainly an important factor, but it was not the only factor. For Tischner, however, the entire problem is reduced to the conflict between Commu-

8. A hard-line Stalinist organization that arose within the Polish Communist Party in 1981.—TRANS.

nism and Catholicism. His book is silent on those people who were cursed from the pulpit before the war and harassed by the secret police afterward. Nor does it speak of those raised in the prewar traditions of Wici and OMTUR, of those who studied the Ossowskis' books as well as Miłosz's *Captive Mind,* or of all the "indomitable" of today who never found solace in any Grand Inquisitor, precisely because they never sought it there.

I have always been intrigued by the type of person, well-known from Polish literature, who professes Christian values but distrusts their official Church guardians, who holds socialist dreams of freedom and justice but distrusts those political parties claiming to bring such ideals to life. Without such people, twentieth-century Polish culture would be barren and gloomy. They restored grandeur to the Gospels and genuine humanist content to the Polish democratic tradition. Such people, present both inside the Church and outside, are the treasure of any society, the priceless capital of any intellectual movement. They are a true bridge between generations, ideological camps, and social milieus. Yet such people are missing from the pages of Józef Tischner's excellent book.

•   •

We are on the road to a new Poland, a democratic and independent Poland. The road we are traveling is a battered one, surrounded by the hostility as well as the admiration of foreigners. They do not understand us. Indeed, it is not easy to understand this extraordinary bloc of social and national solidarity. It is not easy to understand a holy mass in the middle of a strike in the middle of the Lenin Shipyard, and it is not easy to understand why these same striking workers are then deaf to the appeals of a bishop calling for an end to the strikes. No, it is not easy to understand today's Poland, not even for us. Each would like to see it according to his or her own dreams. From the enormity of the social changes that we witness today, a new ideological map of the country is being drawn. On this new map, I feel, there is a place for an intellectual and spiritual tendency that brings together the most treasured values of the Polish Socialist Party and the entire Polish democratic Left with the values and the achievements of Polish Catholicism. I would hope that my book serves such a cause.

Warsaw, July 1981

TRANSLATOR'S NOTE:
The following essay was written in 1987 as
part of a festschrift for Leszek Kołakowski and
is included here at Michnik's request. It deals
with the new relationship between intellectuals
and an increasingly active Church in the period
after the declaration of martial law in December 1981 and prior to the relegalization of Solidarity in 1989. Many intellectuals who had
put their political hopes in the Solidarity
movement now seemed to be putting those
hopes in the Church. Michnik criticizes this as
contrary to the ethos of the intellectual, as he
begins to draw back from his previously favorable accounts of Polish Catholicism.

TROUBLES[1]

Troubles are inscribed in the spiritual biography of the Polish intellectual. Located for years between a totalitarian Communist state and a hierarchical Roman Catholic Church, the Polish intellectual has had to consider the possibilities as well as the dangers inherent in such a condition. He can become a loyal functionary of official state institutions—and then he'll find his dilemmas discussed in the books of Janusz Reykowski and Jan Szczepański. Or he can declare himself a Catholic—in which case the essays of Jerzy Turowicz and Tadeusz Mazowiecki will help him define his place in the world. He can also, however, choose to be *between* these two worlds, as a free-thinking intellectual—as someone who has broken with the totalitarian state but has not, despite his sympathies for the Church, become a Catholic. It is this type of intellectual that I am interested in. With him I feel a kinship as well as a kind of spiritual community. I also feel that I understand the nature of his troubles: while some call him a renegade, others suspect he is a crass manipulator. Meanwhile, this intellectual ponders, seeks foundations, and tries to build anew his own sense of identity. He carefully follows the words and deeds of his mentors—and one of these mentors is Leszek Kołakowski.

I

Sometimes I think that in order to understand the spiritual dilemmas of our intellectual, we need only comprehend and describe the gulf that separates the work of Cardinal Stefan Wyszyński from that of Witold Gombrowicz. It is here that the ideas of Pope John Paul II,

1. From *Obecność* [Presence] (London: Aneks, 1987). This is a compendium of essays dedicated to Leszek Kołakowski for the sixtieth anniversary of his birth. —TRANS.

Czesław Miłosz, Zbigniew Herbert, and of Leszek Kołakowski can be found. For all that is precious in Polish culture has arisen at the crossroads of its great historical paths: in the encounter between the Christian spirit and the free-thinking spirit, in the mutually enriching conflict between these two opposed worlds.

If there is even an iota of truth in this argument, it is worthwhile listening carefully to the voices of critics of the contemporary Polish intelligentsia.

Some say that the Polish intellectual has now abandoned his free-thinking principles, sold out to the Roman Catholic Church, and replaced the red flag of proletarian revolution with the white and yellow banner of the Holy See.

From the Church, however, one hears the following: the motives of such an intellectual aré either tactical or downright insidious. It is only the wish to turn the Church into an instrument of political action that leads this intellectual to the world of Catholic institutions.

Are such suspicions and accusations absurd? No, they are not. Our political context makes it inevitable that the Polish intellectual is susceptible to precisely this kind of temptation, to which he has more than once succumbed. We thus share the fear that the anticlerical radical who was previously connected with the totalitarian power apparatus can be transformed into an apologist of a Church-dominated social order. This would be a great loss for the pluralist dimension of Polish culture and a dubious gain for Christianity. The Church usually has quite enough apologists as is. Nor can it grumble about a lack of enemies. It has always, however, had far too few friendly, well-wishing critics.

By abandoning his true identity and casting his lot with Roman Catholic doctrine and the Church hierarchy, the Polish intellectual is, according to the critics, committing the "second betrayal" of the intellectuals.[2] If support for totalitarian Communism constituted the intellectuals' "first betrayal," then as a result of this second betrayal Poland is being transformed into a unique dualistic country, where a totalitarian Communist facade is countered by a society organized according to hierarchical orthodoxy. In the grip of this political dichotomy, culture will grind to a halt. A *sui generis* Iranization of Poland will occur: a civil society emerging out of a conservative revolution will fight a cold civil war against an autocratic modernizing

---

2. Allusion to French author Julien Benda's 1927 work, *The Betrayal of the Intellectuals.* —TRANS.

state. The state will be ruled by a totalitarian power apparatus while civil society will be ruled by the Roman Catholic clergy. Here we have the return of the old Endek model from the early twentieth century, combining nationalist xenophobia with that special kind of Catholicism that embraces lies and hatred in public life while promoting biblical virtues in private life. No one will call this a "national scandal," and no one will perceive the danger it poses for our national culture. From the teachings of Pope John Paul only empty phrases will remain, while from the ideas of Solidarity—nothing but symbols stained with lies. Poland will be plunged into a provincial kind of nationalism and will grovel in the chaos of ignorant tribal hatreds.

This is the prophecy. One hears it often—increasingly often—often enough that it deserves to be noted and pondered for a while.

II

I look to the past. I reach for the commentary to Pope John XXIII's encyclical *Mater et Magistra,* a commentary written over a quarter of a century ago, in 1961, by Leszek Kołakowski. This was not a friendly commentary. Kołakowski attacked the encyclical for its "philanthropic banalities," "conservative content," "misleading insinuations" and "contradictions," as well as its "utter emptiness."

Kołakowski analyzed the voice of the Holy See from the viewpoint of an antitotalitarian socialist, a supporter of social reforms and the emancipation of labor. What did he find in the words of John XXIII? He noticed, not without reason, that Roman Catholics of all political stripes, even those that opposed each other, could equally embrace this encyclical. Its formulations fit the needs of fundamentalist bishops from Latin America as much as they "allowed the Church in socialist countries to make the political deals necessary for coexistence with the state authorities." They were acceptable to the Christian Democratic Left in Europe and to Christians in the newly decolonized countries, to Salazar as well as to Adenauer—in a word, they were acceptable to everyone. Thus the encyclical, the result of so many contradictory internal pressures, constituted, for Kołakowski, a "zero program, nothing."

In 1961, Kołakowski saw the nature of the Church as follows:

Of the great international institutions of social life, the Church . . . is the one most conservative, most subject to the inertia of its past, and most weighed down by the burden of its own dogma. Thus it is also the institution most closely connected with extreme reactionary social structures, able to change its position only when forced by events to do so.

Kołakowski attributed to the Vatican a "continued desire for the total control of social life," a refusal to cooperate with atheists on even the most basic of worldly matters, and a negative attitude toward all social compacts concluded apart from the auspices of the Church. But even these principles, he noted, are compromised by an ever present ambiguity that allows the various episcopates to "appeal to an obscure text in order to justify every move they make in the fluctuating political context."

What emerges here is a scathing and derisive critique. And yet, as must be emphasized strongly, this was not a critique written "on request from above." On the contrary, the Party line at the time was to praise Pope John XXIII, to favorably contrast his peace declarations and his calls for dialogue to the recalcitrant and "reactionary narrow-mindedness" of Cardinal Wyszyński. Behind every one of Kołakowski's taunting, antipapal remarks stood the genuine passion of a proud foe of the clergy. Such remarks present an accurate picture of the views of a significant part of the secular intelligentsia at the time—including the views of the present author.

This is not the place to demonstrate that Kołakowski's radical anticlericalism is historically rooted in an authentic and important current of Polish culture. There is, however, an increasingly acute need for an honest history of Polish anticlericalism. Only such a history, along with an equally frank history of Polish Catholicism, can facilitate a dispassionate discussion of the transformations of the intelligentsia and the Church in Poland. But Leszek Kołakowski was one of the people who brought about these transformations, and he remains a living example of them. It is for this reason that we reach back to his anticlerical essay of years ago—as the only way to comprehend the enormous distance that this Polish humanist, together with many of his readers, has traveled.

The year 1956 was a crucial turning point. From that time on, Kołakowski unequivocally condemned Stalinist totalitarianism, formulated his own diagnoses of the situation, and judged the world for himself and on his own terms. He became one of the major theorists of a young Polish intelligentsia that was rebelling against Party orthodoxy and seeking new language and ideas.

This new generation searched everywhere for remedies to Stalinist dogma: in new interpretations of Marxism, in existentialism, and in the rationalist spirit of Western democracy. But they continued to look at the Roman Catholic Church critically and distrustfully—critically, since the spirit of the times demanded that every large, hierarchical organization be looked at critically; and disdainfully, since this is how the spirit of the times demanded every orthodoxy rooted in dogma and faith be looked at, too. The anticlericalism of Western Europe—radical and rationalist, Voltairean and Jacobin—corresponded quite well to the anticlerical ethos of the Polish intelligentsia. Newly liberated from the spiritual shackles of Stalinism, Polish intellectuals were well-schooled in the history of the Church, and particularly its black pages. Kołakowski himself treated the Church's *aggiornamento* and declarations of support for pluralism very skeptically. "What is pluralism for the Catholics," he asked. Is it the counterreformation model in which there are "many ways to convert someone and many ways to exercise power"? Does it really imply an attitude of "genuine acceptance of the diversity of human life, open acceptance of everything that may constitute authentic human value, respect of the diversity of ways of living, thinking, and expressing oneself, without giving up the fight for one's own values?"

Kołakowski urged his Catholic adversaries to "clearly and categorically reject the traditional totalitarian tendencies so strongly rooted in the Christian world." The history of the Church, he said, cannot be reduced to the banality that humans are fallible and commit mistakes. "The fact," he continued,

that Catholics themselves often fell victim to intolerance in no way justifies their own intolerance of others. This must continually be emphasized, particularly since the entire history of the Church itself makes one distrustful of Catholicism. The Church is sensitive only to signs that its own rights and ambitions might be curtailed. Yet it is unable to make a clear reassessment of its own past, to renounce—in a way that does not arouse suspicion—all those characteristics that are notoriously typical of the Church in power, and that are difficult to reconcile with the slogans professed by Catholicism. To a certain extent, Catholicism finds itself in opposition to its own foundations.

Did Kołakowski change his views in later years?

III

Of course he changed his views, just as the Polish intelligentsia as a whole changed its attitude toward the Church. I tried to present a picture of these transformations ten years ago in my book *The Church and the Left,* and I will not repeat here my conclusions of that time. For Kołakowski, however, from his article on the papal encyclical and his studies on nondenominational Christianity, through his memorable essays on Jesus Christ as prophet and reformer and on the presence of myth, the road has led to a reconsideration of "the return of the sacred," to reflections on the alleged crisis of Christianity, and finally to a book on religion. This was simultaneously a road of political evolution: from the attempt to reform existing communism from within to a ruthless demasking of the system, from an effort to reinterpret Marxist doctrine (in his essay "Karl Marx and the Classical Definition of Truth") to his magnum opus *Main Currents of Marxism,* the best critical analysis of the Communists' totalitarian faith. Religion and the totalitarian utopia now began to look differently. Our image of the totalitarian state and of the Roman Catholic Church took on new contours.

In *The Presence of Myth,* one can still read that "Christianity created the first models of the totalitarian state in Europe." In later years, this fact became less essential for Kołakowski. His essay "Propitious Prophecies and Pious Wishes," written immediately after the election of a Polish pope in 1978, is a good example of the evolution of Kołakowski's views on the Church: "The Church is perched on the border of heaven and earth. It is at once a repository of grace and a guardian of law, bringing invisible values to the visible world." What kind of Church do people need? They do not need a Church that makes political and sexual revolutions, that "sanctifies our lasciviousness and exalts our passions." They need a Church that will "help them get away from the direct pressures of life, show them the inescapable limits of the human condition and enable them to accept these limits." The Christianity of such a Church "is neither golden, purple, or red; it is grey."

This "greyness" need not be an escape from life, but it must be a firm rejection of all attempts to manipulate the Church for particular political ends. I repeat: *all* attempts, whether by liberationist Catholics or fundamentalist Catholics. To paraphrase Kołakowski, if the tension between God's and Caesar's, between the sacred and the profane, is a permanent feature of the Church in the world, then fundamentalism and liberationism are but two perilous schemes to eradicate this tension.

The fundamentalists, on the one hand, are stuck in the epoch of the *Syllabus.* They long for the bygone era when the worldly authorities protected the dogmas of faith from outside criticism, and the Church was granted license to supervise in detail the administration of worldly affairs. Fundamentalists consequently tend to ally or openly identify with those political forces that promise worldly privileges to the Church.

The liberationists, on the other hand, are those who seek to subordinate faith and the Church to the reformist or revolutionary ideals of the socialist project. They are always ready to identify with movements that declare their "option for the poor," disregarding the fact that such movements normally commence destructive policies vis-à-vis the Church once they come to power.

In each of these two ways the Church is compromised by immoral political ties. The fundamentalists oppose totalitarian Communism for its promulgation of atheism and persecution of religion. They are ready, without much hesitation, to support any military dictatorship committed to fighting communist atheism. The liberationists, however, will ally with the communist opposition against these dictatorships, quite heedless of the fact that, in this way, they contribute to the triumph of a political order that will not only subvert and persecute religion, but trample human dignity and civil rights on a scale unknown to the obtuse reactionary generals. Fundamentalists calmly consent to the violation of human rights in anti-Communist dictatorships; liberationists, accepting communism, act as a catalyst for totalitarian tyranny. Either road implies the abandonment by the Church of a consistent antitotalitarian position. Liberationism means the renunciation of antitotalitarianism in the name of an imaginary world of institutionalized brotherhood, which inexorably becomes just another captive totalitarian civilization. The fundamentalist critique, as noted above, focuses on communism's atheism. In direct continuation of the Church's nineteenth-century attack on liberalism, it makes a doctrinal dispute the heart of its critique. Such a way of thinking only prevents a proper distinction between liberal democracy and the totalitarian ideological state.

As Kołakowski argued,

the despotic form of government, and in particular the persecution of religion, derives not from the atheistic but from the totalitarian nature of communism, which makes it act as if structurally driven to eradicate all forms of collective life and all aspects of culture not imposed by the state.

The distinction is a crucial one. It is not atheism as a philosophy, says Kołakowski, but totalitarianism as a system, "without regard to its ideological costume—racist, communist, or religious—that to-day poses the gravest danger to Christian values and culture."

For Christians, the consequences are obvious. Fighting for their rights in a totalitarian state, they compromise themselves morally "if they do not base their claims on the clear acceptance of pluralistic principles of public life, entailing the consistent rejection of all total-itarianism, regardless of ideology. For although that ideology might be atheistic, it can just as easily be religious."

The belief that atheism is the essential flaw of communism nec-essarily leads to false solutions. Liberationists, who approve the communist project, are satisfied with the right to loyally affirm com-munist beliefs in the language of Christian doctrine. Fundamental-ists, meanwhile, by attacking atheism and ignoring the totalitarian context, "lead people to believe—or at least do not clearly deny—that totalitarianism would not be reprehensible if only its doctrine were based on the Nicean Creed instead of the *Collected Works* of Lenin."

This leads to a paradoxical similarity: the loyal liberationist and the steadfast fundamentalist are united by the belief that their mission is to convert the ruling communists to the true faith, not to resist the destructive policies of the totalitarian state.

Leszek Kołakowski was the first to formulate clearly the nature of these dilemmas that have been gnawing at the mind of the Polish intellectual for years. The precise articulation of what had previously been but a vague intuition seems to be due to long-term changes oc-curring in intellectual circles. The Church has also undergone change. As a result of both processes, we had the Solidarity phenom-enon—an independent self-governing organization of several mil-lion members, born of a workers' rebellion and combining the ethos of Christianity with the traditions of the great freedom-fighting movements.

Solidarity frequently demonstrated its connection with the Church, the guardian of the moral teachings of Christ. Yet it stayed free of the fundamentalist or liberationist temptation to use the Church instrumentally. It offered to meet the Church in truth and in resistance to totalitarianism, yet it simultaneously maintained a plu-ralistic vision of civil society and unflinchingly guarded its own in-dependence. Can such an arrangement last for long? Will it stand the test of time? The shape of the Polish soul depends on the answer to this question.

Let us say only that Leszek Kołakowski was one of the main intellectual architects of this phenomenon.

IV

The encounter between the Polish intellectual and the Roman Catholic Church has now become fact. Let us therefore repeat the question: is it in fact so absurd to say that, by moving toward the Church, the Polish intellectuals have committed the "second betrayal"? We will try to answer this question by trying to understand the present situation. But let us leave aside the wide gamut of collaborationist behavior that has been committed under the Catholic aegis: this belongs not so much to the history of Polish thought as to the history of Polish masquerade.

In the recent conditions of a delegalized Solidarity, some people expected the Church to assume the leadership of the political opposition and to lead the Polish people onto the barricades to recapture the gains of August 1980. The Church was then criticized for not wanting to live up to these expectations. The episcopate was accused of cowardly opportunism, of ungratefully pushing Solidarity aside, of trying to satisfy the particular interests of the Church at the cost of the general interests of the nation. Some people expressed regret, in other words, that the Catholic hierarchy did not want to identify the Church with the short-term interests of the antitotalitarian opposition. We see here a specifically Polish version of the liberationist option.

Yet there is also an opposing tendency, whose adherents take as their starting point the claim that Solidarity is dead. In such conditions, they say, the Church represents Poland's only chance to achieve autonomy. Only via the Church can people come together, and only religion can empower the social organizations of Polish society. Here an ostentatious solidarity with the Church replaces support for Solidarity, and the statements of the Catholic hierarchy are interpreted as political declarations of the opposition party. One also sees an attempt to revive within the Catholic framework all the rotten baggage of the reactionary past, including oppressive chauvinism, aggressive xenophobia, and a conspiracy theory of history. The fundamentals of human rights are rejected in favor of a nationalistic egoism, and the encyclicals of John Paul II are replaced by old Endek brochures, offering a most peculiar model of Polish political theology. Identifying oneself with the episcopate becomes a kind of political test, as well as a way of making the bishops into political leaders of Polish society. What are the possible consequences? The general democratic demand for civic rights turns into a particular demand for the rights of Catholics, the struggle for social autonomy is reduced to a campaign aimed at guaranteeing the Catholic hierarchy a privileged influence on public life, and the conflict between the totalitarian state and a pluralistic society begins to be expressed as a dispute between an atheistic government and a Catholic nation. The shadow of an Iranian syndrome begins to hover over Polish public life: this is the end point of the Polish fundamentalist option.

Reality, of course, comes far more diverse, and all the various viewpoints that actually exist cannot be fit into the model schematically presented above. Our point, however, is that this same Polish reality offers the Polish intellectual two different ways of committing the "second betrayal." Some of us have already chosen, and all of us face such a choice. Whoever is not aware of this will necessarily fall victim to self-deceit.

V

It should be said here that the Communist party publicists have also sounded the alarm about the specter of an Iranian-type theocracy in Poland. From the Party's point of view, the entire Solidarity movement is simply the Eastern European version of Iran's conservative-religious revolution against modernity. Solidarity supporters, in this view, are but "narrow-minded traditionalists feeding off a fanatical spiritual combination of a perverse Catholicism and a chauvinistic Polish romanticism."[3] The union's supporters are said to champion the belief that "for its martyrdom, the nation will be rewarded by guardian supernatural forces" and the "miraculous intervention of mystical factors." They are seen as believers in the "magical rituals of lighting candles, laying crosses, and making pilgrimages to fight off evil forces." They disseminate "collective irrationalism, firm in the belief that an act of faith can overturn relations of power, laws of economics, and all the rules governing the sphere of politics." Solidarity supporters are thus the belated offspring of the Counterreformation's triumph over the Renaissance. In August 1980, just as in centuries past, the Roman Catholic Counterreformation turned the Pole's thinking Renaissance brain into a "stone-age head, set in motion only by greed and superstition, closed to the world of progress."

3. This and other quotations in this section are from Part One of Andrzej Wasilewski, *Wschód, zachód, i Polska* [East, West, and Poland] (Warsaw: PIW, 1985). Wasilewski at this time was Communist Party secretary in charge of cultural affairs.—TRANS.

It made the Pole into a warrior against heresy, a fanatical believer in Polish messianism, and a national megalomaniac "locked up tight as a coffin in a trap of insolent religious bigotry."

Once again, argue the Party publicists, Polish Catholicism has become the source of national misfortune. It is Catholicism, they say, that has turned "the worship of work, rationalism, and practical know-how" into a philosophy of Poland as the Front Line against paganism, into "worship of sword, Providence, and the spoils of war." Returning to haunt us are the Halloween meetings by the graves of the dead, where "patriotic religious commemorations turn into hysterical miracle plays" and the spirit of the "irrational martyrs' crusade" emerges triumphant.

How terrible are these Catholic clergymen! "Swept away by the counterreformationist spirit, their voices filled with a celestial bliss so profound that it seems to elevate them to heaven, these preachers perform true hermeneutic miracles, discovering sections of the Bible that were 'obviously' written about present-day Poland, about the satanic powers that imprison Poland, about Poland's own 'Way of the Cross' to resurrection." In this way the "parochial paradigm" stays intact, entailing a politicized Church with political customs saturated in the cult of ritual and marked by an obsession with mission and a worshipping attitude toward myths and symbols.

Contemporary Polish mythology becomes but a spiritual petrifaction of bygone ages: "a half-secular, half-religious mixture of miracle with mission. The missionary factor leads people to embark on even the most absurd kinds of activism, while the miracle factor allows people to assume that everything will somehow work itself out."

Naturally, the process of recovering national memory, the work of the uncensored mind, is labeled by Party publicists "a crime against the Polish mentality." The opposition's charge of "sovietization" they see as nothing more than "the evasiveness of a self-deceiving consciousness, hardened in an archaic stereotype and hopelessly trying to maintain good feelings about itself by casting blame on an external factor."

"It is strange," concludes the Party publicist, "that the Polish intelligentsia, always calling itself the guardian of progress, opposed by the nature of its vocation to the blind alleys of fanaticism, prejudice, and bias, for the most part still does not perceive the dangerously swelling obscurantist tide, covered as it is with a deceptively romantic gilding."

VI

These comments can be treated in two different ways. On the one hand, we can reject them as evidence of a hypocritical and servile consciousness, intentionally dishonest and necessarily obsequious. On the other hand, we can try to see these comments as a poor caricature of genuine dangers, a kind of distorting mirror of our own authentic fears. We can also see them as a warning, for these words are a logical development of the anticlerical stereotypes held by the Polish intelligentsia—a tendentious and extremely one-sided extrapolation, but a legitimate and consistent one nevertheless. They thus give us a picture of the trap that awaits any intellectual commentary on the clericalization of Polish political thought. It is all too easy, sliding into this stereotypical image, to speak about Catholic obscurantism and say nothing about the power of Catholic faith and hope, to go on and on about Catholic intolerance and pass over the record of Catholic charity and fraternal solidarity, to keep alive the memory of the inquisitorial stakes and erase from memory the images of Catholic martyrdom. We ourselves have witnessed such a stereotypical presentation of history.

This problem has a long and complicated past, where we find both the original model for the Party publicists' vision and an outline of our own present dilemmas. We need only reach for the old issues of *Kuźnica,* probably the most interesting journal of postwar Polish Marxism, that played an important though sad chapter in the history of the Polish intelligentsia. Here we find numerous articles in which enthusiastic supporters of the first years of the Vanguard System speak of Catholicism as a "dead ideology" trying to "delay social progress." It was not without irritation that this group witnessed the formation, around *Tygodnik Powszechny,* of a "paradoxical sect of intellectual friends of the Church." *Kuźnica* considered Stefan Kisielewski the *enfant terrible* of this "sect," which was said to consider the concept of God "the most embarrassing part" of Catholicism, while considering the Church itself as the sole defender of human rights, with Catholic morality allegedly constituting the only hope of salvaging human dignity. "It is amazing how many Catholics there are today," *Kuźnica* needled Kisielewski, "who in the past might have been suspected of everything—except of adherence to biblical morality."

Kisielewski did not seem to mind such attacks. He had chosen to ally himself with the Catholic milieu because he considered Catholicism an idea that was both universalist and deeply rooted in the

Polish national consciousness. It could withstand the test of modernity while boasting a two-thousand-year-old tradition. It had even been able to withstand the test of war and revolution and to reconcile individualism with concern for the social good. Catholicism, therefore, seemed to him the right idea for the struggle against totalitarianism.

Kisiel [as he was affectionately known in Poland—TRANS.] was well aware that his particular brand of Catholicism could be controversial among Roman Catholics. For them Catholicism was a religion, not a way of thinking about politics, economics, or culture. It is true, he admitted, that "Catholicism is first of all a matter of faith, revelation, and grace." And yet "not every individual Catholic knows how to partake of that grace, and not every one is a conscious, practicing Catholic." For many people it is enough just to be formed by Catholicism. "The Church has followers and adherents among nonpracticing Catholics, too," wrote Kisielewski. "A secular journalist wishing to promulgate the Catholic worldview and its political implications has the right to address himself to this group."

Catholicism, in this view, appears as the sole foundation on which to base Polish political thought. According to Kisiel, "It is the Church around which nations gather during periods of great change and catastrophe, when the future appears dark and dismal, traditions are sundered, and the very continuity of national life seems in jeopardy." This is the source of the rising authority of the Church. Many found refuge and solace in Catholicism, including those "who in difficult and complex times want to maintain a clear view of things, who want to keep their calm and control in the face of events, who maintain their respect and admiration of the past while willing to make certain adaptations to the demands of the present, who need authority, hierarchy, and a firm stand on the issues." The Catholic camp is also open to adherents of "secular humanist freedom movements, who consider the defense of individual rights and dignity as their main task." European humanism, after all, arose from the seed of Christian morality. "Although much of the religious ritual and dogma is alien to many secular activists," Kisielewski noted, "the core of Christian morality contained in the Ten Commandments is and will remain the most brilliant and most concise expression of the moral achievements of the European citizen."

It is indeed worthwhile reading Kisielewski's old texts. They help us understand how the Polish intellectual can coexist peacefully with the Church in the face of totalitarian dictatorship.

We can also detect a turn to Catholicism in the *Wiadomości Lit-*

erackie [Literary News] circle, an important intellectual group that found itself in exile after the war. Indeed, a most diverse group of people came to consider the Church the main pillar of Polishness and the chief source of resistance to sovietization. Kisiel, of course, was a tough act to follow. This inimitable mixture of conservative and libertarian brought to Catholic cultural circles the full breadth of his heretical personality: he provoked conflicts, aroused scandals—and was always tolerated. The group of "catechumens" around *Tygodnik Powszechny* (including Zbigniew Herbert, Jan Józef Szczepański, and Leopold Tyrmand) only partially followed in Kisiel's steps. They usually chose their own paths. And it is important, in light of today's dilemmas, to consider these paths, as well as to reflect on editor Jerzy Turowicz's tolerance for these "nonconfessional" collaborators of *Tygodnik Powszechny*.

Yet an equally important task is to think through the caustic words of Witold Gombrowicz. With whom was Gombrowicz quarreling?

VII

Church steeples continued to hover over sovietized Poland. And towering over the Church was the great figure of Primate Stefan Wyszyński. What did *he* think about Communism?

For Wyszyński, the heart of the Polish misfortune was the conflict between "Christianity and godlessness." "If we are to be prepared for this conflict," he wrote in his diary, "we need time to build up God's side." This is how every Catholic bishop understood matters. But Wyszyński went further. He considered the "reform of socioeconomic structures" a necessity. He was ready to support the official reform program, but he felt that the government's "stifling programmatic atheism poses an obstacle." He was, of course, aware of other obstacles, such as "repressive prosecution, the destruction of complex social life, the liquidation of political parties and of free trade unions." Marxism's atheism, however, remained for Wyszyński the main obstacle. In January 1953, soon before his arrest, Primate Wyszyński met for discussions with government representative Franciszek Mazur. Andrzej Micewski, the primate's biographer, summarizes Wyszyński's comments during these discussions as follows:

In the Primate's opinion, Marxism arose on Protestant-Anglican ground and was applied on Russian orthodox ground, and this was one of the factors that made Marxism hostile to Catholicism. Polish Marxists must therefore change their attitude toward Catholicism. Yet because of old nineteenth-century legacies—when struggles between Freemasons and the Church, and between individualism and religion, were fashionable—they cannot do so easily. There is, however, no necessary connection between atheism and Marxism, and even less so between atheism and the new social order. . . . Marxism's atheism only delays social reconstruction and economic prosperity. The struggle against the Church alienates the country's finest people and promotes rigid thinking and spiritual barrenness.

So spoke the primate to the representative of Communist authority. There is no reason to doubt that he was being sincere. Yet there was also a tactical consideration in these words, as the Cardinal wanted to halt the governments's harshly repressive policies against the Church. As he watched the ongoing sovietization of the country, the primate became fully convinced of the "special link between Church and Nation." In this extraordinary situation, the Church, as the sole independent institution, had to take on the role of de facto representative of the nation and defender of the national identity. For millions of Poles, the primate was the leader of the nation, the *inter-rex* in a peculiar *interregnum*. He was the symbol of Polish resistance.

And in this role he told the Polish people: Defend your endangered national tradition, persevere in the Catholic faith of your fathers, and rally together around the Church. Only in this way, he believed, could Poles maintain their own identity. The primate therefore prayed for Poland by recalling its historical destiny:

On this day of thanks for the victory at Chocim,[4] only the Church in Poland offers its prayers to the God who defended us. Do any of the great 'patriots' of today even think of such things? And yet maybe this is what decided the future cultural development of central Europe. . . .

I thank Thee for the force of faith that resisted force, for that laudable idealism that put entire lineages on the battlefields and sacrificed the sons of more than one family. I thank Thee for the strength Thou instilled in the wings of the hussars. I hear their song and I see them galloping to victory. Let all of this sing to Thee, Father of Nations. And while I thank Thee for the past, I beg Thee also remember the struggle we wage today, for a Poland that is not overrun by foreign perfidy, materialist brutality, or semi-educated

4. Refers to an important Polish victory against Turkish Ottoman forces in the seventeenth century.—TRANS.

haughtiness and conceit. A terrible force is gaining, terrorizing even the good and the brave. Father and Lord, lay claim to Thy People.

In writing these words during his imprisonment, Cardinal Wyszyński expressed the emotions of the tormented Polish people. But contrary to the fears of the imprisoned Cardinal, a significant part of the public thought exactly the same way about God and Fatherland.

Witold Gombrowicz, meanwhile, made exactly this way of thinking about Catholicism and captive Poland the object of critical reflection.

VIII

"Today's Poland," wrote Gombrowicz in 1953, "is a piece of stale bread which breaks into two halves with a snap: the believing and the nonbelieving."[5] Yet this dividing line concerned one's attitude toward Communism, not religion. Polish thought had been stopped in its tracks, paralyzed by Communism. "Thus," Gombrowicz continued,

we are allowed to think about Catholicism only as a force capable of resisting, and God has become the pistol with which we would like to shoot Marx. This is a holy secret, which bows the heads of exquisite Masons, drives the anticleric wit out of lay feuilletons, dictates moving stanzas to the Virgin Mother to the poet Lechon, restores a stirring First Holy Communion innocence to socialist-atheist professors, and, in general, is the miracle worker of which philosophers have long dreamed. (*Diary,* 1:27)

A prayer of thanks for the victory at Chocim? For Gombrowicz that is a sign of mental impoverishment. He loved to write about all the anniversary celebrations in Warsaw, where, "having sung the Rota and danced the *Krakówiaczek,*" the participants fulfilled their patriotic duty by extolling the bygone superiority of Polish arms and the deceased Bards, of Chopin and the Wawel, of Copernicus and the May 3 Constitution of 1791. "But I," wrote Gombrowicz,

felt this ritual as if it were born of hell, this national Mass became something satanically sneering and maliciously grotesque. For they, in elevating Mickiewicz, were denigrating themselves and with their praise of Chopin showed that they had not yet sufficiently matured to appreciate him and that by

5. Witold Gombrowicz, *Diary: Volume One,* translated by Lillian Vallee (Evanston: Northwestern University Press, 1988), p. 27. [Hereafter cited in the text with a parenthetical reference to volume and page number. Passages lacking such citation are my own translation.—TRANS.]

basking in their own culture, they were simply baring their primitiveness. (*Diary*, 1:5)

"What," asks Gombrowicz, "does Mr. Kowalski [a Polish John Doe—TRANS.] have in common with Chopin? Does Chopin's composition of the ballads raise Mr. Kowalski's specific weight by even one iota? Can the Siege of Vienna augment Mr. Ziębicki of Radom by even an ounce of glory?" (*Diary*, 1:7). Of course not. Every person answers for himself; each should be proud or ashamed of his own actions. No one is going to judge the Polish people on the basis of Chopin or Sobieski, but on the basis of what they themselves do today. And what do they do? They sit paralyzed by a Polish-Catholic form, which is but a sign of their own immaturity, a symbol of sterility, a way to avoid a creative existence. Polish life in emigration is suffused with a hospital spirit, where patients receive only dietary portions.

Why open wounds? Why add more rawness to the wound life has already afflicted upon us and, after all, shouldn't we behave politely now that we have gotten spanked? Nothing but Christian goodness, decency, temperance, common sense, and virtue reign here so that everything that is written is nothing if not charitable. So many virtues! We were not this virtuous when we were surer of our ground. I do not trust virtue in those who have failed, virtue born of poverty. (*Diary*, 1:4)

Gombrowicz's cutting approach did not mean a declaration of war against Roman Catholicism. He had, he emphasized, no sympathy with Boy-Żeleński's campaign against "the black occupation"[6] (*Diary*, 1:29). He argued only against a specific kind of Catholicism:

If, in my opinion, Catholicism has done great harm to Polish development, then it is because Catholicism was reduced in us to a dimension of too easy and too serene a philosophy, which is at the service of life and its immediate needs. (*Diary*, 1:30)

This was the side of Catholicism represented by the traditional Church hierarchy in Poland, the side that was thoroughly alien to the author of *Ferdydurke*. Yet historical events revealed other sides of Catholicism to Gombrowicz. In an age of wars and revolutions, of political mysticisms and totalitarian faiths, the ideal of human progress—enlightened, humanistic, and rational—became radically relativized. While such values were certainly worth respecting, what

6. Refers to the color of clerics' customary attire.—TRANS.

was most important for Gombrowicz was "that the other man not bite me, spit on me, or torture me to death." Here came the encounter with Catholicism: concerning the "acute sense of hell" present in human nature, and a "fear of man's excessive dynamics" (*Diary*, 1:30). But Gombrowicz was put off by the Church's view that the ideal Catholic is the person "who believes, who wants to believe and will not entertain any other thought except the one that dogma will not include in its prohibitory index" (*Diary*, 1:27–28). Gombrowicz wanted to reverse this perspective: "The question that I put to Catholics is not what kind of God do they believe in, but what kind of people do they aspire to be?" (*Diary*, 1:30).

And what happened?

We were horrified to see that we were surrounded by an abyss made of millions of ignorant minds, which steal away our truths in order to pervert, diminish, and transform them into instruments of their passions. We discovered that the number of people is far more significant than the quality of the truth. That is why we have such a violent need of a basic and simple language, so that it could be the place where the philosopher comes together with the illiterate. And that is why we admire Christianity, which is a wisdom tailored to all minds, a song for all voices from the highest to the lowest, a wisdom that does not have to change itself into stupidity at any level of awareness. Yet, if someone were to tell me that there can be no genuine understanding between a man who is spiritually free and the dogmatic man, I would say to him: Take a closer look at Catholics. They also exist in time and are subjected to its effects. (*Diary*, 1:31)

Unexpectedly, a "profound and tragic Catholicism" was revealed to this secular humanist, this student of Rabelais and Montaigne—a Catholicism that responded to totalitarianism and the crisis of culture with an evolution similar to that of the humanists. And in this way, Christian "teaching, which was the undoing of the Roman Empire, is our ally in the struggle to destroy all those too lofty edifices that we build today and in the struggle to attain nakedness and simplicity and ordinary, elementary virtue" (*Diary*, 1:30–31).

Was Gombrowicz right? And, more important, what exactly did his proposal entail?

For Cardinal Wyszyński it was obvious that in the conflict with communist atheism the coherence of the resisting nation had to be strengthened. Communism, for the primate, was a system based on the corruption of the nation, a system in which an alien power violates and torments the nation, a system in which Poles "continually live like cattle."

For Gombrowicz, communism was a system that "subordinates man to a human collectivity," and thus, for him, "the best way to fight communism is to strengthen the individual against the masses" (*Diary,* 1:18).

The differences are neither superficial nor insignificant. Cardinal Wyszyński sought to sustain the traditional Polish cultural model, which he felt was the source of Polish strength. Gombrowicz sought to lay bare and annihilate this model ("the Polish form"), which he felt was the source of Polish weakness. For Cardinal Wyszyński, Henryk Sienkiewicz was the Polish "commander without a post," teaching the nation to serve "God and Fatherland." For Gombrowicz, Sienkiewicz was the opposite of Catholic profundity, and rather "like a woman who maintains purity in thought and deed not to please God, but because instinct assures her that it pleases men" (*Diary,* 1:228). For Wyszyński, Sienkiewicz was the first "commander" to mobilize Polish youth around the struggle for freedom, the one who aroused the national conscience. For Gombrowicz, he was the one who "beautified history, . . . simplified people, . . . fed Poles the steak of naive illusions, . . . put the conscience to sleep, stifled thought, and impeded progress" (*Diary,* 1:228).

Today, then, when we call Cardinal Wyszyński the Primate of the Millennium, and when no one questions Gombrowicz's towering place in the pantheon of Polish literature, let us ask: Which one of them was right?

IX

The poet Aleksander Wat, author of perhaps the most profound of the many Polish reckonings with Communism, considered Gombrowicz completely useless in the struggle against totalitarianism. It is not rebellion, said Wat, that has been the mainstay of the nation, but rather the Polish practice of

separating itself from the enemy, and that meant precisely this mass Catholicism of the nation—this parochial, obscurantist and so often sordid Polish Catholicism—that purified and strengthened itself "in the catacombs" and found its true pastor in the person of Primate Wyszyński. This Catholicism made the Polish soul impenetrable to the magic of "ideology" and the whip of "praxis." The Polish October was caused not by rebellious writers and revisionists, but, together with the crumbling of the strength and coherence of Stalinism, by the persistent, unremitting, and relentless psychological resistance of the Catholic nation.

Wat formulated this notion in 1965 or a little later. For him, it was the culmination of a long and difficult road from Communism to the truths of the Roman Catholic faith. Was it, however, an accurate description of the situation?

Cardinal Wyszyński, on the one hand, attached the utmost significance to the concept of the "national community," which arose, he said, "from the blood of the sons of the Polish land." The nation strengthens itself not by internal divisions but by "collective love for the Motherland which has suckled us, and which we are sometimes obliged to nourish . . . with our own blood."

Gombrowicz, on the other hand, asked Poles the following: "If you had been told that in order to remain Polish you had to give up part of your humanity—that is, that you could stay Polish only on the condition that you became worse human beings, somewhat less talented, less rational, less dignified—would you make such a sacrifice in order to preserve Poland?" For Gombrowicz, values such as these "have an absolute character and cannot be dependent upon anything. The person who says that only Poland endows him with reason or dignity is in fact just abandoning his own reason and dignity."

In other words, in the conflict with Communism, Gombrowicz did not consider it sufficient to withdraw intellectually into the world of the national-religious tradition. Those bounds seemed too cramped for him. The "Polish-Catholic" form he considered culturally barren, incapable of grasping reality, unable to provide an unqualified defense of fundamental values. While Cardinal Wyszyński was celebrating the tenacity of the national community threatened by communist atheism, and Aleksander Wat was singing the praises of the parochial and obscurantist spirit of a nation that had just endured totalitarianism, Witold Gombrowicz was citing with approval the following diagnosis, by one of his Polish correspondents, of the psychological state of the Polish people:

My God, this Poland is the grim dream of a madman! So gloomy, suffocating, uncertain, and boring. . . . This new *Pol'sza* makes me laugh because, God is my witness, the Saxon period has stayed with us the longest and has left the deepest imprint. The nation is ignorant, Endek, truculent, boorish, lazy, belligerent, half-baked, sanctimonious, and "infantile"—and now a dose of Kremlin communism has been added to this mess. Only now how the dust must fly from those besotted heads! (*Diary*, 2:85)[7]

7. Translation slightly amended.—TRANS.

Gombrowicz wrote these words in 1958. The events of ten years later, of March 1968, force us to look back at these words more closely. The spirit of obscurantism proved to be an ambiguous ally of the Polish cause.

Gombrowicz pointed very early to the dangers hidden in the stereotypical anti-Communism of the Polish Catholic. Thus he appealed to fellow Poles that they learn how to discover a person instead of a Pole, that they free themselves from this oppressive national-religious form, that they replace the moribund conservatism of their fathers with a faith in themselves and in the liberating youth of their sons, that they replace the fatherland with the "sonland."

In rereading today the blasphemies of Gombrowicz, we need to keep in mind the context in which his words were written. Gombrowicz's lampooning of the Polish intelligentsia constituted above all a rejection of totalitarianism and its destructive consequences. The world of Polish affairs seemed to him a battleground between those who had shamefully decided to serve Communism, and those who, in desperation, chose a hollow form of resistance as mindless servants of national-religious stereotypes.

X

Let us disregard the fact that this was a rather simplified diagnosis and focus instead on the conclusions that Gombrowicz drew. At the high-point of Stalinism, he addressed his fellow intellectuals with this characteristic appeal:

Pharisees! If you really need your Catholicism, then gather up a bit more courage and try sincerely to become Catholics. But don't do it for tactical reasons alone. My position is that whatever happens in our spiritual life should happen in the deepest and most honest way. The moment has come in which atheists should seek a new understanding with the Church.

And how did Cardinal Wyszyński perceive the attitude of the intelligentsia in those years? He believed, to quote Micewski,

that Poland has in fact not yet had a Catholic intelligentsia. Its educated circles have always succumbed to moral and intellectual relativism. This has been particularly apparent in key historical moments, when the intelligentsia absents itself in the fight for Catholic ideals.

The intelligentsia, said the primate, places great demands upon the clergy but is itself nowhere to be found. Its distaste for Communism does not prevent it from filling ideological orders, or from writing anti-church brochures. The intelligentsia senses that "only the Church" can save Poland, but it itself stays apart from this Church. The intellectual comes to the Church seeking "political thrills," but does not particularly lead a life of grace. And yet grace is the chief strength of the Church.

How's this for unexpected accord! Cardinal Wyszyński, the architect of a Catholic order in Poland, and Witold Gombrowicz, the agnostic enemy of Polish forms, both criticize Polish intellectuals for a spiritually shallow and politically superficial relationship to the Church. Today, when the question of the relationship between intellectuals and the Church is once again on the agenda, it is worth keeping in mind these two kinds of criticisms. Do they not constitute a different formulation of the same accusation: a "second betrayal by the intellectuals"?

In speaking about this betrayal, we are, of course, not speaking about religious conversion. We are well aware that a practicing Catholic, lay or clergy, need not adhere to a clerical vision of the social order. The encounter with God does not require abandoning one's humanist identity. We speak about "betrayal" only with regard to a particular kind of conversion, political rather than religious. Such conversion means one is rejecting truth, as it is normally understood, for tactical political reasons. It means abandoning pluralism and the principle of inalienable human rights.

One can go to church for various reasons. I might, for example, go because I see the Church as a force playing a key role on the Polish political stage. The problem is that the Church is not and does not want to be a political force. My intentions, therefore, place me in an ambiguous situation. I must disguise my motives, pretend to be a Catholic, and use a language that endows Catholicism with the voice of a political sect. I will then have to say that the specter of an "Iranian syndrome" is but an "invention of the secular Left," that every criticism of the Church is empirical proof of a conspiracy of atheists and Freemasons, and that only cosmopolitans and Bolshevik agents perceive a narrow-minded xenophobia threatening Polish sensibility.

But I can also go to church for quite different reasons. I might seek an ally there for the view that the world needs truth because only truth can set us free, that it needs tolerance and compromise because only thus can a democratic order be born, and that it needs a firm separation between good and evil because only in this way can the moral norms of my culture be salvaged. Going to church for these reasons, I am decisively rejecting the kind of relativism that makes one's moral assessment of reality dependent on the political interests of a party, class, nation, or whatever. There are, of course, different kinds of relativisms: the relativism of Gombrowicz, which is a spiritual search, and the relativism of the nihilist, which is moral capitulation. To quote Leszek Kołakowski:

> If we abandon the view that there is a difference between good and evil—a *real* difference, apparent in the world, that has nothing to do with our own choices and that we cannot continually redefine according to our fluctuating predilections (and it does not matter whether our view derives from a religious conviction or as an imperative of Kantian practical reason)—then there can be nothing to morally restrain us from participating in anything.

Without moral standards, any action can be justified as long as it serves a cause, "whose victory becomes by definition morally justified, even if it bears the name of Hitler or Stalin."

And so I repeat, also following Leszek Kołakowski, that the world needs the realm of the sacred, for perfect rationality is a suicidal ideal.

So even if I am led to church by Kantian moral imperative, I go not to be on the side of force but on the side of truth. And thus I have to speak the truth—even where it concerns the Church.

I should now say something about my own attitude toward the blasphemies of Gombrowicz, as well as toward the moral-patriotic teachings of Cardinal Wyszyński.

It is easier for me to speak about Gombrowicz. I do not agree with Aleksander Wat, who said that people such as Gombrowicz "only nip in the bud" the independent culture reemerging in the vise of totalitarian Communism. In fact, I believe exactly the opposite. Gombrowicz, to quote the words of Jerzy Jarzębski, "inspired the generation that has defended itself against the omnipotence of Doctrine and its Institutions. He is the catalyst of rebellion." Gombrowicz has always inspired resistance against the fictitious cultural life of officialdom. It was he who set in motion the good fight against what Miłosz called the "Polish rituals of nationalist impoverishment." And it is his words that uncompromisingly insist on sincerity and spiritual bravery, on overcoming one's own limitations, and on an authentic and creative existence against the Polish form of "mug" and the Polish form of "fanny."[8]

8. Terms from Gombrowicz's novel *Ferdydurke*.—TRANS.

What would Polish culture be without Gombrowicz? What would it be without his diabolical wit and his devilishly perceptive intelligence? It would be a culture crippled, amputated, with half a brain and half a heart. For Gombrowicz, while questioning everything around him, "never," wrote Miłosz, "doubted one thing: pain, and this wonderful pain made the world real again."

Yet could Gombrowicz's intellectual project have become universally accepted? Could his "interpersonal church" substitute for the real Church? Such questions, though obviously poorly formulated, lead to the more important question of the role of a jester Don Quixote within an endangered Polish culture. Does our culture really need such people?

I consider it highly likely that the Catholic Church *had* to be what it was: somewhat parochial and somewhat obscurantist. Not only could it not be Gombrowiczian, but even a Jerzy Turowicz had to appear in it as some kind of dangerous innovator. And perhaps it was just this kind of Church, unchanging and set in its ways, that could save Polish society from spiritual sovietization. Yet if so, what does this imply for the Polish intellectual?

An intellectual must retain an essential loyalty to his subjugated nation. He may not dabble in theory when a crime is taking place, yet neither may he settle for an elementary moral stance alone.

Witold Gombrowicz stood in solidarity with his nation against totalitarian pressure, never failing to call a crime a crime. And yet he had to rebel against the style of Polish resistance if he wanted to remain loyal to his own artistic conscience. Gombrowicz retained a fundamentally ambivalent attitude toward the Polish and Catholic archetypes of the national consciousness. Could it have been otherwise?

Here we stand before the most troubling questions, those concerning the ambiguities present in the Roman Catholic tradition. For it is easy to see, as we observe the evolution of Church language over the past fifty years, that the previously accursed idea of human rights has now obtained its full civil rights: today it stands at the center of Christian thought. And it is the same in Poland. A certain Franciscan monk, who, in the dark chambers of that model totalitarian civilization known as Auschwitz, sacrificed his own life for that of another, has been canonized and surrounded by a cult. This fact has its symbolic dimension. Professor Father Józef Tischner, a leading figure of Polish Catholicism, sees in this martyr of Auschwitz "a living embodiment of our Polish philosophy of man, a philosophy that lies somewhere deep in our blood, but has never been fully described." It is this martyr, Father Maksymilian Kolbe, who is said to have "discovered the Polish way out of our Polish crisis of hope."

Cardinal Wyszyński, I think, would have agreed. I doubt, however, that Witold Gombrowicz would have accepted this claim—or, for that matter, Czesław Miłosz, Leszek Kołakowski, or Jan Józef Szczepański, or our intellectual who goes to church in search of truth. And the reason they would not accept the claim is not because what Father Tischner says is false, but because it is a truth tainted by what it leaves unsaid.

"The secular world," wrote Jan Józef Szczepański in his essay on Father Kolbe, "probably needs sainthood today more than any time in the past. I suspect, however, that *less* than anytime in the past it needs hagiography."

Maksymilian Kolbe's heroic choice of martyrdom was an extraordinary act, and no murderous dialectic or cunning "demystification" can gainsay that. Not even what we know of Father Kolbe's political record can alter this assessment. And yet that record, whether we like it or not, is also part of our contemporary history. For Szczepański, the prewar activities of Father Kolbe are part of a "rather disturbing" tendency of Polish Catholicism, a tendency associated with "counterreformationist excesses, Sarmatianism, the political activities of the extreme right, . . . and various chauvinist and anti-intellectual movements." Such company, Szczepański continues, "does not at all undermine the boundless respect that Father Kolbe has earned." Nevertheless, he adds, "the qualms that remain— the feeling, which I cannot overcome, that something here is not quite right—should not be ignored."

I agree with Szczepański. If Father Maksymilian Kolbe is, as Father Tischner insists, a symbol of the "Polish horizon of hope," then conscience dictates there be an honest reckoning with the legacy of Polish Catholicism's ties with national-chauvinist doctrines and politics. Times have changed and the post-conciliar Church has changed, and the historical record of that old way of thinking is now just so much troubling baggage for modern hagiographers of the Franciscan saint. Yet contemporary Church teaching still does not include a critical assessment of that reactionary tradition.

I am not quite sure how to react to Father Tischner's observations. His silence concerning this old Roman Catholic baggage of chauvinism and intolerance is striking. Father Tischner finds it easier to dismiss my fears of Catholic obscurantism than to judge, from a

Catholic perspective, the former appeals to boycott Jewish stores, to isolate Jews in university "bench ghettos," and to "pacify" Ukrainian villages. But then it is certainly easier to repeat that "we did not kill our kings" than to remind one's readers of the murder of President Narutowicz, or to say "we did not finish off the wounded" than to say something about the pogroms in Przytyk and Kielce, or to denounce ex-Marxists than to peer deeply and critically into the difficult truth of one's own foundations.[9]

I can understand, although I cannot accept, this kind of selectiveness in the teachings of Primate Wyszyński. But I cannot for the life of me understand why Father Tischner avoids such questions, so essential for the self-examination of our national conscience. Does he too want to sacrifice truth to hagiography?

In polemicizing with Father Tischner, I am not making my life any easier. I am posing these questions to a renowned philosopher and heralded preacher whom I admire and respect. Nevertheless, I wonder whether some small part of the responsibility for the errant paths and wrong choices made by many young people today may not be traced to the silence of such indisputable moral and intellectual authorities like Father Józef Tischner.

And again I wonder, what would Polish culture be without the Quixote-like frankness of Witold Gombrowicz?

XI

I am afraid of "intellectual betrayals," both the first kind and the second kind. Let the spirit of Cardinal Wyszyński protect us from the first, and let the penetrating sarcasm of Witold Gombrowicz guard us against the second. Contemporary Polish culture exists between these two great figures. We too, the Polish "indomitable" intellectuals, live between the prayers of Cardinal Wyszyński and the jeers of Witold Gombrowicz, between the truth of the Priest and the truth of the Jester. And we need both of these truths, because each of them, in its own way, teaches us modesty and humility.

What kind of intellectual strategy ought to be adopted by today's Polish intellectual who rejects the totalitarian government, looks

---

9. Gabriel Narutowicz, Poland's first president in the new, post–World-War-I republic, was assassinated in 1922 one week after taking office. Przytyk and Kielce were sites of anti-Jewish pogroms in Poland soon after the defeat of the Nazis.—TRANS.

hopefully and sympathetically to the Church, and seeks a way to be present in the antitotalitarian resistance movement?

Primate Wyszyński and Witold Gombrowicz would both, I think, say that one must first of all maintain one's modesty. Leszek Kołakowski, who wrote a wonderful synthesis of the Priest and the Jester, could have said the same thing. Our intellectual should keep foremost in mind the various historical moments when European intellectuals joined up with totalitarian movements. He should keep before him the image of all those who donned red or black shirts, whether due to ideological fascination or pragmatic rationalization. He should remember, as Kołakowski put it, that when "intellectuals try to become popular leaders or professional politicians, the results are usually not encouraging. In the end it is the marketplace, with all of its dangers, that is the more appropriate place for them than the royal court." This rule retains its validity even with regard to those elevated to power by revolutionary movements, and even with regard to the Church elite.

And so, you homeless but undefeated intellectual—what are you to be? You can say, following Cardinal Wyszyński, that the people need the sacred, and also, following Gombrowicz, that it is important to mock the sacred, but are you then just one of those who say that the masses need piety while intellectuals need free-thinking skepticism? Are you one of the "born again," motivated, as Kołakowski has written, by an "inconsistent desire to manipulate"? "There is something disturbingly depressing," writes Kołakowski,

about intellectuals who themselves lack faith or religious loyalties, yet who never fail to emphasize the irreplaceable moral and didactic role of religion in the world; people who lament the tenuousness of religion while constituting outstanding examples of this tenuousness themselves. I am not criticizing them for not being religious, or for the fact that they speak about the essential value of religious experiences. I am just not convinced that they can help bring about the changes they feel are necessary. For it is not enough to have an intellectual conviction about the social utility of faith. One must have faith in order to propagate faith.

Here is where your troubles are, lost intellectual. You read in these words a call to convert, and it is indeed hard to read them otherwise. And yet you know how dangerous and treacherous certain kinds of conversions can be for you. You also know that the act of conversion will not automatically solve your troubles. So be grateful if you find God. But also be grateful for the grace of the quest. And answer Leszek Kołakowski in the words of Thomas Mann: that religious conviction for you means

recognizing and obeying: recognizing the inner changes of the world, the reforming of the ideals of truth and justice; and obeying the call to make life and reality conform to these changes, in order to satisfy the spirit.

The point, you should explain, is not to flatter your own epoch, whose favors you can obtain only at the cost of lies. It is a matter of "not living in sin," since, as Mann noted, "to live in sin means to live against the spirit, to hold onto outmoded and backward things due to inattention and disobedience."

Since Thomas Mann was himself an ironical skeptic, you know that his words are not unproblematic. Skepticism and irony, after all, can lead either to base capitulation or to a heroic duel with the world. Deaf to the callings of God, the ironical skeptic may find the Kantian imperative within and can fashion it into a weapon against the abject might of totalitarian civilization. Such skepticism is a child of pride as well as of humility. It is a Mannian "piety that is a kind of wisdom."

Be pious then, proud intellectual, but do not renounce your skepticism—at least not in the sphere of political involvement. Participate in the antitotalitarian community, but do not abandon your homelessness. Remain loyal to your national roots, but do not give up your eternal unrootedness. Bring the stark simplicity of biblical commandments (where yes means yes and no means no) into a world swimming in moral norms, but treat the deadened world of officially codified values to the laugh of the jester and the doubts of the skeptic. It is not your lot, after all, to commemorate political victories or flatter your own nation. It is for you to maintain faith in defeated positions, to say unpleasant things, to arouse objections.

You are supposed to get flogged by friend and foe alike—"because this alone is how you will attain the good you will not attain."

GLOSSARY OF NAMES

ABRAMOWSKI, Edward Józef (1868–1918)

Philosopher, sociologist, professor of psychology at Warsaw University, and influential socialist theorist. With anarchist leanings inspired by French syndicalists, Abramowski became the major theorist of Polish cooperativism and non-statist socialism and was extremely influential for Michnik.

AJDUKIEWICZ, Kazimierz (1890–1963)

Philosopher, logician, and founder of Polish logical-positivism.

ANDERS, General Władysław (1892–1970)

Imprisoned by Soviets soon after World War II began, Anders became commander-in-chief of a new Polish army, formed on Soviet territory in 1942, that went on to fight in the Middle East and Italy. After the war, he came to symbolize anti-Communist hopes and resistance.

ANDRZEJEWSKI, Jerzy (1909–1983)

Novelist. While his prewar novel, *Heart's Harmony,* was inspired by Catholicism and drew critical acclaim, Andrzejewski was quickly drawn to Communism after the war and became one of the most important pro-regime writers until he left the Party in 1957. Model for "Alpha" in Czesław Miłosz's *The Captive Mind.* Active in the opposition in the 1970s and one of the founders of KOR (Workers' Defense Committee) in 1977. Works include *Ashes and Diamonds, Gates of Paradise,* and *Pulp.*

ANEKS

Political quarterly founded in 1973 by group of young, left-leaning intellectuals who left Poland after 1968, edited by Aleksander Smolar.

ASKENAZY, Szymon (1866–1935)

Historian, diplomat, and minister plenipotentiary at League of Nations (1920–23). Author of books on eighteenth- and nineteenth-century Polish history.

BARAŃCZAK, Stanisław (b. 1946)

Poet and literary critic, active in student movement of 1968. A PZPR member in his youth, Barańczak became active in the opposition movement of the 1970s as a leading contributor to the underground press and as a founding member of KOR. Professor of Slavic Literature at Harvard University since 1981, he is the editor of *Polish Review* and a frequent contributor to *Salmagundi* and *Partisan Review*.

BECK, Józef (1894–1944)

Polish Minister of Foreign Affairs from 1932 to 1939.

BIAŁOSZEWSKI, Miron (1922–1984)

One of the most prominent and innovative Polish poets. Began publishing in 1956.

BIEŃKOWSKI, Władysław (1906–1991)

Politician, writer, revisionist Marxist. Played key role in normalizing relations between Church and state in 1956, served as Minister of Education in Gomułka's government from 1956 to 1959, after which he lent his support to democratic opposition. Author of *Motor and Brakes of Socialism, Sociology of Defeat,* and other works.

BIERUT, Bolesław (1892–1956)

Communist leader of Poland during Stalinist years. Consolidated his power with ouster of Gomułka in 1948. Died in Moscow in February 1956, just after Khrushchev's "Secret Speech" at the Twentieth Congress of the CPSU.

BOREJSZA, Jerzy (1905–1952)

Communist militant and publicist entrusted by the Party with organizing Polish intellectual life after war.

BOROWSKI, Tadeusz (1922–1951)

Writer and poet; prisoner of Nazi concentration camps (1943–45) and author of *This Way for the Gas, Ladies and Gentlemen,* harrowing stories from his camp experiences. Became an eager advocate of social realism until his death by suicide. Model for "Beta" in Czesław Miłosz's *The Captive Mind*.

BRANDYS, Kazimierz (b. 1916)

Novelist and essayist, author of socialist realist works and strong supporter of Communist regime until 1956. Later, as a revisionist oppositionist, his novels depicted the tragedies of idealistic Communists who submitted to Party discipline in all aspects of their lives.

BRANDYS, Marian (b. 1912)

Author of historical essays, chiefly on Napoleonic era.

BRUS, Włodzimierz (b. 1921)

Leading Polish economist and supporter of market socialism, member of PZPR until his expulsion in 1968 for supporting student protests. Emigrated to England, where he has continued to write on economic reform in socialist countries.

BRZOZOWSKI, Stanisław Leopold (1878–1911)

Philosopher, novelist, and literary critic influenced by Catholicism and Marxism and considered by some to be a precursor of post-Leninist Western Marxism. A very influential figure in Polish socialism. His novel *Flames* inspired a generation of prewar and wartime socialist activists.

BUREK, Tomasz (b. 1938)

Critic and essayist, who contributed to the literary review *Twórczość* and taught at the clandestine "Flying University" in the 1970s.

CATHOLIC INTELLECTUALS' CLUBS (KIK)

Founded in 1957 during the thaw in Church-state relations under Gomułka. Connected with *Znak* and *Więź*, KIK provided a forum for independent public discussion groups. People connected with these circles would play a key role in the new Church-Left dialogue discussed by Michnik. In 1980, independent trade union representatives often used KIK offices before Solidarity had space of its own.

CIOŁKOSZ, Adam (1901–1978)

Prominent PPS activist of the interwar period who left Poland during World War II and stayed in exile as leader of PPS in Great Britain. Author of many works.

CYRANKIEWICZ, Józef (1911–1989)

Prewar activist in PPS, joined PZPR after the war, and served as Prime Minister from 1947 to 1952 and from 1954 to 1970.

CYWIŃSKI, Bohdan (b. 1939)

Historian and literary critic. Author of extremely influential *Genealogies of the Indomitable* in 1974, which attempted to show the centrality of both socialist and Catholic nationalist traditions for the modern Polish intellectual. Coined notion of "Julianic Church" as a Church that speaks of democratic values but seeks only to recover lost privileges for itself. Active in opposition movement of 1970s, taught history in the "Flying University" (lecture series in private homes).

CZESZKO, Bohdan (b. 1923)

Author of novels about Nazi occupation, strong supporter of Communist system.

DĄBROWSKA, Maria (1889–1965)

Renowned writer, frequently nominated for Nobel Prize. Considered the conscience of the secular intellectual Left after 1956.

DEJMEK, Kazimierz (b. 1924)

Theatrical director of National Theater in Warsaw where, in 1968, he staged Adam Mickiewicz's classic *Forefathers' Eve*. Cancellation of this play led to the widespread student protests.

DEMBIŃSKI, Henryk (1908–1941)

Politician and publicist. Leader of the leftist Catholic organization "Renaissance" until he joined the Communist Youth Association in 1934. Imprisoned from 1937 to 1938; executed by the Nazis.

DMOWSKI, Roman (1864–1939)

Founder and leader of National Democrats, leading nationalist political party of prewar era, and one of the most important political figures of modern Poland. A key strategist of the Polish independence movement who favored an alliance with Russia. Became increasingly pro-fascist in 1930s, penning many violently anti-Semitic tracts. Author of numerous works on Polish politics.

DOJCZGEWANT, Józef (b.1946)

Radical student activist in 1968. Arrested with Michnik and served several months in jail, after which he emigrated to Sweden. His name frequently cited by official press in 1968 as "evidence" of "Zionist conspiracy" against Poland.

DYGAT, Stanisław (1914–1978)

Popular satiric writer in postwar period, "a pupil of Gombrowicz," according to Miłosz, with his "nose-thumbing at shibboleths" and "colloquial, nonchalant language"; author of novels *Constance Lake* (1946) and *Disneyland* (1965), the second of which has been translated into English as *Cloak of Illusion*.

DZIŚ I JUTRO [Today and Tomorrow]

Pro-regime weekly published from 1945 to 1956 by Bolesław Piasecki and PAX organization, aimed at "reconciling" Catholics with Communist "reality."

ELZENBERG, Henryk (1887–1967)

Philosopher of ethics and aesthetics. Quite influential in liberal Catholic circles.

FELIŃSKI, Zygmunt Szczęsny (1822–1895)

Archbishop of Warsaw. Spent twenty years in Siberian exile for supporting 1863 Insurrection against tsarist rule.

GOMBROWICZ, Witold (1904–1969)

One of the greatest (the word would make him wince) and easily the most controversial of Polish writers of the twentieth century. Fiercely irreverent in his attitude toward accepted standards of all kinds, he loathed literary rules and national shibboleths alike. His method was one of constant provocation: a recurring theme is a relentless mocking of the notion of "Polishness." He has been championed by radical intellectuals and denounced by Catholic conservatives, making his work quite a sensitive topic in Poland. Originally studied law, philosophy, and economics. Left Poland on a cruise to Argentina in the summer of 1939 and never returned.

GOMUŁKA, Władysław (1905–1982)

Leader of postwar Polish Communist movement. With a reputation for defending Polish sovereignty, supporting national rights, and being sympathetic to prewar socialist traditions, he was expelled from the PZPR in 1948, charged with "right-wing deviations," and remained under house arrest until 1956. Demands for radical change in that year led to Gomułka's return to power in October, with wide support among the people. After working with liberal and revisionist elements in the Party and liberalizing relations with the Church, he largely abandoned his reform program by 1958. He was removed from his position as leader of the Party in December 1970, days after army and police forces violently suppressed strikes and protests on the Baltic Coast, killing dozens of workers.

GROT-ROWECKI, Stefan (1895–1944)

Military commander of Home Army (AK) from 1940 to 1943. Betrayed to the Gestapo and tortured.

GRZĘDZINSKI, January (1891–1976)

Writer and publicist. Active in Polish Legions of 1918 and in campaign against Soviet Russia in 1920; supporter of Piłsudski's coup d'état of 1926; left Poland with army in 1939, but returned in 1957. Eight years later he published a memoir of 1926 in the émigré journal *Kultura* for which he was expelled from the Journalists' Union. Continued to publicly speak out against regime and publish under his own name in *Kultura*.

GRZYBOWSKI, Konstanty (1901–1970)

Historian, legal expert, and professor at Jagiellonian University in Kraków. Author of *History of Political and Judicial Doctrines* (1967) and a collection titled *Skeptical Essays*.

HANDELSMAN, Marceli (1882–1945)

One of the most prominent historians of the interwar period. His focus was on nineteenth-century Polish politics. Died in Nazi concentration camp.

HERBERT, Zbigniew (b. 1924)

Perhaps the most important and influential poet in contemporary Poland, writer of works rich in moral and philosophical reflection. Unlike many of his contemporaries, Herbert always kept his distance from the postwar Communist system, refusing to join the party and shunning socialist realism.

HERLING-GRUDZIŃSKI, Gustaw (b. 1919)

Prominent liberal writer and essayist. Deported to a Soviet prison camp in 1939, and author of a book on that subject *(A World Apart)*. Author of many volumes of fiction and a regular contributor to the journal *Kultura,* published in Paris.

HERTZ, Paweł (b. 1918)

Poet, novelist, essayist, and editor of many anthologies and of a critical edition of the works by Dostoyevski. Close to *Kuźnica* circle in postwar period.

HOCHFELD, Julian (1911–1966)

Sociologist and politician, claimed by socialist and communist traditions alike. Activist in prewar PPS, then joined Polish United Workers' Party in 1948.

HOME ARMY (A.K. or ARMIA KRAJOWA)

Military organization of anti-Nazi resistance movement in World War II, subordinate to the Polish government-in-exile. Trying to oust the Nazis and prevent a Soviet occupation, the AK launched the unsuccessful Warsaw Uprising in August 1944. While formally dissolved by its own command in January 1945, many AK soldiers were imprisoned after the war by Communist authorities.

INFELD, Leopold (1899–1968)

Theoretical physicist, professor in Toronto and Warsaw. Author of many works, occasional co-author with Albert Einstein.

IRZYKOWSKI, Karol (1873–1944)

Literary critic, playwright, novelist, film theorist, and exciting innovator in prewar Polish avant-garde. Some consider his novel *Pałuba* (1908) to be a precursor of the works of Joyce.

JASIENICA, Paweł (1909–1970)

Essayist and historian; Home Army soldier during occupation. Played important role in Polish opposition movement of 1956, serving as vice-president of the influential discussion group, the Club of the Crooked Circle. Violently denounced by the Communist press and by Władysław Gomułka in 1968.

JASTRUN, Mieczysław (1903–1983)

Prominent poet, active in modernist avant-garde of 1920s, with a wide range of interests and expertise, ranging from Virgil to Kafka. Translator of French, Russian, and German poets, author of essays on European civilization.

KACZMAREK, Czesław (1895–1957)

Bishop from Kielce, one of nine bishops arrested between 1948 and 1953. Arrested in 1949 for "collaboration" and put on show trial four years later, where he "confessed" to being a "neofascist" spy for the United States and Germany. Sentenced to twelve years in prison and released in late 1956.

KAMIEŃSKA, Anna (b. 1920)

Poet and essayist inspired by Catholicism; author of a number of works for adolescents.

KISIELEWSKI, Stefan (1911–1991)

One of Poland's leading journalists for over fifty years, beginning in the 1930s; also a composer, music critic, and irreverent novelist. He was a liberal who supported the Church, but only insofar as it defended individual freedom against communism. A regular contributor to *Tygodnik Powszechny* and a member of parliament from 1957 to 1965 as part of the Catholic group *Znak*. He wrote the Preface to the original Polish edition of *The Church and the Left*.

KLISZKO, Zenon (1908–1989)

Prewar Communist activist, close associate of Gomułka, and member of the Politburo from 1956 to 1970. Confronted intellectuals in 1964 over the "Letter of 34" that demanded an end to censorship. Lost power together with Gomułka in 1970.

KOCIOŁEK, Stanisław (b. 1933)

Leading official of Polish United Workers' Party in late 1960s and one of the youngest members of the Politburo. Most widely known as Party Secretary of the Gdańsk region during the massacre of shipyard workers in 1970.

KOŁAKOWSKI, Leszek (b. 1927)

Philosopher, historian, essayist, and probably the most influential scholar for Michnik's generation of intellectuals. A prominent Marxist revisionist in 1956 who then turned against Marxism, he was expelled from Warsaw University in 1968. Since then, he has taught philosophy at Oxford and at the

University of Chicago. Author of numerous books, including *Towards a Marxist Humanism, Conversations with the Devil, Religion, Modernity on Endless Trial,* and the three-volume *Main Currents of Marxism.*

KONWICKI, Tadeusz (b. 1926)

Novelist, script writer, and film director. A Home Army soldier who joined the PZPR after the war, then became part of the democratic intellectual opposition after 1956. On the editorial board of *Nowa Kultura* from 1950 to 1958. His books include *Dreambook for Our Time, A Minor Apocalypse,* and *Moonrise, Moonset;* among his films are *Salto; How Near, How Far;* and *Issa Valley.*

KORBOŃSKI, Stefan (1901–1989)

A leader of the prewar Peasant Party and of the Polish resistance under Nazi occupation. Forced out of Poland in 1947 and settled in the United States.

KOTARBIŃSKI, Tadeusz (1886–1981)

Philosopher and logician, known for his work in "praxeology" (a theory of efficient action). President of the Polish Academy of Sciences from 1957 to 1962 and a towering authority among Polish intellectuals.

KOTT, Jan (b. 1914)

Literary and theatrical critic, author of *Shakespeare, Our Contemporary* and many other books. Supporter of PZPR in early postwar period, on editorial board of *Kuźnica,* revisionist opponent of regime after 1956. Since 1967, he has lived in the United States and is Professor Emeritus of Comparative Literature at State University of New York at Stony Brook.

KOWALSKA, Anka (b. 1932)

Poet and novelist, member of KOR (Workers' Defense Committee) and an editor of the underground press in the 1970s.

KRYNICKI, Ryszard (b. 1943)

Poet of the "young generation" who advocated moral and social commitment (though not "socialist realism") as a reaction against the "hermetism" of the preceding generation of poets.

KUCHARZEWSKI, Jan (1876–1952)

Historian and politician, Polish Prime Minister in 1918. Author of seven-volume work on Russia, *From White to Red Tsarism.*

KUŁA, Witold (1916–1988)

World-renowned economic historian, professor at Warsaw University.

KULTURA (Paris)

A monthly journal of cultural, political, and social affairs founded by liberal Polish émigrés in 1947 and published since 1948 in Paris under the direction of Jerzy Giedroyć. It is also an independent publishing house and in this role has issued several hundred books by émigré authors (including Gombrowicz and Miłosz) as well as by writers living in Poland whose books could not appear there.

KUROŃ, Jacek (b. 1933)

One of Poland's most prominent democratic activists. Originally a radical communist and pedagogue; considered a "mentor" by Michnik both for his writings and his role as leader of the scout group in which the teenaged Michnik and other future radical student activists took part. A historian at Warsaw University in the early 1960s; author, with Karol Modzelewski, of the 1964 "Open Letter to the Party," a left-wing attack on the Communist system that brought him a three-year prison sentence. Abandoning his Trotskyist views, Kuroń became a major theorist of "anti-politics" and the "civil society" opposition movement of the 1970s. A founder of KOR, an adviser to Solidarity, and, in 1989, elected congressman and Minister of Labor in first postcommunist government. Cited by opinion polls in 1992 as one of the most popular politicians in Poland.

KUŹNICA [The Forge]

Important postwar literary weekly, taking its name from a prominent political association of the Polish Enlightenment. Intellectually close to György Lukács, the journal championed Marxist criticism, advocated realism (of the Balzac, not Soviet, variety), and conducted a wide-ranging debate on the purpose of literature in the new society. Its circle included the writers Kazimierz Brandys, Paweł Hertz, Mieczysław Jastrun, Jan Kott, Adam Ważyk, and Zygmunt Żuławski; edited by Stefan Żżółkiewski. Merged with *Odrodzenie* in 1950 to form *Nowa Kultura*.

LANGE, Oskar (1904–1965)

Economist and politician, theorist of PPS, author of 1938 classic *On the Economic Theory of Socialism*. A professor of economics at the University of Chicago from 1945 to 1948, Lange returned to Poland to work with the Communist government. Served on the Central Committee and as Polish ambassador to the United States.

LEŚNODORSKI, Bogusław (1914–1985)

Legal scholar and historian of the Enlightenment, co-author of *History of State and Law in Poland* (1977).

LIPIŃSKI, Edward (1888–1986)

Economist, socialist activist, and author of many works on the history of Polish economic thought. A founding member of KOR (Workers' Defense Committee).

LIPSKI, Jan Józef (1926–1991)

Literary critic and opposition activist. A member of the PPS after World War II, Lipski was chairman of the revisionist "Club of the Crooked Circle" in 1956, as well as a chief sponsor of the "Letter of 34" in 1964 that demanded an end to censorship. A founder of KOR (Workers' Defense Committee) and its historian. Instrumental in reviving the Polish Socialist Party in 1987. Active in Solidarity, elected senator in 1989.

ŁUBIEŃSKI, Konstanty (1910–1977)

Politician, soldier in Home Army. Joined PAX, then left PAX in 1956 to join liberal Catholic intellectuals around *Znak*. Member of Parliament from *Znak* group, then joined ODISS, alternative Catholic opposition group founded by Janusz Zabłocki.

MACIEREWICZ, Antoni (b. 1948)

Historian of Mayan Indians, important contemporary political activist. Organized demonstrations against war in Vietnam in his youth, then organized campaign against changes in Polish constitution in 1975. Co-founder of KOR (Workers' Defense Committee) in 1977, adviser to Solidarity. Originally influenced by socialist ideas of Abramowski, he moved toward the Right in the late 1970s, closer to Catholic, nationalist, and populist circles, thus becoming a political rival of Michnik's. In 1990, he became vice-president of the Christian National Union; in 1992, he served as Minister of Internal Affairs.

MALEWSKA, Hanna (1911–1983)

Writer, author of historical novels. Directed Catholic monthly *Znak* (affiliated with group of the same name).

MAZOWIECKI, Tadeusz (b. 1927)

Essayist, Catholic activist, and, in 1989, first Prime Minister of postcommunist government. Affiliated with PAX after the war, he then broke with PAX during the "Polish October" of 1956 and founded and edited the monthly *Więź*—very influential for Michnik and his co-thinkers. Went to Lenin Shipyard during the strikes of 1980 and became adviser to Lech Wałęsa, then editor of *Solidarity Weekly*. Continued close association with Solidarity circles until he became prime minister. He was defeated by Wałęsa for the presidency in 1990, then formed his own party, Democratic Union, which won fourteen percent of the seats in the 1991 parliamentary elections (largest percentage for any single party).

MIKOŁAJCZYK, Stanisław (1901–1966)

Leader of the Polish Peasant Party and the prime minister of government-in-exile during World War II. Returned to Poland as vice-premier in 1945, but, increasingly constrained by Communists, forced to flee in 1947.

MILLER, Jan Nepomucen (1890–1977)

Modernist literary and theater critic and PPS activist. Took an active part in postwar literary life, until his opposition to Communist control of literature left him unable to publish. He worked in provincial theater for ten years before returning to Warsaw in 1957. Put on trial in 1965 for publishing essays in an émigré British publication.

MIŁOSZ, Czesław (b. 1911)

One of the greatest contemporary Polish poets, enormously influential in opposition circles of the 1970s, winner of the 1980 Nobel Prize for Literature. An avant-garde poet in the prewar era, Miłosz joined the PZPR and served as cultural emissary for the postwar government until he left for the West in 1951, when he published *The Captive Mind*. Author of numerous books of poetry, essays, novels, and a *History of Polish Literature;* professor emeritus at University of California, Berkeley.

MOCHNACKI, Maurycy (1803–1834)

Publicist and literary critic, took part in 1830–31 insurrection against Russian occupation. Emigrated after the collapse of the uprising.

MOCZAR, Mieczysław (1913–1986)

Hard-line Communist activist and official, Minister of Interior from 1964 to 1968 and a member of the Politburo. Considered leader of national-chauvinist "Partisan" faction of the Party and mastermind of "anti-Zionist" campaign of 1968.

MODZELEWSKI, Karol (b. 1937)

Historian, prominent Left activist. Author, with Jacek Kuroń, of "Open Letter to the Party" in 1964, for which he served three years in prison. Rearrested in 1968 and served another three years. He became an accomplished medieval historian, but maintained ties to opposition circles. In 1980, he was a leader of Solidarity from Wrocław; he served on Solidarity's National Commission and was jailed for three more years after the imposition of martial law. Elected senator in 1989. Critic of free-market "shock therapy" program; a leader of the social democratic "Solidarity of Labor" party.

MROŻEK, Sławomir (b. 1930)

Playwright and satirist, one of the most popular and influential contemporary Polish writers. Lives and works in Paris since 1963.

NORWID, Cyprian Kamil (1821–1883)

One of the great Polish poets, unrecognized in his lifetime, rediscovered early in the twentieth century and hailed as the precursor of modern poetry. Lived in Paris after 1849.

NOWA KULTURA

Leading literary journal published from 1950 to 1963, a main organ for revisionist writings.

ODISS

Center for Documentation and Social Research, a Catholic research organization founded by Janusz Zabłocki in 1967 within the framework of *Znak*, but which soon positioned itself close to the regime. Published monthly journal, *Christian in the World*. Opposed *Znak*'s decision to challenge the government over proposed constitutional changes in 1975, then replaced *Znak* in the new parliament of 1976 while maintaining, against Church orders, the same name. Tries to become recognized Christian Democratic Party, but never succeeds.

ODRODZENIE [Rebirth]

Social and cultural weekly published from 1944 to 1950, edited by Jerzy Borejsza. Close to the journal *Kuźnica;* these two publications were merged in 1950 to form *Nowa Kultura*.

ONR

A radical right-wing nationalist group founded in 1934. Anti-Communist, anticapitalist, and fiercely anti-Semitic. Organized attacks on Jews at the university, demanding a *numerus clausus* and the segregation of Jewish students.

OSSOWSKA, Maria (1896–1974)

Sociologist, author of many books on ethics. Together with her husband Stanisław, this couple embodied the intellectual integrity of the secular Left by refusing to compromise with Stalinism.

OSSOWSKI, Stanisław (1897–1963)

Prominent liberal sociologist and cultural theorist, author of the antiracist work *The Social Bond and the Blood Heritage* (1939) and of *Class Structure in the Social Consciousness* (1957), the second of which is still widely read in universities throughout the world. A towering moral authority for Polish intellectuals.

OZGA-MICHALSKI, Józef (b. 1919)

Member of the Peasant Party who helped arrange its capitulation to the Communist movement in 1947. Later occupied high state posts. Prominent pro-government spokesman in 1968.

PAX

Pro-Communist Catholic organization founded by Bolesław Piasecki in 1945.

PIASECKI, Bolesław (1915–1979)

One of the founders of the prewar fascist group ONR. Imprisoned by Soviets, then released after proposing the creation of PAX. Became a major official in Communist Poland, including being a member of the State Council.

PIŁSUDSKI, Józef (1867–1935)

The leading figure of interwar Poland. A founder of the Polish Socialist Party and an organizer of its armed battalions, or Legions. Soon reduced his ties to PPS to concentrate on struggle for Polish independence. Virulently anti-Russian, he tried to work with Austria and Germany to secure independence during World War I, but was imprisoned by German authorities. Freed in 1918, he became the undisputed leader of the independent Poland created in November 1918. He was the head of state from 1919 to 1922, but he refused to formally become president or prime minister. Led successful 1920 military campaign against Soviet Russia. Announced retirement from politics in 1923, but returned to lead coup d'état against right-wing government in May 1926, winning both the praise and the suspicions of many leftists. A strong critic of parliamentarism for its slow pace and proclivity to talk, he allowed parliamentary government to continue but with the pervasive threat of intervention. In 1930, he arrested and interned numerous parliamentary rivals, who were then freed and allowed to resume their activities, but from 1930 through 1935 his rule became increasingly repressive, especially as he personally became less involved. A very complex figure: authoritarian, but no fascist; hostile to anti-Semitism, but unable to create a stable institutional democratic polity.

POMIAN, Krzysztof (b. 1934)

Philosopher and historian expelled from Warsaw University in 1968 for his liberal views. Settled in France.

PO PROSTU [Simply Speaking]

Weekly of the Polish Youth Association which, after 1955, came to epitomize the critical spirit of the "Polish October." Closed down by authorities in 1957; resumed publication in 1989.

PPR

Polish Workers' Party, official name of Polish Communist Party from 1943 until 1948, when it took over PPS to form PZPR, or Polish United Workers' Party. The earlier Communist party, or KPP, was dissolved in 1937 by orders from Stalin's Comintern.

PPS

Polish Socialist Party, founded in 1893, played instrumental role in securing Polish independence in 1918. One of the most dominant parties of interwar period, laying claim to both socialist and patriotic traditions. Formally dissolved by its own leaders in 1939 just before the Nazi takeover and revived in postwar period with pro-Communist bent; dissolved again in 1948 as it merged into PPR to form PZPR. Attempted revival in late 1980s, so far with little success.

PRUSZYŃSKI, Ksawery (1907–1950)

Writer, journalist, pro-Republican reporter from Spain during Civil War, Polish ambassador to Holland from 1948 to 1950.

PRZEGLĄD KULTURALNY [Cultural Review]

A major Warsaw literary journal published from 1952 to 1963; a champion of revisionism during 1955–57 period.

PRZYBOŚ, Julian (1901–1970)

Avant-garde poet and theorist. Joined PZPR and helped organize literary life in postwar Poland; sympathetic to revisionist opposition.

PUTRAMENT, Jerzy (1910–1986)

Novelist and Communist activist, born in Vilnius. Ambassador to France from 1945 to 1950, then member of the Central Committee and the Party leader of the Polish Writers' Association. Model for "Gamma" in Czesław Miłosz's *The Captive Mind*.

PUŻAK, Kazimierz (1883–1950)

Activist in Polish Socialist Party beginning in 1904. Imprisoned by tsarist authorities; became secretary general of the PPS in 1921. Organized armed units for the Socialist resistance during Nazi occupation. Arrested in Warsaw by Soviet authorities in 1945 together with other non-Communist Polish political leaders. Tried in Moscow and sentenced to a year and a half in prison. Tried again in Poland in 1948 and given a five-year sentence. Died in prison.

PUZYNA, Konstanty (1929–1989)

Theater critic and, from 1972, chief editor of journal *Dialog*. Author of numerous essays on Mrożek, Gombrowicz, and the contemporary theater.

PZPR

Polish United Workers' Party, acronym of Polish Communist party, 1948–1990. From 1943 until 1948 known as PPR, or Polish Workers' Party. The first Communist Party of Poland, KPP, was liquidated on Stalin's orders in 1937.

REJKOWSKI, Janusz (b. 1929)

Professor of Social Psychology, and a harsh but very insightful critic of Solidarity. A reformist, anti-Stalinist Communist, he sat on the Politburo in the late 1980s and played a key role on the government side in the Round Table negotiations of 1989.

RUDNICKI, Adolf (1912–1991)

Novelist with both a realist and psychological orientation, his first novels were published in the 1930s. A Jew, he survived the war outside the Warsaw ghetto thanks to false documents; much of his later work sought to explain the hellish dynamic between Poles and Jews during this period. Active in *Kuźnica* circle.

SIENKIEWICZ, Henryk (1846–1916)

Novelist, winner of Nobel Prize for literature, author of *Quo Vadis* (1896) and other novels dealing with Polish history. Attacked by the Left and modernist avant-garde for conformism and conservatism.

SKARGA, Piotr (1563–1612)

Jesuit theologian and supporter of strong royal authority to counterbalance anti-statist tendencies among Polish nobility.

SŁONIMSKI, Antoni (1895–1976)

Poet, playwright, essayist, associated with prewar liberal Left. President of Polish Writers' Association from 1956 to 1959 and a prominent and prestigious moral authority for Polish dissidents. Michnik, who worked as Słonimski's personal assistant in the early 1970s, refers to him as "my teacher."

STEMPOWSKI, Stanisław (1870–1952)

Writer, archivist, and one of the leading figures of Polish freemasonry. Exercised great authority among leftist intellectuals in prewar period.

STOMMA, Stanisław (b. 1908)

Legal expert and Catholic publicist; an editor of *Tygodnik Powszechny;* member of Parliament from the Catholic group *Znak,* 1957–1976.

STRUG, Andrzej (1871–1937)

Novelist and publicist allied with PPS and a leader of Polish freemasonry. His novels deal with revolutionary themes.

STRZELECKI, Jan (1919–1988)

Sociologist, socialist activist. Organized militant underground socialist youth organization during Nazi occupation. After the war, he joined PZPR and became an advocate and theorist of "socialist humanism," one of the first postwar leftists to rethink the Left's traditional hostility toward the Church. In 1976, Michnik called him a "controversial figure" for insisting on working for change inside the PZPR, but added that Strzelecki's role in bringing about Church-Left dialogue was "impossible to exaggerate." In 1980, he became adviser to Solidarity and remained a figure with great moral authority in intellectual circles.

STWOSZ, Wit (Veit Stoss), (c.1447–1553)

Sculptor and painter of German origin who worked in Poland. His masterpiece is the high altar of St. Mary's Church in Kraków.

ŚWIĘTOCHOWSKI, Aleksander (1849–1938)

Writer and publicist, critic of Polish romanticism, theorist of Polish positivism, founder of concept of "organic work."

TRZECIAK, Stanisław (1873–1944)

Priest and extreme right-wing essayist known for anti-Semitic writings. Executed by German firing squad.

TUROWICZ, Jerzy (b. 1912)

Editor of independent Catholic weekly *Tygodnik Powszechny,* 1950–53, 1956–present. A towering authority for Michnik and other secular intellectuals of the Left for his consistent loyalty to democratic values. Signer of "Letter of 34" against censorship in 1964; published essays of liberal and Jewish intellectuals purged in 1968 and of pro-Solidarity writers (including Michnik) after declaration of martial law in 1981. Sympathetic to Christian socialism, he wrote a glowing eulogy to Dorothy Day in 1982. Author of *Christians in the Contemporary World* (1963), with a preface by Cardinal Wojtyła, and other works.

TYGODNIK POWSZECHNY [Universal Weekly]

Independent Catholic weekly edited by Jerzy Turowicz. Began publication during the Stalinist years; a consistent defender of democratic Catholic ideas. Extremely important for Michnik's reassessment of the Church.

WARSKI, Adolf (1868–1937?)

One of the founders of prewar Polish Communist Party. Summoned to the Soviet Union in 1937, arrested and shot as "fascist agent."

WAŻYK, Adam (1912–1982)

Poet, essayist, one of the main figures of the prewar Polish avant-garde, and supporter of Marxism in postwar years. In 1955, he published the extremely influential *Poem for Adults,* attacking Stalinism in the name of socialism and heralding the events of October 1956.

WERBLAN, Andrzej (b. 1924)

Activist in postwar PPS who helped "unify" it into the PZPR; became one of the youngest leaders of the new Polish United Workers' Party. Considered one of the more sophisticated defenders of the regime among those who joined after the war.

WICI

Prewar association of peasant youth with over 100 thousand members; aligned with Peasant Party. Founded in 1928, liquidated in 1948.

WIĘŹ [Links]

Influential Catholic monthly, philosophically rooted in Catholic personalism; founded in 1958 by Tadeusz Mazowiecki. Played key role in facilitating new Church-Left dialogue.

WITOS, Wincenty (1874–1945)

Founder of the Polish Peasant Party, himself a farmer and self-taught public figure; repeatedly served as Poland's prime minister (1920–21, 1923, 1926). Arrested by Piłsudski government in 1930. Left Poland but returned in 1939 and was imprisoned by Germans until 1940. Died soon after end of war in Poland.

WOROSZYLSKI, Wiktor (b. 1927)

Poet, essayist, translator. Specialist in Russian literature, author of *Life of Mayakowsky* (1966), editor of samizdat literary journal in 1970s.

WOŹNIAKOWSKI, Jacek (b. 1920)

Art historian and essayist, professor at Catholic University in Lublin, affiliated with *Tygodnik Powszechny,* directed *Znak* publishing house.

WYŚPIAŃSKI, Stanisław (1869–1907)

Poet and painter, author of poetic dramas (including *The Wedding)* that are absolutely central to modern Polish theater.

WYSZYŃSKI, Cardinal Stefan (1901–1981)

Cardinal Primate of Poland. Spent occupation at institute run by Franciscan nuns, which became a center of Catholic intellectual resistance. Named primate of Poland in 1948 and cardinal in 1952. Under house arrest from 1953 to 1956. Next to Karol Wojtyła, he is the dominant figure of twentieth-century Polish Catholicism.

ZABŁOCKI, Janusz (b. 1926)

Catholic publicist; initially associated with PAX, joined editorial staff of *Więź* in 1958, then left to found ODISS, a Catholic organization trying to find a middle ground between PAX and *Znak.*

ZAŁUSKI, Zbigniew (1926–1977)

Colonel, hard-line Communist and nationalist, fierce critic of liberal intellectuals in 1960s, known for his praise of Polish military.

GLOSSARY OF NAMES

ZAREMBA, Zygmunt (1895–1967)

Leading official of prewar PPS; editor of *Robotnik* [The Worker]; one of the founders of WRN (Freedom, Equality, Independence), an underground socialist organization during the Nazi occupation. Left Poland for France in 1946.

ZAWIEYSKI, Jerzy (1902–1969)

Prominent writer and cultural figure, an actor in prewar era, a liberal Catholic activist afterwards. Head of Warsaw Catholic Intellectuals' Club in 1957, member of Parliament from *Znak* group and member of the State Council from 1957 to 1968, after which he fell into official disfavor for his support of student protests.

ZDZIECHOWSKI, Marian (1861–1938)

Literary historian who wrote on Tolstoy, Soloviev, and Berdyaev; a conservative thinker influenced by Spengler.

ŻEROMSKI, Stefan (1864–1925)

Influential writer and novelist who tried to link socialist and nationalist traditions in his writings.

ZIEJA, Father Jan (1896–1990)

Military chaplain during Polish-Russian war of 1920; taught in seminary in Minsk and was active in Wici movement during prewar era. Helped efforts to rescue Jews during Nazi occupation. In 1953, one of the few priests to publicly denounce the arrest of Cardinal Wyszyński. A co-founder of KOR (Workers' Defense Committee) in 1977.

ZNAK [Sign]

Group of Catholic parliamentarians admitted into parliament by Gomułka in 1957; also the name of a liberal Catholic monthly and an affiliated Catholic publishing house based in Kraków. Important actor in new Church-Left dialogue discussed by Michnik.

ŻÓŁKIEWSKI, Stefan (b. 1911)

Literary critic, prewar Communist, editor of *Kuźnica*.

ŻUŁAWSKI, Zygmunt (1880–1949)

Socialist and trade union leader in prewar period and member of parliament from 1919 to 1935. Coordinated socialist underground movement in Kraków during Nazi occupation; after the war, he refused to participate in either PPR or the revived PPS. Elected independent delegate to parliament in 1945; tried to create Polish Social Democratic Party, but the authorities refused permission. One of the most interesting socialist activists in the 1930s and early postwar period.

INDEX